HELL
AND THE
MERCY
OF GOD

HELL AND THE MERCY OF GOD

ADRIAN J. REIMERS

The Catholic University of America Press
Washington, D.C.

Design and composition by Kachergis Book Design

Library of Congress Cataloging-in-Publication Data
Names: Reimers, Adrian J., author.
Title: Hell and the mercy of God / Adrian J. Reimers.
Description: Washington, D.C. : The Catholic University of America
Press, 2017. | Includes bibliographical references and index.
Identifiers: LCCN 2016056228 | ISBN 9780813229409 (pbk. : alk. paper)
Subjects: LCSH: God (Christianity)—Goodness. | Hell—Christianity. |
Catholic Church—Doctrines.
Classification: LCC BT137 .R45 2017 | DDC 231—dc23
LC record available at https://lccn.loc.gov/2016056228

For
Marie (Warrington) Reimers

CONTENTS

The remote inspiration for this present work on hell and God's mercy dates to my childhood. Attending Catholic schools, learning about sin and its consequences, being taught by the sisters on how to go to confession and why it was important, attending my Grandpa's funeral, receiving First Communion, and going to Mass every Sunday, I was continually aware of and concerned about the "last things"—death and judgment, heaven and hell. Like most Catholics of my generation (as far as I know), I learned to "dread the loss of heaven and the pains of hell," to borrow the words of the Act of Contrition. There were mortal sins that I could commit—anyone could, even Monsignor—and if I should die not having committed and not confessed one of these, I risked eternal damnation. Of course, as one grows older and more educated, these ideas call for a more refined understanding of what hell is, why it may constitute an appropriate punishment for misdeeds in this life, and what is the nature of the mercy by which one avoids hell. In the background of these considerations lies the question of legalism and a divine system of rewards for those who do what God wants and punishments for those who cross his demands.

The proximate inspirations for this book are twofold. The first was my research on happiness, during which I examined St. Thomas Aquinas's account of God as the ultimate end for human life in relation to Karol Wojtyła's account of the good of the human person.[1] Logically—that is, according to its concepts and argumentation—St. Thomas's account of the ultimate good for the human being is wonderfully satisfying. However, its formal structure leaves the more experiential and practical questions unanswered. If the vision of the Divine Essence is the perfect fulfillment of the human intellect, how does this redound upon the human person as a whole? Assuming that Wolfgang Amadeus Mozart and King Edward the Confessor are currently enjoying the intellectual vision of the Divine Essence, it would seem strange that they both enjoy this experience in the same way. Should there not be something *musical* to Mozart's eternal happiness? Would not Edward (who, for all we know, may have been tone-deaf) take a particular personal interest in God's reign, aware that he was himself a king? Particularly troubling is the question of how one attains to this end, which by his own efforts he cannot attain. And, of course, the troubling question remains concerning the state of those who may not attain to that vision, whether this be the unbaptized paradigmatic philosopher Socrates or—perhaps, but we do not really know— the notorious bank robber John Dillinger, who was surprised by federal law-enforcement agents and gunned down outside a Chicago movie theater.

The second proximate inspiration has been the young, in particular those whom I encounter at the university. How do I answer this question: "Why would a good God consign those who disobey him to unending torment in hell?" If God really

1. My research eventually resulted in Adrian J. Reimers, *An Analysis of the Concepts of Self-Fulfillment and Self-Realization in the Thought of Karol Wojtyła, Pope John Paul II* (Lewiston, N.Y.: Edwin Mellen Press, 2001).

is good, then eternal torment for a series of missteps in time seems to be all out of proportion. If, as both Pope St. John Paul II and Pope Francis have insisted, God's dealings with us are to be understood in terms of his mercy, then may we not charge him with a kind of schizophrenia?

The guiding image recurring throughout this present work is the death of Dismas, the crucified thief whose wicked life ended with mercy. Having deserved execution by the state, he probably deserved the wrath of God for his crimes, but he found salvation instead. In an important sense, the story of Dismas tells us what we need to know about God's judgment.

An important conceptual leitmotif is the character of Satan and the other demons. A purely spiritual being, Satan expressly refused God's mercy. On the basis of his nature and this refusal, we can characterize Satan's psychology and hence his motivations. We see that having refused mercy, the devil has refused his own proper happiness and consequently lives in resentment and envy. So far as sinful human beings are concerned, hell is simply to fall within Satan's reign and under his governance. This analysis is complemented by an analysis of the human being as a spiritual being that is necessarily not entirely confined to space and time. An important part of this analysis is my account of the forms of human suffering and an account of the soul in relation to the seven deadly sins. An especially important conclusion here is that the *hell* of hell lies not in the physical pains, but in spiritual desolation and abandonment to merciless torment.

To address the question of eternal damnation, significant discussion is devoted to the goodness of God as paradigmatic of all goodness in order to answer the troubling question of whether, say, a good mother can enjoy heaven knowing that her child is damned to eternal torment in hell. Because we are bodily, and therefore finite, beings, we do not fully understand what constitutes the fullness of goodness, and therefore we lack a fully adequate understanding of evil.

A third and especially important theme is that of idolatry and its relationship with the work of evil spirits. In this context a critique of utilitarianism and (following John Paul II) the consumer culture is essential. By looking at the devotion of human beings to our idols, it is possible to see the structures of hell on earth. Indeed, it is my contention that anyone who disbelieves in the reality of hell is simply not paying attention to the full underlying dynamics of earthly life.

Finally, as the story of Dismas makes clear, the salvific key to the entire work is mercy. Satan's issue is with God's mercy. Human beings are saved by mercy. The book's fundamental theme is the dynamic economy of mercy.

As my account of the inspirations for this work indicates, this is very much a personal work arising from my own reflections on our ultimate good, evil, mercy, and condemnation. As such it does not strive directly to engage the state of scholarly discussion and debate on these issues. The intellectual core of the book is philosophical, but some of the arguments are, necessarily, theological. Because the genesis of the work is also personal, parts of it may even have a somewhat devotional character. My intention throughout, however, is to present a well-founded logical and conceptually coherent account of the topics under consideration.

ACKNOWLEDGMENTS

For this reason a man shall leave his father and mother and be joined
to his wife, and the two shall become one.

—Ephesians 5:31

When we academics write our scholarly books, after listing
the colleagues to whom we owe some scholarly debt for the
contents, concepts, presentations, and arguments, those of us
who are married usually acknowledge the contributions of our
spouses for their patience with our mental distraction, their
helpful suggestions on style, help in proofreading, and their encouragement for our work. Indeed, such acknowledgments are
appropriate. Because of the nature of this present book, I owe a
deeper debt to my wife, Marie Reimers. As St. Paul notes in the
citation from Ephesians, husband and wife are one. This unity
is forged not only or even primarily in the marriage bed but in
the daily building of a life of love, which necessarily requires
direct mutual confrontations with evil, sin, and suffering, for

Unless otherwise indicated, all scriptural citations are from the Revised Standard Version—Catholic edition (New York: Oxford University Press, 2004).

xiii

evil is constituted by this—that it undermines love. If one is to write intelligently and meaningfully about love and mercy, it is necessary to have lived them. To be married is to live these together, jointly confronting the evil in our own hearts, in the neighborhood and city we live in, among our friends, and among our children's associates. We learn judgment and mercy in the daily struggle for goodness. We talk, my wife and I, and as we talk with each other we refine each other's perspectives and help each other to think through the drama that is our life together. Therefore, before all else it is appropriate to acknowledge my wife, Marie's, contribution to this work, not so much as a helpful observer to its composition, but rather as coauthor, having shared with me the dynamics of the life of love for each other and for God in the face of the evils that have beset us and, of course, all humankind. Besides all this, she spent many hours carefully reading and proofreading this manuscript. For these reasons I dedicate this book to her.

There are others who have looked at drafts of this book and provided helpful comments. Catherine Gropp, a former fellow parishioner, provided astute comments on my composition of the original version, and Fr. Grzegorz Hołub, a philosophical colleague from the Pontifical University of John Paul II in Krakow, read my first draft and encouraged the project. Kelly (Mason) Lindquist is a former student of mine who did me the courtesy of reading the initial version and offering comments.

I thank also the editorial staff of the Catholic University of America Press and their copy editors and reviewers, who have made this a better and more readable book than it was when it came off my computer.

HELL
AND THE
MERCY
OF GOD

Prologue

THE MAN ON THE CROSS

Crucifixion is an ugly thing. The victim hangs suspended by nails driven through the wrists, arms pulled unnaturally far back, the pressure of the nails on the wrist bones pinching the nerves and sending excruciating pain through the arms. The hanging body's weight stretches the chest muscles; breathing is almost impossible. Desperate for breath—and to stop the sharp pain that burns the arms—the victim straightens his legs to put his weight on his feet, which are held in place by nails. This "relief" is not real, though, because it sends pain through the feet, and the legs soon tire. Normally death on a cross takes a long time. There is not enough blood loss for a quick death. Instead, the crucified person dies of exposure and thirst. The crucified would often curse with such blasphemies that the Roman executioners would cut out their tongues simply to silence them. The victim hangs there for hours or even days, until his muscles and power to resist give out and he dies.

In one case three men were crucified: Dismas the criminal, his unnamed sometime partner, and Jesus of Nazareth. They knew that they would die before evening, simply because the morrow was the day of the Jewish great feast. Already the cursing had started. Dismas could hear his partner:

Are you not the Christ? Save yourself and us.[1]

From everything Dismas had heard, Jesus was a good man, something of a prophet whom people had hoped to be the Messiah. Dismas rebuked his colleague:

Do you not fear God, since you are under the same sentence of condemnation? And we indeed justly; for we are receiving the due reward of our deeds; but this man has done nothing wrong.[2]

In his heart Dismas found room for mercy. Having wasted his life in crime, in the end he could at least speak out for someone worse off than himself. He spoke to Jesus: "Jesus, remember me when you come in your kingly power" (Lk 23:42).

Why did he say that? Did he really believe Jesus to be the Messiah? He himself may not have known, not exactly. Jesus did not look like a king, especially now as he hung, bloody, on that cross. In months past he had worked miracles. They said that God was with him. And so perhaps, if this really was a man of God and if God really did vindicate him, then somehow he might remember Dismas. The criminal's life would not have been a complete waste, even if it did end like this. Then Jesus answered him: "Truly, I say to you, today you will be with me in paradise" (Lk 23:43).

1. Lk 23:39.
2. Lk 23:40–41.

The most Dismas could hope for now was an end of this pain in a quick death—and Jesus spoke of paradise. The afternoon wore on. Mercifully—for the hot sun could be brutal—it became very dark. He had ceased to hear anything from Jesus' cross, although the other criminal would occasionally moan and curse. Finally the soldiers came up with their clubs. Breaking their legs would mean terrific pain, but then the ordeal would be over.

There was indeed that searing pain as his legs broke and his body collapsed. Darkness came over him. He was dead. But then in his death he experienced an unexpected and unimagined light and joy. It was somewhat like that joy he had felt a long time ago when he was a boy, and again later when he realized what his wife's love meant to him. (This was before he had turned away and broken her heart.) It was the joy he wanted most. He was in paradise.

This story tells us, in a way, almost everything we need to know about God's mercy and the "four last things": death, judgment, heaven, and hell. Most people will say that hell (if there really is such a place) is for bad people and heaven is for the good. But Dismas was a bad man. He himself admits it: "You are under the same sentence of condemnation. And we indeed justly." If on the way up Calvary a band of zealots had set him free, he might well have returned to his life of crime. But without even proving that his repentance was genuine, *"this day"* he entered paradise. Here is a man whom Roman justice, from which our own justice system is ultimately drawn, had condemned to execution. Granted that Roman justice was far from perfect—consider Who was hanging on that middle cross—nevertheless it was pretty good, all things considered. Dismas had his chances, and he chose crime. But his condemnation and execution notwithstanding, he entered paradise. Why? *He asked Jesus to remem-*

ber him. He showed *mercy* and had *faith in Jesus,* who remembered him when he assumed his kingly power.

Dismas asked Jesus to save him. So did Jairus and the woman with the hemorrhage (Lk 8:40–56). So did the leper (Mk 1:40–44) and the Syrophoenician woman (Mk 7:24–30). So did the two blind men in Jericho (Mt 20:29–34). Whenever someone approached Jesus believing that he could help them—save them— he did. They did not need to recognize his divinity. Surely Jairus, an official in the synagogue, would not have claimed him divine. Nor did they have to acknowledge him as Christ. A Syrophoenician would not care about a Jewish Messiah. The Lord's standards are actually very low: what is necessary is to turn to Jesus, believing that he has the power to save—not necessarily the whole world, but *me* from the evil I am suffering now—and ask him. A person is saved simply by asking Jesus for help.

The Question of Judgment

"How can a good God send anyone to hell?" This is more than a rhetorical question. Its answer appears to be clear enough. A good God, one who is truly merciful and who loves sinners "warts and all," could never send his own creature to a place of brutal punishment, of undying flames and endless cruel torment. A loving God might be "put out" somewhat by his creatures' obtuse and even selfish foibles, but he will never punish with hellfire the mistakes arising from simple human frailty. This question is the theme of our book. And let us begin by answering the question.

To believe that a good God could not send a sinner to hell is to understand neither the wickedness of sin nor the goodness and mercy of God. Furthermore, to misconceive hell is to misconceive heaven. We do not believe in judgment on sin, because we do not understand the reality of our situation. What the scriptures and Christian doc-

trine make clear is that we have a serious, dramatic choice between good and evil. How a person chooses will make him to
be good or evil. But we of the twenty-first century are blind
to the reality and gravity of this choice. Enjoying remarkable
wealth, prosperity, and comfort, as well as a level of peace
and civic order almost unique in human history, we have not
eradicated the evil from our own hearts. Indeed, our wonderful
material and social advantages serve to veil our eyes from our
true condition. We are Auden's "faces along the bar" in the dive
on 52nd Street, for whom "The lights must never go out / the
music must always play / . . . Lest we should see where we are
/ lost in a haunted wood / children afraid of the night / who
have never been happy or good."[3] Auden addressed his poem to
an isolationist America far removed from "the unmentionable
odor of death [which] offends the September night." Indeed,
as we shall see, our situation is far worse than Auden's "dive."

On the other hand, corresponding to our blindness to evil
is the abundant mercy of God, a mercy that far surpasses what
we imagine. God's mercy is not an easygoing, divine congenial-
ity that is willing to pass over our crimes as so many missteps.
The God of mercy is not the kind heavenly grandfather who
clucks his tongue and gently picks us up when we have stum-
bled and scraped our spiritual knees. Indeed, the reward that
God grants to those who accept his mercy is a good far beyond
our imagining. God's mercy is serious and severe, so much so
that it is found not in the Elysian Fields, but on Calvary as God
himself takes on the true burden of our sins.

The story of Dismas tells us, in a way, almost everything
we need to know about hell . . . and about the mercy of God.
In the course of these reflections, we will return to Dismas. His
too is one of the "faces along the bar."

3. W. H. Auden, "September 1, 1939," in *The Major Poets: English and American*, by Charles Coffin (New York: Harcourt, Brace and World, 1954), 518–20.

The Place Prepared by My Father

The classic scriptural text on God's judgment is surely Christ's teaching in Matthew 25:31–46, where Jesus says to the blessed, "Come, O blessed of my Father, inherit the kingdom prepared for you from the foundation of the world."[4] And then Christ the Judge commands those on his left, "Depart from me, you cursed, into the eternal fire prepared for the devil and his angels."[5] And in pain and despair they obey the devils who drag them into hell. How can the loving Savior, Jesus of Nazareth, who preached "blessed are the merciful" and who gave us wonderful parables about lost sheep and a prodigal son, damn these people to everlasting torment? Let us more closely consider Christ's words as he assigns each group their destiny.

Christ's words to the two groups are not quite in parallel. He invites the sheep into a "kingdom *prepared for you*," while he consigns the goats to "the eternal fire *prepared for the devil* and his angels." Our mental habit is to see heaven and hell as two parallel and equally available options. God sets up his rules, and, depending on whether one keeps or breaks them, Christ sends him to the one place or the other. This is a serious theological and philosophical error. It is an unscriptural view of heaven and hell. Neither is it about God's paying off or getting back at the people depending on how they responded to his rules. It is also philosophically inadequate. If the reward of the afterlife is simply that—a reward—then it bears no real relation to this life. Similarly, we might add that an eternal punishment seems to be a disproportionate penalty for the finite and temporal acts performed for a very brief period in one tiny corner of the universe. But this notion of heaven and hell as two parallel options is not what Christ speaks of.

4. Mt 25:34.
5. Mt 25:42.

Let us examine Christ's words more closely. At the moment of judgment, Jesus welcomes the just into the place that God has prepared for them "since the foundation of the world." The night before he died, Jesus spoke at length with his disciples at the Last Supper. At the beginning of this "Farewell Discourse," the Lord tells them:

In my Father's house are many rooms;... And when I go and prepare a place for you, I will come again and will take you to myself, that where I am you may be also.[6]

Christ's words mean that God does not intend hell for us. That promised mansion that he is going on ahead to prepare has no counterpart in hell. God does not want anyone to be damned. Rather, "since the foundation of the world"—that is, from the moment of creation—God has prepared a place with himself for each human being. God has created human beings for himself, eternally to enjoy his love and fellowship.

Human Destiny to Salvation

St. John of the Cross tells us that God wants to give himself to us and will do so for anyone who opens his heart to him, for what God wants is to divinize us.[7] The Second Vatican Council taught that "the root reason for human dignity lies in man's call to communion with God. From the very circumstance of his origin man is already invited to converse with God."[8] What this conciliar teaching implies is that far from being merely another life-form on the earth, humanity is ordered directly to God, that human beings exist for and are destined to intimate friendship with

---

6. Jn 14:2–3.

7. Juan de la Cruz, *Cantico Espiritual* (Madrid: Avapiés, 1996), canto 38:3.

8. Second Vatican Council, Pastoral Constitution on the Church in the Modern World, *Gaudium et spes*, §19.

their Creator. And this is certainly not a new theme in Christian teaching. In his analysis of human happiness, St. Thomas Aquinas asks about the ultimate end or good of human life and determines that the perfect good, the ultimate goal *for every human person*, is the eternal vision of the Divine Essence.[9] His entire discussion of happiness starts from Aristotle's discussion of human happiness in his *Nicomachean Ethics*. A pagan who lived about 350 years before Christ, Aristotle argues in his *Ethics* that a reasonable analysis of human nature reveals that a good life, a happy life, is had by living virtuously and nobly in a well-ordered society (rather like ancient Athens). The crown of such a life will be the leisure in one's later years to contemplate the highest truths, the most divine things.[10] Aristotle was well aware, of course, that things can go wrong. Like the noble King Priam of Troy, one can have lived well and nobly, only to lose everything to an invading army.

Aquinas starts with Aristotle, using his definitions and manner of analysis, but he gives a radically different answer. It is important for us to understand *why* his answer is different from Aristotle's. The easy explanation is to say that Aristotle (or any other wise secular thinker) teaches us about the *natural* end (or purpose) of human life and that Aquinas teaches us about the *supernatural* end. But Aquinas himself does not allow this option, as though there could be a natural destiny for most people and heaven for Christians who want it. Each and every human being, from Adam to King David, from Socrates to Genghis Khan, from Boëthius to Tolstoy, is called to the same destiny, which is the vision of the Divine Essence. The reason for this is the

---

9. St. Thomas Aquinas, *Summa theologiae* (henceforth *ST*), Ia-IIae, q. 3, a. 8 corpus, in *Great Books of the Western World*, trans. Fathers of the English Dominican Province, vols. 19–20 (Chicago, London, and Toronto: Encyclopedia Britannica, 1952).

10. Aristotle, *Nicomachean Ethics*, trans. David Ross, rev. J. L. Ackrill and J. O. Urmson (New York: Oxford University Press, 1988), Book X, chap. 7.

insatiability of the human desire for good, an insatiability that Aristotle recognized.[11] It is not enough to say that the human heart always wants more, although that is true. The human person wants what is truly good. If we simply reflect on our experience, we see this in a variety of ways that are centered on three fundamental questions: Is this really good? In virtue of what is this thing good? Is there anything better?

The dynamic these questions raise is constantly at work in the development of technology and art. Music is good. George Gershwin's first job was to peddle sheet music around New York City by performing it for vendors. If someone wanted to hear the latest songs, he could buy the sheet music and play it on his own piano. But in the meantime, Thomas Edison developed a technique for scratching wax cylinders so that sound could be stored on them. The cylinders were replaced with vinyl disks and those with cellulose tapes. Today a card smaller than a matchbook can hold all of Gershwin's music. If listening to music is good, then human beings have sought for and discovered technologies to make it possible to enjoy it more often and more easily. From quite a different angle—but remaining in the realm of music—"Twinkle, Twinkle, Little Star" is a nice song to sing to children. Mozart knew the tune, too, but in it he found musical possibilities that he developed as the "Theme and Variations on a French Folk Song." Mozart found within the simple tune resources to develop a richer sense than is found in the original. Music is a good that we can deepen and extend more widely.

These questions become especially important if one considers his own life and its direction. My life is proceeding daily, but where is it going? What is the good for which I live? Is that good the best thing for me? These are not abstract questions,

11. Ibid., Book I, chap. 7.

but commonplace issues that confront young persons as they choose their futures—"I can make a good living as a physician, but I hated my chemistry course," or "a program of advanced study abroad will make it impossible for me to marry this person to whom I am drawn." At issue is the good that is most truly good, that will most completely fulfill the person's life. In choosing the goals of one's life, a person chooses himself and the kind of person he will be. This is easy enough to see with young people, but older persons face it, as well. We read often enough of the "midlife crisis," which can induce a middle-aged man or woman to leave a prosperous career and turn to teaching or some form of public service. We all want the good, the fullness of good, so that our lives can be worthwhile.[12]

All that we love and enjoy in this life, all the goods of food and wine, of nature and the creations of culture, of love and friendship—all find their origin and their fulfillment in God himself. St. Augustine wrote, "You made us for yourself, and our heart is restless until it rests in you."[13] We are destined for a perfection and a love far beyond those that our imaginations can grasp in this life. One of the big mistakes we make—both when we are doing theology and when we are chatting casually—is to think that it is pretty much indifferent to God whether we go one way or the other. He has a reward for those who do as he commands and punishment for those who do not, but regarding those things that are not a matter of divine command—planting a garden, marrying this particular person—God is fundamentally indifferent. On the contrary, God created human beings for fellowship with him. God is very happy being God—all-perfect, all-knowing, magnificent in his

12. John Paul II, Encyclical *Fides et ratio* (Vatican City: Libreria Editrice Vaticana, 1998), §§1, 4.

13. Augustine of Hippo, *Confessions*, Book I, chap. 1, trans. John K. Ryan (New York: Image, 1960).

beauty—and he wants to share his joy. His idea all along has been that we be like him, that we participate in his divinity. A sign of how much he wants us is the great length he went to in order to save us and win us back after Adam sinned. "For God so loved the world that he gave his only begotten Son."[14] God does not intend human beings for hell.

Nevertheless, as the gospel makes clear, some persons can be damned. They can fail to take possession of the place reserved for them. Instead, they are condemned to the "eternal fire prepared for the devil and his angels." Our common conception, which is in fact seriously misleading, is that God has established a certain place of punishment for those who do not obey his rules, his law, a place called "hell" where sinners burn forever. Thus for the damned, God is remorselessly punitive—even if he is generous with those who obey him—and he deliberately inflicts great pain on his enemies forever. This is not, however, what the scriptures say. Later we will reflect on what this "fire" must be like, but right now we must think about "the devil and his angels," those for whom this place is intended, after which we can reflect on what God has intended for human beings.

14. Jn 3:16.

CHAPTER 1

The Fall of Satan

Angelic Nature and Demonic Psychology

The scriptures are clear that devils exist. Christian theology tells us that these are fallen angels, members of the heavenly court who rebelled against God and were therefore cast out of the Divine presence. By nature angels are pure spirits, incorporeal intelligent personal beings upon whom God calls to deliver messages to human beings; the word "angel" comes from the Greek word for "messenger." Foreign and indeed contrary to our contemporary mindset, the concept of spiritual, immaterial beings requires an account.

To understand spiritual being we have to follow St. Augustine's lead and reject sensual and physical images. That is to say, by "spirit" we do not understand some sort of ghostly physical-but-not-quite-physical sort of entity, like a humanoid apparition that one can faintly see but that passes through closed doors. Clarence, in the film *It's a Wonderful Life*, is not really an angel, but a kind of ghost.[1] Augustine warns us that the natural bent of our imaginations to conceptualize spiritual realities in some kind of physical form lay at the root of the errors of Manichaeism; that only when he rejected the implicit physicalism of his notion of the spiritual was he able to understand immaterial being: "I did not know how to love you, for I knew only how to think on gleaming corporeal things."[2] Shortly after this he clarifies: "This was because I had, thus far, no conception of mind, except as a subtle body diffused throughout local spaces."[3] Whatever a spiritual being might be, we err when we conceive of it along the lines of material being. This same kind of error recurs subtly in our discussions of the human self or the soul when conceived as a kind of entity, not quite physical but spatiotemporal, which interacts causally with the body. The common error is to consider spiritual being along the lines of material being, but with some physical properties missing.

We do well to follow Karol Wojtyła's lead as he characterizes the spiritual life precisely in terms of its focus on truth and the good.[4] A spiritual being is one capable of knowing and understanding truth and of loving (or desiring) the good. Since we define any being capable of these acts as a spiritual being, it is clear also that the human being is a spiritual as well as a physical being. The theory of nonmaterial spiritual beings originates not within Christianity, however, but in ancient Greece, spe-

1. *It's a Wonderful Life*, directed by Frank Capra (1946).
2. Augustine, *Confessions*, Book IV, chap. 16.
3. Ibid., Book V, chap. 10.
4. Karol Wojtyła, *Love and Responsibility* (1959), trans. Grzegorz Ignatik (Boston: Pauline Books, 2013), 5. (Wojtyła was elected to the papacy in August 1978 after the death of Pope John Paul I. He was a prolific writer, both before and during his papacy. His pre-papacy writings are listed under "Wojtyła" in the notes and the bibliography; his writings during his papacy are listed under "John Paul II.")

cifically with Aristotle, who in *Metaphysics* XII attributes the governance of the world to nonmaterial intelligences. On the other hand, rather like Plato, we conceive the world to be governed by Forms, which we call invariant laws of nature. If this is so (and I believe that this thesis is thoroughly defensible), then Aristotle's critique of Plato's theory is to the point. "Nothing, then, is gained even if we suppose eternal substances, as the believers in the forms do, unless there is to be in them some principle which can cause change; . . . for if it is not to act, there will be no movement."[5] In other words, even granted the reality of invariant principles or laws governing the world, these are useless to explain unless we grant the existence of some active principle by which the law-governed motion is caused. "Further, then," adds Aristotle, "these substances must be without matter; for they must be eternal, if anything is eternal." As eternal, these substances stand outside of the realm of material change, whose measure is time. How, then, do these substances act, if they are not physical? Proceeding with his analysis of the movement of the heavens, Aristotle writes:

Therefore the first heaven must be eternal. There is therefore also something which moves it. And since that which moves and is moved is intermediate, there is something which moves without being moved, being eternal, substance, and actuality. And the object of desire and the object of thought move in this way; they move without being moved. . . . For the apparent good is the object of appetite, and the real good is the primary object of rational wish. . . . And thought is moved by the object of thought.[6]

Shortly after this text he classifies beauty together with truth and the good, and all three produce movement through

5. Aristotle, *Metaphysics*, trans. W. D. Ross (Chicago and London: Encyclopedia Britannica, 1952), Book XII, chap. 6.
6. Ibid., Book XII, chap. 7.

being loved. Such are nonmaterial substances. They are intelligent beings that move the heavenly spheres and are themselves moved by truth, beauty, and the good that they contemplate in the First Cause, the unmoved mover, which is identical with thought-thinking-itself. Subsequently, Christian thinkers identified these immaterial intelligences with the angels spoken of in the scriptures.

As an entity that can know truth and desire or love the good, a spiritual being is one that operates according to and is governed by ideas. By "idea" we do not mean what Hume wrote of, a mental image or a conscious thought. Rather we mean a principle in virtue of which images, thought, and symbols have meaning.[7] An idea is a principle by which a variety of other realities can constitute a unity. We subsume Fido, Rex, and Rover under the common concept, designated by the term "dog," and Fuffy-T, Cuddles, and Tiger under another, represented by "cat." "Dog" and "cat" are related meaningfully to each other through ideas represented by "mammal," "domestic animal," and "carnivore," among others, and with such concepts we can construct arguments. Concepts or ideas relate meaningfully to each other not according to material relationships but logically, according to the principles of reason.[8] Spirits relate rationally to reality. Human beings, who are embodied spirits, relate rationally while remaining subject also to physical influences and determinants.

It is characteristic of spiritual beings to bring unity, in particular the unity of order, out of multiplicity and disorder (or chaos). A paradigmatic example is the scientist's work as he seeks the laws underlying physical interactions. For example, Isaac Newton showed how the apparently complex and intricate mo-

7. Adrian J. Reimers, *The Soul of the Person* (Washington, D.C.: The Catholic University of America Press, 2006), 76–78.
8. Ibid., 250–59.

tions of the sun, moon, and planets can be accounted for in terms of two equations, one stating the relationship among mass, force, and acceleration and the other showing how the force of gravity between two bodies is determined. Another, and perhaps even better, example is artistic creativity, wherein we find the intelligent mind at work as it combines disparate elements to create something new. Sophocles works the myth of Oedipus into a tragic play contrasting the well-intentioned pride of a great man with the inexorable logic of the obligation to uncover and punish hidden crime. An intelligence, whether embodied as human or angelic, is a source of new ideas as it creates order among disparate realities. Such beings are the angels—free, intelligent beings capable of knowing truth and loving the good. As such, they fashion beauty within the ordered cosmos.

In this context it is helpful further to consider the relationships of the spiritual and the material as they are found in the human being. The common dualist error is to conceive the spiritual as a kind of nonphysical being that somehow occupies a specific organism. This is precisely the model that Gilbert Ryle parodied as the "dogma of the ghost in the machine."[9] However, not only is it unnecessary but it is positively misleading to conceive the spirit as a motive entity within or somehow attached to the organism, moving the organism by its own spiritual power. Rather, all the motive power of the human being, all the forces by which he acts, is physical. Whatever the human being does, be it mental or muscular, is physical. The will is not a kind of immaterial power that sets a body in motion; neither is the intellect a nonphysical center of consciousness that is somehow in touch with the brain. Even our thinking is physical, requiring as it does the activities of neurons whose minute electrical charges are transmitted across

9. Gilbert Ryle, *The Concept of Mind* (New York: Routledge, 1949), xx.

synapses. What makes thinking spiritual is not that it is mental, but rather that it is meaningful, relating to truth and goodness. Playing the violin, serving a tennis ball, making an omelet, and solving Diophantine equations are all spiritual activities. The human soul is not a source of motion separate from the body. Rather it is that which forms the body's actions. It is in virtue of the soul's power to bring the motions of the body into unity that the movements of the violinist's right shoulder, elbow, and wrist unite with those of the left hand's fingers to produce music. The work of the spirit is to form the matter at its disposal according to some ideal. So, just as the human spirit (the soul) forms the actions of the body, so too do the intelligences, or angels, have the power to form and direct material bodies. By this we do not mean that angels are, so to speak, pushing planets and satellites out of their orbits, but that the very laws that govern physical nature have their origin in intelligent beings.

As an intelligent, spiritual being, the devil is by his nature a source of meaning and order, rather as the tyrant's minister of torture plans his dungeons and equipment. Aristotle had no conception of evil incorporeal Intelligences. The Stagirite understood human evil, vice, to result from human weakness. As he understood it, to achieve human excellence it is necessary to control one's behavior by the rational part of the soul so that the desire for pleasure and the fear of pain do not control one's life and behavior.[10] Immaterial intelligences, however, neither experience passions nor fear harm. According to Aristotle's thought, evil as such is not constituted by passion or fear, but by an *unreasonable* passion or fear—or rather a passion or fear that diverts one from his true good. Here we must keep in mind that the angel is outside the realm of physical interactions. Evil is a turning from or against the true good. What

10. Aristotle, *Nicomachean Ethics*, Book I, chap. 7.

Aristotle could not conceive, that of which he had no inkling, was the possibility of a direct personal relationship between the First Cause and other intelligent beings. Satan fell not because of some congenital inner perversity nor from a concupiscent weakness, but because he would not relate reasonably to God's love.

Angelic sin must therefore be of a different sort than human failings, misdeeds resulting from particular choices to steal, kill, commit adultery, and the like. Angelic sin must be completely spiritual, a misconception of the true good, not motivated by bodily passion or fear of loss. Because he is immaterial and not subject to interactions with the material world, he does not experience himself as existing in time; Aquinas speaks of "aeviternity," which, as a mean between time and eternity, has no beginning and allows for neither before nor after.[11] Therefore, Satan cannot make a specific unfortunate choice at a particular point in time. Brutus may, at Cassius's urging, decide to make one with the conspirators, changing at that moment from Caesar's friend to his enemy.[12] Satan's "choice," however, is not in time but aeviternal. As a spirit, the angel is ordered rationally to truth and goodness, and his evil must consist in a perversion of these concepts.

Ultimately the whole of creation finds its origin, plan, and destiny in God, the Author of all truth and the ultimate Exemplar of all goodness,[13] whose essence is beyond all created power to know, no matter how powerful.[14] Therefore, absent the grace of a direct vision of the Divine Essence (such as is granted to the blessed in glory), the created intellect can only know of God that he is but not what he is in himself. Human

11. *ST* Ia, q. 10, a. 5.
12. William Shakespeare, *Julius Caesar*, act 2, scene 1, in *The Complete Works of Shakespeare*, ed. W. J. Craig (New York: Oxford University Press, 1919).
13. *ST* Ia, q. 2. a. 3.
14. *ST* Ia, q. 2, a. 4.

intelligence can and does know about God by the powers of reason: "For what can be known about God is plain to them, because God has shown it to them. Ever since the creation of the world, his invisible nature, namely his eternal power and deity, has been clearly perceived in the things that have been made."[15] This principle is the basis for Aquinas's Five Ways to show God's existence.[16] By his experience of the world and reasoning from fundamental principles, the human being can determine that the whole finds its unity only if there is an Uncaused Cause, a First Mover, an Ultimate Intellect that brought this whole cosmos into being.

St. Thomas argues that the human desire for happiness is at root the desire to know this Being who is the Author of all truth and the Exemplar of all good.[17] Having prepared his argument by citing 1 John 3:2, "When He shall appear, we shall be like to Him; and we shall see Him as He is," Aquinas proceeds to present an argument that at best appears strange to the devout believer seeking an account of his hope. It runs thus: our will (rational desire) remains restless as long as there remains something to desire. Because the highest power of the human soul is the intellect, the human cannot be satisfied so long as his intellect lacks what it desires to understand—namely, the ultimate cause of things. Even though the intellect may know *that* the Ultimate Cause exists, it remains dissatisfied until it knows the essence of this Cause. But the only way that it can know this cause is by direct intellectual vision, which can be attained only by the free gift (or grace) of God himself. That means that our human fulfillment must ultimately consist in an intellectual—and hence spiritual—fulfillment. And indeed the fulfillment of any intellectual being can consist only in this same vision of the Divine Essence.

15. Rom 1:19–20.
16. *ST* Ia, q. 2, a. 3.
17. *ST* Ia-IIae, q. 3, a. 5.

Just like the human being, an angel (or immaterial intelligence) cannot by his own powers attain to the direct knowledge of the Divine Essence. However, his intellect, operating as it does by direct intellectual insight into the natures or essences of things, is immensely more powerful than the human. Therefore, the angelic intellect can grasp the fact that God exists, and it does so with far greater depth and certainty than can a human being. Indeed, such an intellect can attain to a much clearer conception of what can be known of the divine nature. Nevertheless, the angelic intellect does not, by its own power, see God; he cannot know the First Cause of things in its essence, and precisely here is the rub. Satan, who, according to the theological tradition, was the most brilliant and powerful of the intelligences, was constitutively ignorant of the First Cause and ultimate principle of everything. He knew that God exists, that he is one and identical with his own essence and existence, eternal and unchanging, full in his perfection. Whatever the human mind can know of God by philosophical reasoning, the angel knows too. But by his own natural powers the angel does not know God himself. He does not see God. If he is to enjoy the vision of God, which is his true happiness, the angelic being must receive this as a favor from God himself. Like the human being, he must turn to God and ask for this gift to attain to that which surpasses the powers of his nature.[18]

As intelligent personal beings, angels can turn to or away from God, the eternal and perfect good. Satan and the angels who followed him turned away. It is worthwhile to see how St. Thomas Aquinas explains this turning away.

Without doubt the angel sinned by seeking to be as God. But this can be understood in two ways: first, by equality; secondly, by likeness. He could not seek to be as God in the first way [i.e., by equal-

18. *ST* Ia-IIae, q. 5, a. 5 ad 1.

ity].... One may desire to be like unto God in some respect which is not natural to one; as if one were to desire to create heaven and earth, which is proper to God; in which desire there would be sin. It was in this way that the devil desired to be as God.... But he desired resemblance with God in this respect—by desiring, as his last end of beatitude, something which he could attain by the virtue of his own nature, turning his appetite away from supernatural beatitude, which is attained by God's grace. Or, if he desired as his last end that likeness of God which is bestowed by grace, he sought to have it by the power of his own nature; and not from Divine assistance according to God's ordering.[19]

The knowledge that the created intellect, whether human or angelic, has of God is metaphysical; it presupposes a "God's-eye" view of the world. Metaphysical reflection seeks to discover more than the connections and relationships that may exist within the world. It seeks the underlying principles, the causes, of the world as a whole. This is why the discoveries of astronomical cosmology concerning the Big Bang, the development of matter and space-time from the primordial singularity, and the origins and nature of "dark matter" bear only incidentally (at most) on arguments such as those St. Thomas presents in his Five Ways. Like the physicist—but also like the prisoner released from Plato's cave—the metaphysician seeks a kind of "theory of everything." In the human being, a profound understanding of the nature of things can inspire humility. But it can also inspire pride to the point of arrogance (a failing common among us who hold doctoral degrees and are addressed as "Professor"). Satan, who was preeminent for intellect among the angels, grasped the "why" of things, the principles of the created universe, with an unparalleled depth and thoroughness.

19. *ST* Ia, q. 63, a. 3.

Here is the great temptation. To know the First Cause as it is in itself, to know the divine Essence directly, the angelic intellect needs to turn to God himself, to ask this of him and receive his offer of this vision. The angel had to acknowledge his own incapacity to understand the ultimate truth of things. But he could—and did—refrain from this. So powerful was his own vision and understanding of the nature of things that he desired "something which he could attain by the virtue of his own nature, turning his appetite away from supernatural beatitude." Satan was, as it were, so taken with his own power, based on his own profound intellect, that he turned away from the offer to receive the fullness of goodness and understanding from God. He chose to embrace his own wisdom and beauty as the ultimate, rather than God. If we understand this, then we can begin to understand the demonic psychology and the mystery of evil.

Love's Twofold Character

At this point we do well to examine more closely the nature of love and its twofold character as erotic and agapic. On the one hand, all love seeks a kind of union with the object of its love.[20] We may even speak appropriately of a love for steak to the extent that one desires to consume it and is concerned that it be cooked and served properly. On the other hand, love also has the character of a gift, as one goes out toward the beloved for the beloved's own good. Both aspects, desire and gift, are essential for an intellectual being to love.

Only God, who is perfect in his being, is without need. Every living creature needs and desires (even if without knowing it) something that is not itself. Sunflowers need moisture

---

20. Wojtyła, "Thomistic Personalism," in *Person and Community: Selected Essays*, trans. Teresa Sandok, OSM (New York and San Francisco: Peter Lang, 1993), 173.

and the sun. Birds desire the seeds from the sunflower. More to the point, human beings need not only the resources of nature, but also other human beings. This need is not only practical—no one can live long without the help of others, without the helps and resources that others can bring into his life—but also moral, spiritual. To be human one must live in some community. Even to think one needs a language, which is inherited from his forebears. To learn his way around the world, how to understand it and to work in it, one needs others to pass on knowledge and traditions. Even the most individualistic life depends deeply on others, on immediate neighbors and on a cultural heritage. Aristotle tells us that we might want friends for utility, because they can provide us with things and services that we need or want. Certainly there is truth in this. We may also want friends for their pleasantness, to enjoy good times and pleasures with them. The happy person, however, wants friends primarily neither for pleasure nor utility but for virtue, to admire the friend's virtue and to practice virtuous acts with him.[21] In other words, the basis for friendship is not utility or pleasure alone, but is rather some worthy good to which the two direct themselves and each other. Friends help each other to be good, to attain to the authentic good.

Karol Wojtyła develops this point at some length in his analysis of love and its stark difference from utilitarianism.[22] Love exists where two persons unite their minds, affections, and wills under a common good, under some good that transcends them both and that they mutually recognize as a good for both. Essential for such a love is the moment of goodwill (*benevolentia*), the directing of one's will to the other's genuine good. Precisely in this we find both moments, the erotic and the agapic. On the one hand, the lovers desire union with

21. Aristotle, *Nicomachean Ethics*, Book IX, chap. 9.
22. Wojtyła, *Love and Responsibility*, 12–15.

each other, a union that may (in the case of marital love) include physical union, but that will always involve a desire to be together, involved in the same activities, a union of feeling as they enjoy the same things. Lovers and friends find that they are drawn together in part because they feel a *need* for each other. Toward the other each feels that "you are *good* for me." From this proximity and union flow various benefits such as mutual aid, pleasure, enlightenment, encouragement, and simple companionship.

To describe love simply in terms of the desire for union proves to be inadequate because our primary analogate for union is physical. Such a metaphor for the union of persons is too static and indeed simplistic. The union of spiritual beings, such as human persons, is much more complex than a physical joining of bodies or emotional resonance and agreement on activities. Authentic union of spiritual beings is constituted by the union of that which makes them spiritual beings: intellect and will. The two are one in virtue of their embracing the same truth and ordering themselves toward the same good. Let us consider these elements in turn.

Union in Truth

If truth is the agreement of understanding and its object, the correspondence of the intellect and thing,[23] the knowledge of truth actually forms the soul. We often err about this, because we conceive the operation of understanding as a kind of copying or a reception of data such as happens in a camera. We imagine that just as the visual image of an object impresses itself

---

23. Thomas Aquinas, *The Disputed Questions on Truth*, vol. 3, trans. Robert W. Schmidt, SJ (Chicago: Henry Regnery, 1954), q. 1, a. 1; Aquinas, *Commentary on the Gospel of St John*, ed. James A Weisheipl, OP (Toronto: Pontifical Institute of Medieval Studies, 1998), chap. 18, lecture 6, no. 2365.

upon the eye (although this actually misrepresents how visual perception works), the essence or form of the object known is impressed upon the intellect. Rather, what actually happens is that the intellect actively *proceeds outward* toward that which it seeks to understand, experimenting with it and comparing its various aspects with what it already understands in order to come up with a vision or intellectual account of the object's nature and unity. This is why teachers cannot force their pupils to learn, but must instead propose definitions, illustrations, examples, and exercises in the hope that the pupils will come to grasp the concept in question.

To know anything the mind must go out to that thing in order to learn from it, as it were, what its truth is. The logical form of this action is that of hypothesis, as the intelligence tries to make sense of the unknown by comparing it with what is already known. We create mental or imaginary models of the reality under consideration and compare the implied behavior and reactions of those models with what we find experientially. The whale looks like a fish, but it has lungs like a mammal, and this requires the mind to conceive of a kind of mammal different from dogs and bears and antelopes. Until Galileo turned his new telescope on it, the moon was understood to be a very shiny celestial body, made of heavenly matter different from that of earth. Having found mountains and craters on the moon's surface, Galileo realized that he was looking at a body remarkably like the one he was standing on. By such means our knowledge is corrected and our intellectual understanding is refined and purified. We come better to know them as they are.

Integral in this process of gaining knowledge is the role of beauty, which is the mind's grasp of the idea, the principle of unity of a thing as a whole.[24] Perceiving and cognitively grasp-

24. Reimers, *The Soul of the Person*, 79–85.

ing the totality of some thing, the harmony of its parts in relation to the order of the whole, the person is struck with admiration of this harmony. Admiration is the normal human response to beauty. Attracted by beauty, the mind is drawn into further investigation to uncover the sources of that beauty and to grasp more perfectly the beauty at hand. Admiring its beauty, one falls in love with the beautiful object. This may be a person, of course, or an artwork, a piece of music, a machine, or a scientific theory. Sometimes this exploration of beauty may turn out badly. The beautiful theory may turn out to be inadequate and even misleading. A physically beautiful man or woman may turn out to be morally corrupt. The proper and normal effect, however, is that a beauty discovered leads to deeper and richer beauties, and for this reason the mind invests itself in its object, seeking to understand its structure, the various facets of its being and how they interrelate, its behavior and the reasons underlying it.

The work of understanding is an intellectual investment in the object of love as the lover seeks to know the beautiful object of his love "from within." Where another person is concerned—and this is clearly the paradigmatic case of personal love—this project of understanding entails an entering into the beloved's mind, seeking to understand as she understands and to love as he loves. The love that stops short of such an effort is simply the self-indulgent enjoyment of the physical, an enjoyment that eventually degenerates into the admiration of a fantasy rather than love of a person. True union in love requires the investment of one's own mind, his intellect, in the reality that the other is. Because the human person is inexhaustible, this knowledge of the beloved can never be complete. The beloved is an intellectual creature whose own mind is capable of grasping any truth, of understanding reality on its own. Therefore the beloved's mind cannot be fully understood. Indeed, it may be seriously misunderstood. Our knowledge of another person is always and necessarily incomplete.

Union of Wills

Because to love another is to will the authentic good of another, love demands a harmony of will. This is not a matter of simply submitting one's own will to the beloved's, of resigning one's own will to his. Nor can it amount to an insistence that the other conform her will to one's own. The good in virtue of which an authentic union of persons is formed can only be one that transcends both persons and toward which they move together in harmony. Central to this unity is the concept of *common good*. Karol Wojtyła writes that "love between persons is unthinkable without some common good which binds them. This good precisely is the end which both of these persons choose."[25] Indeed, the common good lies at the heart of any communion or community of persons.[26]

It is a fundamental truth that what a person loves forms his life. The love for science or literature, for baseball, for one's country, or for God defines and determines the person's life by shaping his activities and commitments, indeed by shaping his personality. When two persons love the same thing—a common good—that good shapes them together. In sharing this common transcendent good, for which they both strive, they come closer together, each entering as much as possible into the other's mind and heart. The lover *wants* to love what his beloved loves, and in this way the two come to be increasingly part of each other's life and self.

25. Wojtyła, *Love and Responsibility*, 12.
26. Wojtyła, "Thomistic Personalism," 247–50; see also Wojtyła, *Persona e atto*, in *Metafisica della persona: Tutte le opere filosofiche e saggi integrativi*, trans. Giuseppe Girenti and Patricja Mikulska (Milan: Bompiani, 2003), 1191–94.

Regarding this, Karol Wojtyła identifies two attitudes that are essential for authentic participation in any community, including the union constituted by two persons.[27] The first of these is *solidarity*, which, far from being an emotion, is a commitment to the realization of the good for the other, a good to be attained together by common effort. The second attitude, *opposition*, is almost counterintuitive because it implies a resistance to the will of the other, a working-against the friend's or beloved's efforts. It is sometimes necessary, however, when the beloved's acts seem to run counter to the shared goals that define the relationship and in terms of which the two are one. "The attitude of opposition is a function of the vision of the good of the community and also of the living need to participate in the common existence and in particular in common action."[28] Both attitudes and the virtues to which they give rise are founded on the common good for which both parties live and act.

The union of intellects and wills—or, if one prefers, of hearts and minds—is far from being a mere event that happens to two persons. Rather it requires that each proceed creatively and generously toward the other, each contributing from the richness of his own interior life to the other. This inevitably entails a receptiveness and vulnerability toward the other, as well as a courageous strength in holding to the truth, especially the truth about the good. In love there is neither compulsion nor manipulation as the lovers mutually offer each to the other the fruits of their understanding and love of the good. This spiritual dynamic necessarily requires a love that freely gives of itself. In this way erotic love, which desires union, cannot be attained between spiritual beings without agapic love, which gives disinterestedly of self.

27. Wojtyła, *Persona e atto*, 1195–1200.
28. Ibid., 1199.

It is love in this sense that Satan rejected, a love that is incompatible with his decision against seeking God's love.

The Mystery of Evil

At root, the *mystery* of evil is its inexplicability. How and why did Satan choose himself rather than God? We want to know the process by which he abandoned his natural vocation for the sake of pride. Where human beings are concerned we can point to bodily and environmental processes, to some form of concupiscence—perhaps the urging of the sexual faculties—and to some source of temptation—perhaps a sexually desirable and willing coworker—and we can understand how an incautious word or gesture, a protracted moment of contact, a couple of drinks after work all lead to the adulterous liaison. We may even find an explanation for the wrongdoing, although upon further reflection we recognize that our explanation is not complete. With an angelic being such an account is impossible. He has no body, no physical desires to distract him. Indeed, to arrive at truths he does not even have to *think*. There is no mental process that he goes through; angels have no brains. He does not have to pass through various stages of reasoning and examine their logic. His understanding, his grasp of truth, takes place outside of time. Therefore we cannot properly speak of Satan's having been innocent at one moment and fallen in the next. His choice, his decision, is atemporal and inexplicable in terms of temporal causes or relationships.

This atemporality becomes clearer when we consider that the spiritual being's relationship with the good is not physical. Many goods, such as food to a hungry man, may be physical, but the relationship between good as such and desire is not material or physical. For a variety of reasons medical, religious, ascetical, a man may determine that in a particular circumstance food is not good, hunger notwithstanding. Physical or material goods are such only within the context of a particular physical situation of causal interactions. For the rational being, good must satisfy the rational appetite. It must admit of recognition by the intellect as something perfect and perfecting. As Plato intuited in his allegory of the cave, the good is the eternal principle in virtue of which all other things may be in some way good and be recognized by the rational being as such.[29] Concerning any good thing, the rational being can (and often does) ask, "But is it really good?" and "In virtue of what or in what respect is it good?," two questions that of themselves presuppose a transcendent and atemporal standard of good. This principle is recognized and in play whenever a person, whether human or angelic, determines that *this* is good. Satan's decision not to turn to the mysterious God whose mind (or essence) he could not penetrate entailed that he must locate this standard of good within his own intellect, in himself. We who try to think of this with time-bound human minds might call this an instantaneous decision; more accurately, it is a decision outside of time. It has to be, because there are no material factors involved in it. As we shall see, this truth about angelic evil becomes important for understanding human wickedness.

God's Rival

God is the Supreme Being, the Creator, who in virtue of his absolute supremacy deserves our worship and love. St. Thomas Aquinas tells us that we cannot even conceive what God is like, that on their own our minds are incapable of devising an image or a concept of God.[30] This is no doubt why the ancient Hebrews believed that no one can see God and live,[31] and why

29. Plato, *Republic*, Book VII, 514a–17c.
30. *ST* Ia, q. 3, Prologue.
31. Ex 33:20.

St. Paul tells us of God that he "dwells in unapproachable light, whom no man has seen or can see."[32] God is truly awesome, overpoweringly so. And yet, as Dismas can attest, he welcomes whoever seeks his mercy. The almighty and all-powerful God is pleased with any response of love we give to him. Let us recall the surprise of those on the King's right in the final judgment. "When did we see you hungry and give you to eat?" If you give even a glass of water to one of those who belong to Christ, you will receive your reward (see Mt 10:42). In one sense, God has no pride and very low standards. He will do anything—to the point of becoming one of us and letting us torture him to death—and will welcome almost any positive response, even a last-minute "Jesus, remember me." And this marvelous Being wants to share his glorious life with us.

The fall of those angels who followed Satan is the direct consequence of their refusal to turn to God for his love. Entranced by their own magnificence and beauty, as it were, they chose to rely on their resources rather than on God's offer of his life and love. As a result, Satan and his minions must rely on their own inner resources to understand and to guide their acts. Because only God, who as the Creator of all things knows all things, fully understands the structure of reality, Satan's understanding of creation—however great it may be—is necessarily incomplete and imperfect. He may well know more than any human being can—indeed, he certainly does—and by this impress the mind of any who should follow him, but his limited knowledge is, in virtue of its limitation, based on a flawed understanding. Furthermore, having rejected the love of God, the devil has no grasp of authentic goodness. The only good he can know is the good that he conceives. For Satan, he himself is the good, and everything else is good to the extent that it serves

32. I Tm 6:16.

his will. His followers can conceive goodness only in terms of themselves.

The highest good, whatever it may be, is what deserves admiration and obedience. The highest good must be most perfectly formed, as it were, harmonious and bright, hence attractive, and as such deserves admiration of rational beings, who are capable of admiring beauty. Indeed, we do not really choose to admire beauty; rather, beauty elicits admiration. Whatever is good in any respect is, in that respect, desirable.[33] The will, or rational appetite, is rightly ordered, therefore, whenever it is ordered to the true good. This is why the fundamental moral responsibility of every rational being, including human persons, is to seek out and pursue the highest good. By rejecting God's offer of his love for himself, Satan has, as it were, supplanted God in his own mind and will, finding his own beauty to be most admirable and not a reflection of a higher beauty. Furthermore, having rejected the highest good, which is God himself, Satan has no option but to regard himself as the highest good, whose satisfaction is the obligation of every other being. From this it follows that Satan and his minions can find no other order than that constituted by their own rebellion. Among themselves they are ruled by Satan and collectively constitute an association of self-admiration, subjected in everything to the most magnificent of their kind, to whose will the highest honor and obedience must be given. And regarding human beings, the only possible role they can play in Satan's realm is in subservience to the demons. They must worship and serve the devils to whom they have turned rather than God. To the satanic mind they deserve no further reward.

Scripture says that Satan is a liar and a murderer from the

33. *ST* Ia, q. 6, a. 1; Aquinas, *The Disputed Questions on Truth* (henceforth *De veritate*), vol. 1, ed. Robert W. Mulligan, SJ (Chicago: Henry Regnery, 1952), q.1, a. 1.

beginning.[34] He is opposed to the truth and to life itself. Furthermore, he resents God and his prerogatives. The Prophet Isaiah satirized the death of the king of Babylon, and the church fathers have seen in this satire a revelation of Satan's character.

How you are fallen from heaven, O Day Star,[35] son of Dawn!... You said in your heart, "I will ascend to heaven; above the stars of God I will set my throne on high.... I will ascend above the heights of clouds; I will make myself like the Most High." But you are brought down to Sheol, to the depths of the Pit.[36]

According to this text, the satanic wish is to outdo God, to supplant him. Satan envies God. He will rival God, but his way of "being god" is very different from God's. If God is the Creator and giver of life, Satan claims to be master of life. Since, unlike God, he cannot give life, he exercises his mastery by taking life. He is a "murderer from the beginning."[37]

God is the Author of all truth, because all things were created according to his eternal Word.[38] Satan has no power to create according to his own plans, so instead he lies. He creates an imaginary world according to his laws and tempts us to believe it. "You will not die!"[39] In fact, to those under his power he *insists* that they repeat and hold fast to his lies. The totalitarian tyrant who demands that his people be indoctrinated in *his* "truth" and who insulates them from any other source of information is a true disciple of the satanic father.[40]

God is the highest good, full of mercy and love for those who seek him. Satan sets himself up as the standard of good

---

34. Jn 8:44.
35. Or "Lucifer."
36. Is 14:12–15.
37. Jn 8:44.
38. Jn 1:3.
39. Gn 3:4.
40. Václav Havel, "The Power of the Powerless," in *The Power of the Powerless*, ed. John Keane (Armonk, N.Y.: M. E. Sharpe, 1985), 23–96, and Havel, "Dear Dr. Husák," in *Open Letters: Selected Prose, 1965–1990* (New York: Alfred A Knopf, 1991), 72.

and threatens those who do not obey him. Here is a subtle but important point. If we ask, "Why should I love God?" the answer is that God is so very *good*. God by his very nature is beautiful, admirable, and lovable. To know him really is to love him. Satan wants that love. In fact he *demands* that love, primarily in the form of obedience. The devil offers good things—wealth, fame, pleasure, glory—while hiding his evil will. The satanic demand is for an obedience that mimics love. (Here we may think of the overwhelming margins of victory by tyrants in "free" elections. Saddam Hussein regularly gained at least 99 percent of the popular vote, so much was he "loved.") The closer one gets to God the more lovable he seems to be, as the testimony of his greatest lovers among the saints and martyrs makes so clear—"For me to live is Christ and to die is gain."[41] Satan wants the adulation God receives but without God's attractiveness, and so when he has lured a soul into his company, he must crack the whip, as it were, to keep that person in line. The first taste of his fruit may be sweet, but afterward there is the constant demand to meet his expectations, as one never again tastes the sweetness that was once promised.

Psychology of Satan

The nature of demonic evil opens the door to understanding demonic psychology. In the Book of Wisdom we read, "Through the devil's envy death entered the world, and those who belong to his party experience it."[42] He understood everything, and if not everything in all its depth and richness, then as well (at least) as any other angel possibly could. His intellect, which was itself capable of forming worlds and systems, of teaching other intellectual creatures,[43] was, albeit by his own choice, denied the

---

41. Phil 1:21.   42. Ws 2:24.

43. We will turn to this subject of one intellect's power to illuminate another later.

vision of the Ground of the understanding he had. There was (so he could have understood) a level of understanding deeper even than his, a level not to be attained by superior intelligence, but simply by asking God for it, by submitting himself to the order of the Creator. This *gift* of immediate vision of the Divine Essence was not to be a reward to his superiority, for the greatness of his understanding, but a simple gift to be received. Lesser beings than he had gained that vision of God, which was denied him, simply by their asking. His own glory was relativized to insignificance by a glory that others enjoyed but of which he had only secondhand awareness. Envy came naturally to Satan as the logical and inevitable consequence of the nature of his sin.

From his envy flows hatred. Excluded from divine intimacy and glory, Satan *needs* to rule. He craves admirers and seeks disciples of his magnificent intellect. As a principle of order, intelligence naturally seeks to communicate itself. That is, every intellect is creative, originating ideas, integrating them, and directing other things according to them. If Aristotle's analysis is right, then the respective orders of the heavens derive not directly from the First Cause but from the lower intelligences. On the earthly level, the Bible locates the work of some angels in a kind of governance of nations,[44] and the gospel suggests that he has a significant influence on the relationships among nations.[45] The "prince of Persia" referred to in Daniel 10 is presumably a fallen angel that oversees that particular land, forming its ethos and influencing its governance. This impulse to rule is implicitly required by the angelic intellect. It is of the very nature of intellect to bring order out of chaos, unity out of multiplicity. Spiritual beings work directly with ideas, and the essence of an idea is to be a principle of unity and order. In the countryside we recognize the presence of human beings by

44. Dn 10: 13, 20.
45. Mt 4:8–9; Lk 4:5–7.

the regular rows of corn, well-defined fields, animals in pens, and so on. Similarly, the angel seeks to impose unity and order according to his understanding.

An angel's intellectual operation is difficult for us to understand. The angel is not a motive power within the physical universe, as though besides the workings of gravity, electromagnetic fields, and physical impact, there are spiritual entities that push material things around. Rather, the angelic beings must work by imposing form on material things. Addressing the question of angelic governance, St. Thomas writes:

> It is generally found both in human affairs and in natural things that every particular power is governed and ruled by the universal power; as, for example, the bailiff's power is governed by the power of the king.... Now it is manifest that the power of any individual body is more particular than the power of any spiritual substance; for every corporeal form is a form individualized by matter, and determined to the "here and now"; whereas immaterial forms are absolute and intelligible. Therefore, ... so are all corporeal things ruled by the angels.[46]

Just as the human soul informs the physical behavior of the human being, so can the angel inform the behavior of some corporeal thing, superseding, as it were, the existing form of that thing. How this angelic behavior relates to the physical universe is a topic for another time and place. What is pertinent to our study is the influence that the angelic being can have on the human being by his power to rule over material aspects of the human organism. The human mind works through a physical organ, the brain (or perhaps the brain and nervous system), whose thoughts develop discursively through phantasms (mental likenesses of experienced things), which correspond to specific events in the brain. Whenever the mind thinks, the brain is in action, and whenever the brain is in action, there is mental ac-

46. *ST* Ia, q. 110, a. 1.

tivity. Whenever we feel something or think, call to mind past events, recall sense or emotional experiences, decide upon something, or even "let our minds wander," the neurons of the brain are in motion, transmitting signals among the various sectors of that organ. And whenever neurons in the appropriate parts of the brain fire, even without our willing it, thoughts pass through the mind. This seems to be what happens in one way when we dream and in another when we experience an "earworm," a song that keeps running through the mind. The activities of the mind, and hence the events in the brain, can be and often are formed by the intellect as we control and discipline our thoughts according to the laws of reason and understanding we have of the truth. What St. Thomas's text indicates, however, is that another spirit can also influence the signaling networks and mechanisms of the brain according to its own conceptions. Teachers do this when they repeat lessons to their pupils and require them to memorize, say, the Gettysburg Address in order to improve their understanding of Lincoln's presidency. An evil spirit can do much the same as this, but from within, molding, as it were, the random thoughts of the imagination into a lesson or understanding that he wants to impart. This is what we call "temptation." Strictly speaking, the spirit does not gain control of the intellect and will, but by influencing the activities of the brain he powerfully proposes his own ideas, understanding, and desires.

Why does the spirit do this? The reasons are twofold. First, it is natural to any intelligence to create order—by its own power of understanding to bring order into things. There is a natural order rooted in the wisdom of the Creator that the created mind—be it human or angelic—can grasp to a greater or lesser extent. In doing so, it becomes a kind of co-creator.[47] Satan has this same impulse or innate desire. As an intellectual being, his

47. Wojtyła, "Thomistic Personalism," 171.

natural inclination is to understand and apply that understanding. A realm that is particularly susceptible to his operation is that of intellectual creatures—in particular, human beings. Through his power to influence the formation of human knowledge and understanding, he can try to induce humans into participating in a realm or world of his own design. Hence it follows that Satan has his own regime, which rivals God's. He offers an alternative to the divine order, which for his part he seeks to subvert and destroy. In a way, Satan envies God his divinity and makes it his business to supplant the Creator as God.

With a necessity that follows logically from the foregoing, Satan's attitude necessarily stands opposed to God's love. If the intimacy implicit in the beatific vision of the Divine Essence is absolutely beyond the natural powers of any created intellect, then such an intellect—be it angelic or human—attains to this vision only if God grants it as a gift. But the gift is an act of love. In the fullness of his perfection, his utter actuality, God does not need other beings to admire, appreciate, or assist him. Whatever God gives, whether to angels or to human beings, he gives completely freely. God gives himself in love to any intellectual creature who will but turn to him. There is no other way to make sense of God's creation and interaction with intelligent beings. (Recall that for Aristotle, the First Cause can have no such interaction with lower beings. All they can do is to admire it from a distance, as it were.) For his part, Satan does not stand in such a relationship with other rational beings. He must give what a god can give, to be sure, but neither to the degree nor with the freedom with which God gives it. Having rejected the order of the gift—he did this by his refusal of the gift offered him—he is himself incapable of giving freely. His intelligent disciples must submit to him in his rejection of God. Any angel may lead another angel or a human being toward some ideal, but the demon cannot situate that ideal in relation to

God. Satan (as well as his angelic followers, of course) insists on loyal followers. He cannot be a helper for others in their search for God, nor can he brook any rivals. In particular, his demonic mind cannot abide another mind's allegiance to God. Every other intelligence, to the extent that Satan can affect it, must be turned away from its Creator, from the source of all goodness and truth. Hence he truly is a "liar from the beginning."[48]

The Fires of Hell

As nonphysical, immaterial beings, the devil and his angels have no senses and are therefore incapable of physical suffering. Fire may cause a human being or any other animal extreme agony, but it will not bother an angel. Whatever sufferings they undergo must be of a very different sort. From what we have already said, the explanation for angelic suffering is clear. Satan lives in and by hatred. He suffers from the lack of love. Paradoxically, in his theology of the body St. John Paul II offers us the key to understanding this. In his discussion of concupiscence, he notes that "the man *whose will is occupied with satisfying the senses* does not find rest nor does he find himself, but on the contrary '*consumes himself*.'"[49] The desire of the man for the woman and hers for him becomes insatiable because the satisfaction of the flesh does not even approach satisfying the spiritual desire for loving communion.[50] How does this tell us anything about a purely spiritual being? Material and sense desires are satiable. Animals in their natural state do not become obese (an overfed and pampered dog might, because he is bored and not properly provided for). The glutton or drunkard, the sexually promiscuous person is using sensible stimuli to meet a spiritual need. The advantage

---

48. Jn 8:44.

49. John Paul II, *Man and Woman He Created Them: A Theology of the Body*, ed. and trans. Michael Waldstein (Boston: Pauline Books and Media, 2006), 284.

50. Ibid., 252–54.

of sensual satisfactions is that they offer immediate gratification that is recognized as such. An ignorant person will have to study and learn for some time before realizing the satisfaction of having gained understanding. Similarly, it is not always immediately evident how much one may be loved by another. But sweet foods or those high in fat give immediate satisfaction. How often do the lonely resort to sexual activity to hide their sorrow at being unloved? Sensual excess expresses a spiritual dearth.

Purely spiritual beings experience their spiritual pain much more keenly than do we embodied spirits. The "fire" that pains them is the insatiability of their desires, of their will for what is truly good. To understand this better we must consider what love is. St. Thomas Aquinas tells us that love is the desire for union with that which is loved.[51] If I love pizza, I want to eat it. If I love my friend I want not only to be with him, but to talk and work and play with him. The love of husband and wife is realized in a complete sharing of life in the mutual gift of self, one to the other. The love of the spiritual being for God is the desire for union with him, a union that takes the form of a beatific vision. This spiritual vision is realized by God's informing the intellect. That is, if the spirit "sees" by understanding, by conforming itself to that which he knows—Aristotle said that "the mind is, in a way, all things"—then the spiritual being, whether human or angelic, sees God by being conformed to God. The Eastern Christians, the Orthodox and Greek Catholics, speak of divinization. The love of God is realized and fulfilled by the mind's direct possession of God, or better, by God's direct possession of the mind.

Satan—and this applies to all who have followed him— wants to love God, in a way. He wants to understand God fully and know him completely, but on his own terms, so that he

51. *ST* Ia, q. 60, a. 4.

can, as it were, say to himself, "There I have figured out this much more about God. Soon I will know the First Cause of everything and will have done so *on my own terms*." Were he to do this, then he would necessarily be equal to God. But he cannot do this. God is not commensurable with the created mind, not even the highest of angelic minds. And so Satan is in constant dissatisfaction, in fundamental and irremediable frustration. His desire for God (hence, his love), which is greater than any other desire because it is fundamental to all other desires, is constitutively frustrated. He is spiritually restless to the depths of his being. The restless human being, because he has a body, can at least distract himself from his spiritual disquiet, but Satan's being is transparent to himself. And these profound and thorough spiritual frustrations and restlessness constitute a raging inner fire that he cannot escape.

"The Place Prepared ..."

We can now draw a significant, indeed fundamental, conclusion. When the King consigns the damned to their destiny, it is to this place prepared for the devil and his angels, which is to the company of those who have rejected God, both angels and humans. Having turned from the offer of mercy and salvation, which is eternal communion with God, they have no option but to enter the society of Satan and those who have embraced his rebellion and refusal of God's offer. The fires of hell, then, are not an inferno created and stoked by a vengeful God to punish those with whom he is angry but a state of torment that arises on one side from the inner hunger of the damned for the love of God and on the other from the contempt of the envious one whom they have followed.

At this point it is fitting to turn to the question of Satan's interaction with the human race and to our own sinfulness. We now consider the evil that men do.

CHAPTER 2

Original Sin and the Fall

At the beginning of the human race, the devil insinuated himself into human thinking and understanding. As he spoke to
the woman in the garden, his appearance was reptilian but his
personality and actions, demonic.[1] If we look not at his anato-
my but at his character, we see clearly the enemy of God and
of humanity. The man and the woman were happily settled in
the garden, in a created world that God had made to be "very
good."[2] They had a pleasant, abundant land to live and work in.
They had each other in an untroubled mutual love: "And the
man and his wife were both naked, and were not ashamed."[3]

---

1. Gn 3:1–5.   2. Ibid., 1:31.
3. Ibid., 2:25.

And they knew that God had given them but one command: they were not to eat of the tree of the knowledge of good and evil, lest they die.

Precisely in this situation, the serpent speaks to the woman, suggesting to her that God was deceitful. "You will not die. For God knows that when you eat of [the tree] your eyes will be opened, and you will be like God, knowing good and evil."[4] This is not a temptation of the flesh, a suggestion that here was delectable fruit of unsurpassed sweetness. Eve had no concupiscence, no weakness of the flesh to lead her astray. Satan's appeal was to her pride. The serpent was challenging God himself by questioning God's truthfulness, his power, and his goodness:

God's truthfulness: God had told the man that if he were to eat the fruit of that tree, he would die.[5] In their dealings with him to that point, the man and the woman had never had reason to question God, because he had given them nothing but good. The serpent, however, insinuates that God had lied and that he relies on lying threats to keep his creatures in line.

God's power: When the serpent appeals to envy—"your eyes will be opened, and you will be like God"—he implies that God is deceiving them in order to protect his own prerogatives. If these two human beings will but eat the fruit, then they can have some of the power that God keeps to himself.

God's goodness: Here is the most wicked part of the serpent's words. He brings God down to his own level, as if to say, "God is like the rest of us. He plays things to his own advantage. When it comes down to it, God looks after God. *You* have to look after yourself, because if you don't then no one else will." Concerning this, St. John Paul II writes:

4. Ibid., 3:4–5.
5. Ibid., 2:17.

This is the dimension of sin that we find in the witness concerning the beginning, commented on in the Book of Genesis.... According to the witness concerning the beginning, sin in its original reality takes place in man's will—and conscience—first of all as "disobedience"— that is, as opposition of the will of man to the will of God. This original disobedience presupposes a rejection, or at least a turning away from the truth contained in the word of God, who creates the world. This Word is the same Word who was "in the beginning with God," who "was God," and without whom "nothing has been made of all that is," since "the world was made through him." He is the Word who is also the eternal law, the source of every law that regulates the world and especially human acts.[6]

The lesson of Genesis about the origins of human sin is this: a spiritual agent, the devil, planted suspicions about God's goodness, truthfulness, and power into the minds and hearts of the first human beings, and they believed it. Jesus calls him a "murderer from the beginning" and the "father of lies,"[7] and throughout his ministry he fights against Satan. In Jesus, God intends to undo what Satan plotted to ruin. As Jesus was about to begin his public ministry, Satan tempts him,[8] and the plot to kill Jesus is, in the final analysis, coordinated by Satan.[9] Preaching to the first gentile convert to Christianity, St. Peter said, "Jesus went about doing good and curing all who had fallen into the power of the devil."[10] Jesus' ministry is to undo the work of Satan.

Granted that the serpent was a mythical feature of the biblical narrative, his personality is real. We can *recognize* him. Even if the first human beings appeared in southern Africa 100,000

6. John Paul II, Encyclical *Dominum et vivificantem* (Vatican City: Libreria Editrice Vaticana, 1986), 33.

7. Jn 8:44.

8. Mt 4:1–11; Mk 1:12–13; Lk 4:1–13.

9. Lk 22:3; Jn 13:2, 13:27, 14:30.

10. Acts 10:38.

years ago and even if the first woman never met a talking snake, a new and insidious point of view was planted and took root in her mind and that of her husband, an attitude that put "me first," that decided not to trust the good God who had made the earth and provided abundantly for them, that would not submit even to the Creator of all things. The first human couple had no reason to believe the demonic temptation. Their own experience of God's love and generosity had been good. Life was good, and they had much to be grateful for. These suspicions came from someplace else.

This kind of temptation is common in human experience. In Shakespeare's *Othello*, the general and war hero Othello enjoys the faithful love of his beautiful bride, Desdemona. By the end of the play, he has strangled her out of jealousy, not because of anything she had done but because Othello's aide, Iago, had persistently planted suspicions, twisting words and manipulating situations to make it appear that Desdemona was unfaithful. And so, rather than to believe his own eyes and experience of his wife's goodness, Othello believed the scenario suggested by Iago's machinations, turning murderously against his wife. Shakespeare's story is fiction, of course, but such suspicion is a common enough experience. We might know and like—maybe love—someone, but we hear suspicions and innuendos, and then we are not so sure. If the suspicion is encouraged and allowed to ripen, then in time a friendship is ruptured. Desdemona never hurt Othello. But the seed was planted and the suspicion—suspicion about truth and goodness—grew. While Iago's plot was unfolding, the lies all made sense. Only when the relationship is destroyed do we see how we have been duped. It is the work of wickedness, a destructive hatred of the truth and the true good. What Shakespeare describes has been true of human sin from the very start. Envying Othello's glory and the love he enjoyed, Iago plotted to undermine his commander and ruin him. So it is with Satan. The Book of Wisdom makes the tempter's motivations clear:

God created man for incorruption, and made him in the image of his own eternity, but through the devil's envy death entered the world, and those who belong to his party experience it.[11]

That God should love these material beings, with bodies like the animals and intelligence far inferior to his own, was intolerable to a brilliant spirit like Satan. He resented it that God should favor them with his company. Envying God's glory and his love for humanity, Satan plotted to undermine the first couple and ruin them.

The Intolerable Human Will

Because of their free will, human beings are an intolerable offense to Satan and his angels. Angels (and Satan himself is an angelic being) are phenomenally intelligent beings. They have an instant "see-it-and-know-it" kind of intelligence. If we humans are to come to know something, we must work hard—practicing and studying books and doing problems at the end of the chapter, running experiments, practicing again, and finally after much work we understand. Angels grasp things immediately so that just to see something is to know it. The citizens of hell are therefore much smarter and more intelligent than the human beings who will be condemned there. To be a devil is to understand things very well. What a human being thinks counts for nothing. And this brings us to what makes the human being so offensive to the devils. These inferior beings, who come nowhere near the intelligence of any ordinary devil, have *free will*. They can make up their own minds on

11. Ws 2:23–24.

things and decide for themselves what to do. For Satan this is simply intolerable.

To God's mind, free will is essential. "Only in freedom can human beings direct themselves toward goodness."[12] Only a free being can respond to God's love by loving in return. (This is something galling to Satan. He spent all his freedom, as it were, in his rebellion against God. His mind is set, and he cannot change it.) We sometimes think that God gave us free will just to see if we would pass his tests and qualify for heaven, but this is not so. The reason for free will is that only a free being can love.[13] Only a free being can turn to God's goodness. Love is meant to be a gift, and what is forced is not a gift. God put himself in the vulnerable position of awaiting our gift of ourselves back to him. He will lead us to him by giving us good things and warn us of the evils that result when we turn away from him. But he does not force our love.

The vanity of Satan cannot allow itself to wait for the free gift. He sees homage and obedience as things that are owed him. For a human being to assert his freedom in the face of Satan's greatness, intelligence, and power is intolerable. Here is a common enough earthly example. During the times of William Wallace, Scotland's "Braveheart," many Scottish nobles opposed England's King Edward I, "Longshanks," and his dominion over Scotland. Some of them even betrayed him, but Longshanks could tolerate them. He knew that by using a callous but crafty "carrot and stick" approach with most nobles, he could attack their land and castles, then buy them off and keep them in fear of him in the future. But Wallace was different. He could not be threatened or bought off. He had his own principles, and the one thing he wanted was freedom for

---

12. Second Vatican Council, *Gaudium et spes*, §17.
13. Wojtyła, *Love and Responsibility*, 117.

Scotland. And this kind of principled defiance was intolerable to Longshanks. This Scots noble dared to defy the king's authority, grandeur, and power on the basis of his own principles, his assertion of his own inner freedom, and in defense of the freedom of others. And so not only did Edward I seek Braveheart's death, but that death had to be as painful and humiliating as possible.[14] Similarly, the laws in the antebellum Southern American states forbade teaching black slaves how to read and write. A literate slave would be punished severely and quite possibly killed, because to be educated is to become equal to the white man. It was a dangerous thing in those times and in the Jim Crow era following the emancipation for a black man to assert his own freedom.

Temptation

If there was no talking serpent, how did the devil do this? To understand evil, we must understand how angels, including demons, work on and in our minds. We must beware of a simplistic conception here, the kind often represented by the little devil sitting on the left shoulder as a good angel sits on the right, each whispering advice into an ear. The serpent in the biblical narrative speaks words that Eve can hear, and she in turn speaks words that her husband can hear. But what made this temptation come alive? Even if in the actual event there was no snake—we may recognize this element of the story as mythical[15]—and therefore no sensible voice, the woman was tempted. Whether an audible voice is heard or not, the spiritual problem remains. How does one spirit influence another? How does a pure spirit (such as an angel) influence an ensouled

14. D. J. Gray, *William Wallace: The King's Enemy* (New York: Barnes and Noble, 1991), 133, 150–53.
15. John Paul II, *Man and Woman He Created Them*, 138 (3:1); 157 (8:2).

bodily being? For an answer we turn to Thomas Aquinas's account of the human intellect.

The intellect, the power of understanding, is a power of the soul in each individual. (It is not, as the Arabian philosopher Averroes argued, a superior power from without that affects individual souls.)[16] However, comparing the intellectual power with the power of sight, the human intellect needs a kind of light if it is to perform its work. This light is from above, from some higher being. Aquinas argues that "we must needs suppose a superior intellect, from which the soul acquires the power of understanding" (supra animam intellectivam humanam necesse est ponere aliquem superiorem intellectum, a quo anima virtutem intelligendi obtineat).[17] The human soul "is called intellectual by reason of a participation in intellectual power; a sign of which is that it is not wholly intellectual but only in part."[18] Therefore it is necessary that there be some higher intellect by which the soul is helped to understand, an act by which the soul abstracts universal forms from particular conditions. The separate intellect, by which the soul is illuminated, is the creator of the soul, which is God himself. In relation to this, Thomas and the ancient fathers quote the scriptural text: "The true light that enlightens every man was coming into the world."[19]

To understand things the human mind has to abstract the forms of things around him to acquire intellectual concepts by which these things can be known. Looking at Rover, Fido, and Rex, the human thinker forms the concept "dog," and with this he is able to think and talk about dogs, as well as to

16. Ralph McInerny, *Aquinas against the Averroists: On There Being Only One Intellect* (West Lafayette, Ind.: Purdue University Press, 1993), 29, 35, 45, 147, and in passing.

17. *ST* Ia, q. 79, a. 4.   18. Ibid.

19. Jn 1:9.

act intelligently regarding dogs in general. This is, of course, not an infallible process, as we know well from experience. A child may confuse wolves with dogs, and adults long confused whales with fishes. This work of abstraction is the process of discerning the interpretive unity among singulars by which they can be understood in themselves and in relation to other things. It is, by way of analogy, a matter of putting on the mind of the Maker, to discern what his plan has been, what his intention for this being may be, analogous with the thinking that anthropologists carry out when trying to make sense of some artifact whose design is unusual and purpose not immediately evident. To abstract is to discern the principle of unity underlying certain phenomena or experiences. The scientist applies rigorous rules for abstracting as he designs experiments that will isolate only what he expects to be the relevant factors for measurement. If abstraction is the mental act by which the form of the thing is discerned and recognized, then the fruit of abstraction is the application of a common term to individuals and the relating of that term meaningfully to other terms.

Things in the environment are not the only realities regarding which we abstract forms. An essential aspect of understanding another person's communications is this selfsame process. For a simple example: both Plato and David Hume speak of ideas, but after having grasped, for instance, Plato's *Republic* or *Phaedo*, when we try to understand Hume's writings we find him unintelligible until we realize that his conception of ideas is radically different from Plato's. How do we know? We find that this word token, "idea," plays a different logical role in the writings of the two thinkers. Similarly, we may discover that Aristotle and John Stuart Mill mean different things by the word "happiness." If I try to read Mill's definition of the term back into the *Nicomachean Ethics*, then Aristotle's thoughts no longer make sense. In other words, the process of interpreting another's language utterances is essentially the same as that of interpreting the world about the individual. In order to understand another person we abstract forms (or concepts) from what we read or hear. As with the process of interpreting the world about us, this process is not infallible; we can misunderstand. For this reason, teaching is never the simple imparting of understanding directly from one mind to another.

The key to the act of abstracting lies in the principles by which one discerns the forms of things. What interpretive or hermeneutic rules does one apply? For a simple example: a marketing professional maintains "nothing happens until somebody sells something."[20] The marketer provides a series of examples, after which he deftly dismisses his audience's counterexamples by showing how, even where we least expect it, a sales transaction is at work. This slogan, "nothing happens until somebody sells something," becomes an interpretive key for all human interactions. The marketer proposes and argues that through the lens of *sales* we can interpret and understand our neighbor's and our own behavior. This paradigm is proposed as the interior intellectual principle for abstracting concepts, a kind of intellectual "light." Indeed, the study of philosophy itself involves a kind of search for intellectual lights, whether these be Aristotle's four causes, Aquinas's notion of participation, or Hume's reduction of experience to sensation and the memories of sensations. I maintain that these principles are proposed whenever one intellect influences another. Among human beings, this is paradigmatically seen in the case of the teacher's influence upon his students. However, angelic beings can also propose interpretive principles. When a demonic being does so, this is a temptation.[21]

20. It is worthwhile simply to Google this phrase to see how important it is in the realm of marketing.
21. *ST*, Ia, q. III, aa. I and 3.

Discerning the Good

The moral task of the human being is to determine which acts are those that will realize his true good. For this, it is necessary to have a clear conception of the good. One of the conceits of modern thought is that "good" is without meaning; that to know the objective realm—and this is the realm known by science—*good* plays no role. All we have are facts and relationships determined by invariant scientific laws.[22] In truth, however, the concept "good" is essential and inevitable to human beings. The proof of this is simply that we want things and know that we want them. Whatever one wants constitutes value, or apparent good, for him. Not only does he desire that thing, but he is capable of knowing that he desires it. The infant desires milk and soon enough learns that mother's breast will satisfy his want. We say then that every object of every desire constitutes a value and can be recognized as good. It is well known, however, that not everything that a person desires is actually good. More specifically, the satisfaction of the senses does not adequately satisfy the requirements of the true good for the human being.[23] As Aristotle shows in his *Nicomachean Ethics*, to attain his proper excellence (or virtue) the human being needs to act in accordance with reason, restraining his appetites and temper. Unlike the nonrational animals, the human being cannot trust his sense appetites to lead him infallibly to his appropriate good.[24] The good for the human being has to be known and understood by reason. Therefore, *good* is a spiritual category linked with the intellect. Because the authentic good for the human being can be known only with reason's discernment and not by sense alone, the human being is morally responsible.

22. Adrian J Reimers, *The Truth about the Good: Moral Norms in the Thought of John Paul II* (Ave Maria, Fla.: Sapientia Press, 2011), 24–27, 49–84.
23. Aristotle, *Nicomachean Ethics*, Book I, chap. 7, 1098a1–b17; chap. 8, 1098b6 ff.
24. *Love and Responsibility*, 89–90.

When the teenager whines that "I didn't know," his mother responds, "Well, you should have *thought* about it before you acted."

Because human knowledge is not infallible, the judgment on which the moral good is discerned may err. Different persons, judging according to different facts and different criteria, may evaluate specific choices differently. This need not entail that the good is not to be known. Indeed, if the good truly cannot be known, then it makes no difference how one acts. The abiding human conviction, however, has been that the good can be known, perhaps imperfectly to all and but vaguely to some. Nevertheless, human beings can confidently know the most fundamental truths about the good. Precisely here is the knowledge of God pertinent. Imperfect as our knowledge of God may be, we can know that God is good. Indeed, careful reflection reveals that God is *the* good, that he is goodness itself.[25] From this it follows that it is ultimately in relation to God that the good is known and further that the one who knows God as he is in himself—this applies to the blessed and to the angels that did not fall—enjoys exact and accurate knowledge of the good. Unfortunately, Satan and his followers, because they refused God's invitation into his intimacy, are programmatically, systematically blind to the truth about the good. For Satan himself, who is the leader and chief intellect behind the angelic rebellion, the only good can be Satan's own conception, which arises within his own intellect. One of the most sophisticated and powerful intellects in creation is incapable of recognizing the true good.

---

25. Thomas Aquinas, *On the Truth of the Catholic Faith: Summa contra Gentiles*, trans. Anton C. Pegis, vol. 1, *God* (Garden City, N.Y.: Doubleday, 1955), chaps. 37–38.

The "Society" of Sin

Hell is the place God created for the angels who rebelled against him.[26] We say "place," but since angels are spirits the word "place" is metaphorical. Hell is a condition and also a society of those who are separated from God. Having rejected God and lost his angelic privileges to God's company, the devil in his envy has made it his aim to seduce human beings away from God and into his own dominion. And the place of that dominion is hell. Hell is Satan's society.

In the Genesis story, after Eve ate the fruit the serpent disappeared from the scene. With the woman and Adam left alone before God, the ancient text presents a stunningly accurate psychology of sin. Immediately the man and woman are ashamed to be naked in front of each other, and they sew fig leaves to cover up.[27] Why? Although comfortable and at ease in their original nakedness just a few minutes earlier, having mistrusted God they no longer trust each other. When they hear God coming, they hide. The serpent's insinuations notwithstanding, they know they have done wrong. God was truthful, and the serpent was not. *What they had known all along about truth and goodness* is brought into the light.

Then the "blame game" began. Adam lamely attempted to shift at least some of the blame through his wife onto God. "The woman whom thou gavest to be with me, she gave me fruit of the tree, and I ate."[28] Earlier it was the delighted exclamation, "This at last is bone of my bones and flesh of my flesh!,"[29] and now he complains about "the woman whom thou gavest to be with me." For her part, Eve blames the serpent. God then pronounced his sentence: the two are expelled from the garden, their lives will become hard, and finally they will

26. Mt 25:41.   27. Gn 3:7.
28. Ibid., 3:12.   29. Ibid., 2:23.

die.[30] The good they had enjoyed was lost, and it was their own fault. We can only imagine the frosty relationship between the two as they left their home, the place that the Lord God had provided for them. Satan had planted the seeds of suspicion—the lies—that had damaged not only their relationship with God but also the friendship they had enjoyed with each other. Instead of a free and generous love, the first couple is plagued with mistrust, resentment, recriminations, and domination.[31] The next generation, according to the story, took this social breakdown to its most serious level, as Cain killed Abel. Satan had impressed his own image on human society.

In a sense, we do not need the scriptures to tell us about the impact of sin on human society; all we need do is open our eyes. In the Bible, however, we see all our patterns of sin. Jacob cruelly deceived his own father in order to defraud his brother Esau of his rights as firstborn.[32] His uncle, Laban, then swindled Jacob.[33] After this we read of rape,[34] treacherous vengeance,[35] envious men selling their brother into slavery,[36] callous efforts at seduction by a bored and powerful woman,[37] and so on. To this day we lie to each other. We defraud, seduce, cheat, hurt, abuse, rape, and murder each other. We sinners hurt each other, and we hurt our societies.

Nevertheless, even after the Fall, human beings were not without God. Indeed, even as he pronounces his sentence on the sinning couple, God hints at a coming redemption,[38] the Offspring who will crush the serpent's head. And in the meantime, to prepare the human race for the coming Savior, God forms a people of his own to whom he gives a law and whom

30. Ibid., 3:16–35.
32. Ibid., 27.
34. Ibid., 34:1–5.
36. Ibid., 37.
38. Ibid., 3:15.

31. See ibid., 3:16.
33. Ibid., 28:15–30.
35. Ibid., 34:25–31.
37. Ibid., 39:7–20.

he teaches to worship him, to turn back to him. The whole of salvation history recounts God's response to sin and his provisions to undo the effects of Satan's death-dealing lies.

After the Fall, the serpent slid away. He has his place, however, where the damned are sent. Those who have turned away from Christ are condemned to the "eternal fire prepared for the devil and his angels," within the spiritual society of lies and murder, of shame and humiliation, where true goodness has no place. The "hell" of Hell is this: to live in a realm without justice, without friendship, without kindness, but rather one whose governing principle is its ruler's own power, as he relies not on truth and goodness but on lies, suspicion, and death. It is a realm whose founding act was the rejection of goodness offered as a free gift for the sake of subjection to the rebel's rule.

God has a place for each of us, a place that he has prepared from before we were even conceived. It is a place for our good, for our perfect happiness. Hell is to lose that place. Satan, who envied Adam and Eve's good life in Eden and so tempted them to lose it, seeks to deprive each human being of his rightful place with God. Those whom he manages to seduce away from God have no place to be but with him, his angels, and those human beings who have followed him.

Criteria of Judgment

In Jesus' parable of the Last Judgment, both the sheep and the goats seem to be surprised at his verdict on them: "Lord, when did we see thee hungry and feed thee, or thirsty and give thee drink?"[39] God had given a law, the Ten Commandments, and Jesus reiterated its importance. Indeed, in his Sermon on the Mount he went beyond the external observance of the law and required his disciples to observe the law in their hearts.[40] When

39. Mt 25:37, 44.
40. Ibid., 5:17–48.

the rich young man asked what he must do to have eternal life, Jesus first directed him to the Commandments.[41] Only when the young man says that he has observed these does Jesus call him to something higher, to renounce all and follow him. We would expect that the King would pass judgment based strictly on the law, for a king is one who enforces the law. But in the Last Judgment, he judges according to their respective responses to his hunger and thirst.[42] Here is an important lesson. It is common to think of God's judgment in terms of the rules: those who obey the rules, doing what God commands and saying their prayers, get into heaven. Those who break the rules, disobey God, and neglect prayer are sent to hell. This is very much the way our civil justice system works: "Keep your nose clean, do your work, and your life will be good. Break the law and you pay a fine or go to jail." The Final Judgment, however, is based on a very different criterion: how we have treated Jesus. It is about a personal relationship, not merely about rules. When one loves another person very important to him, then he shares food with him. When a friend is alone in prison he will visit him. The criterion of judgment is manifest in practical love for Jesus. This does not mean that the Commandments have ceased to be important, of course. Jesus also said, "If you love me, you will keep my commandments."[43] His commandment, however, is to love: "If you keep my commandments, you will abide in my love.... This is my commandment, that you love one another as I have loved you."[44] Speaking of Christ's conversation with the rich young man, Pope St. John Paul II explains further:

The commandments of which Jesus reminds the young man are meant to safeguard the good of the person, the image of God, by

---

41. Ibid., 19:17–19.   42. Ibid., 25:35, 43.
43. Jn 14:15.   44. Ibid., 15:10, 12.

protecting his good.... The commandments thus represent the basic condition for love of neighbor; at the same time they are the proof of that love. They are the *first necessary step on the journey towards freedom*, its starting point.[45]

Those are saved who have loved Jesus by loving the least of his brethren. The "rules" of the Ten Commandments are simply the "bare minimum" and "starting point" for the love of neighbor.

And what about the damned? Granted, they could have done better, but is it really all that bad to have ignored the hungry and the thirsty, the naked and imprisoned? Dismas knew that he deserved punishment under Roman law because he had violated it. But the Lord's parable of the Last Judgment gives us no indication that the "goats" had committed any crimes. Here we should call to mind Jesus' parable of the rich man and Lazarus.[46] The rich man dressed in "purple and fine linen." He feasted every day. We do not read that he had gotten his wealth illegally or that he ate and drank too much or was unfaithful to his wife. At his gate lay Lazarus, who had nothing but "desired to be fed with what fell from the rich man's table." The rich man died and found himself in torment, while Lazarus rested in Abraham's bosom. Where did the rich man go so badly wrong? This parable parallels that of the Good Samaritan.[47] In both stories we see someone in serious need, one whom others—except, of course, the Samaritan—ignore. Jesus tells the parable of the Good Samaritan in direct response to the lawyer's question, "Teacher, what shall I do to inherit eternal life?" As he would later do with the rich young man, Jesus directs the lawyer to the law, which the lawyer knows well. But, being a

---

45. John Paul II, Encyclical Letter *Veritatis splendor* (Vatican City: Libraria Editrice Vaticana, 1993), §13.

46. Lk 16:19–31.

47. Ibid., 10:25–37.

lawyer, he wants his terms defined: "And who is my neighbor?" Since it is only one's neighbor that a person is required to love as himself, we need to know who that neighbor is. The lawyer's legalistic approach here is noteworthy. He wants to know the requirements. Who is it that he *is required to* love as himself?

Jesus' answer is somewhat strange. He does not say, "Every battered and bloodied crime victim is your neighbor," or even "everyone who is in trouble or need." Jesus says to the lawyer, "Which of these three, do you think, *proved neighbor* to the man who fell among the robbers?" (emphasis added). Jesus turned the lawyer's perspective on its head. Your responsibility, he seems to say, is not to discern whether this or that person is your neighbor. I do not need to find criteria to recognize who it is that I am supposed to love. Rather, to obey the commandment "Love your neighbor as yourself," I must *make myself* a neighbor to the person before me. *If I want to inherit eternal life*, I must become the neighbor to those I meet. I must love them as myself. There are no rules about it. The Good Samaritan seems to have been pretty prosperous. He had coins in his pocket, and his credit with the innkeeper was good. When someone is suffering, even if one does not know what to do—even if there is in fact nothing that he *can* do—he can show mercy, a bit of human kindness. Dismas showed mercy. He appealed to his partner in crime to stop mocking Jesus.

Those on Christ's left in the Last Judgment—the "goats"— were not aware that they had failed to feed him when he was hungry or give him drink when he was thirsty. Nor were they aware that those they had ignored were the "least of Christ's brothers." We can contrast this with a legal situation in which St. Paul found himself.[48] As he and Silas were preaching in Philippi, they were seized by the authorities, flogged, and

48. Acts 16:16–40.

jailed. Now Roman law—the Lex Portia—absolutely forbade the flogging of Roman citizens. And both Paul and Silas carried Roman passports, as it were. When the authorities realized that in their haste they had flogged Roman citizens, they were horrified and *very* apologetic. Having failed to check on Paul and Silas's citizenship, they left themselves open to severe penalties under Roman law. By contrast, the *least of Christ the King's brethren* carry no passports. I am to be a neighbor to the person in front of me; I must love him because he too is one of the least of Christ's brethren.

The logic behind these criteria of judgment is as inevitable as it is impeccable. The primordial root of judgment is God's offer of his love, his offer to welcome into his company anyone, whether angel or human being, who would turn to him and look for that love. Satan and his angels refused this offer. Those men and women who are "blessed of my Father" and welcomed to the place prepared for them are those who imitate God in his mercy and generous love. St. Thomas Aquinas writes, "When one understands a thing, there results in him a conception (word) of that which is understood. When one loves a thing, an impression results of the thing loved in the affection of the lover. Thus that loved is said to be in the lover as that understood is in he who understands."[49] Those on the King's right hand do not see God in his essence and hence are incapable of having in their minds a conception by which God is understood. Quite literally they do not know God (save through grace, but this, as St. John of the Cross shows, is a kind of hidden knowledge in a "dark night of the soul"). But they have loved God, which results in an impression of the thing loved in their affections. One who truly loves God, even in the darkness of faith, finds his affections drawn toward God, and

49. *ST* Ia, q. 37, a. 1.

loving God he desires to imitate God, to be like him. Although it is impossible to imitate God's power and omniscience, one can imitate his love and mercy, albeit imperfectly. To participate in God's love means, therefore, that one loves as God does, generously and mercifully. Those who have ignored their neighbors' sufferings and needs have, even if they do not realize it—and the parable suggests precisely that they do not—turned away from love. They try to approach God by another way, a way that, because of God's utter transcendence, is impossible. All their knowledge and efforts fail of the goal of attaining to God, of imitating him. The only true imitation of God is by loving Christ (God Incarnate), particularly as he is encountered in one's neighbor. The "passport" to the place prepared by the Father is one's likeness in love, evidenced by mercy toward the neighbor.

Those, on the other hand, who are consigned to the "place prepared for the devil and his angels" are those who have chosen the way of the devil. They are genuinely puzzled: "When did we see thee hungry or thirsty or a stranger or naked or sick or in prison, and did not minister to thee?"[50] They seem to object that had they been told of the requirement to feed the hungry and thirsty, visit the sick and imprisoned, and so on, they would have done so. They might believe they have followed the rules, but never from the very start was it about rules. At stake in the initial fall from grace, in Satan's original sin, was the rejection of the offer of love. When the tempter approached Eve in the garden, he did not offer her pleasures and rewards, but rather independence from God and his order of love: "Your eyes will be opened, and you will be like God, knowing good and evil."

50. Mt 25:44.

The "Good Life"

The rich man who ignored Lazarus might be one of us. Like him, we eat well. By the standards of most of the world's population throughout history, Americans and those in other developed nations today feast at mealtimes on meat, fruits, and vegetables imported year round from warmer climates, desserts sweetened with cane sugar, safe milk products—all in abundance. Except for the very poor among us, we eat very well. And we dress well. Not only do we have comfortable and warm clothing, we can vary the style of our dress from day to day. I could go on, but the main point is this: we live as comfortably and well as did the rich man in Jesus' parable. With CDs and iPods we can have music with us all the time. Even Louis XIV of France, the "Sun King," did not have such reliable and comfortable transportation as a modest automobile with its CD player and air-conditioning. Compared with most people around the world today and with almost everyone who has come before us, we live very good and comfortable lives.

All these good things do not, of themselves, make us deserving of damnation. The problem is the attitude that so often goes along with the good life, an attitude that Pope John Paul II identified as "consumerism"—believing that what a person *has* is more important than what he *is*. To have the good life, we have to look out for ourselves and our own interests. The Rich Man almost certainly had his own problems; he had investments and properties to care for and competitors to worry about. He did not *hate* Lazarus. He simply did not care about him. In his parable of the Last Judgment, Christ is telling us about our attitudes, how we regard those we meet. Whether we are wealthy or poor, how we regard the person we meet is how we regard Christ. This section of Matthew's Gospel is often applied (and rightly so) to the importance of charitable endeavors. But it is not only about them.

Seeing the Suffering Christ in the Suffering Neighbor

As many people were astonished at him—his appearance was so marred, beyond human semblance and his form beyond that of the sons of men—so shall he startle many nations.[51]

A king should be regal, magnificent, imposing, but that man carrying the cross is disgusting—skin scarred, torn and bloody, hair matted and unruly. What do I make, then, of the cognitively disabled person who slurs his words and stands too close to me, whose repeated questions make no real sense, as he holds with me what he takes to be intelligent conversation?

He had no form or comeliness that we should look at him, and no beauty that we should desire him. He was despised and rejected by men, a man of sorrows, and acquainted with grief.[52]

It is easy to ignore the import of these texts, to see others in terms of their capacity to help us attain our own goals and to realize our own purposes. From the anticipation that this particular encounter may well prove profitable, one slips easily into viewing every encounter in such terms so that those that plainly will not yield advantage are avoided or at least shortened. Popular magazines and online sources offer advice on how to get out of unpromising conversations at social events. Experts tell us that in every gathering the hierarchies of influence follow the same patterns; that by the end of the event— the cocktail party or reception—the truly influential will have established their positions toward the center of the room and others take up positions around them. It is vital, then, to maneuver oneself into that group, to identify the key players and to be near them.

51. Is 52:14.
52. Ibid., 53:2–3.

Surely he has borne our griefs and carried our sorrow; yet we esteemed him stricken, smitten by God, and afflicted.[53]

This man carrying the cross must have done something wrong ... there have been rumors ... even if some people say he was good and helped many people, we don't know the whole story ... best not to become associated too closely with him. After Argentina's "Dirty War," in which many innocent people "disappeared" at the hands of their own government on suspicions of disloyalty, a young man was asked if he didn't find the arrests and disappearances disturbing. He replied that he did not, because if anyone was arrested (and he knew some who were), they must have done something wrong. If you were not doing anything wrong you had nothing to worry about.[54]

In the final analysis, those on the left, the "goats"—like the rich man who feasted every day and dressed in purple and linen—used other persons to meet their own desires. Other persons in their world were contacts to be used, resources to be taken advantage of. They lived in a world in which if you scratch my back, then I'll scratch yours. But if you will not scratch my back, then you are of no use to me. They had friendships and were capable of kindness. They were not all ruthless and grasping. But the friendships were friendships for advantage alone. I surround myself with people who are pleasant to be with, who can help me out. But isn't this what we all do? We love those who are pleasant and whom we find useful in living our lives. Christ is saying that these are the criteria for the society of the damned.

Dismas was in pain—in great pain. His former companion did what most crucifixion victims did: he cursed and blas-

53. Ibid., 53:4.
54. This story appeared in an edition of the *National Catholic Register* in the early 1980s. Unfortunately, I no longer have the paper or access to the story.

phemed. He ridiculed the innocent man hanging next to him, the one who said, "I tell you solemnly, insofar as you did this to one of the least of these brothers of mine, you did it to me." Neither Dismas nor the other knew who Jesus truly was. To them, Jesus himself appeared as "one of the least of these brothers." The one criminal cursed and ridiculed him. Bathed in his own agony, Dismas showed the little mercy of which he was capable. By doing so he proved himself unfit for hell. He was welcomed into the place prepared for him by the Father.

The Immortal Soul

The Lord promised Dismas, "Today you will be with me in paradise," and shortly afterward, Dismas died. The soldiers took him down from the cross, and his corpse was buried. With his body in the grave, Dismas was nonetheless "in paradise." According to the church's teaching, immediately after dying the soul undergoes a private judgment at which its eternal destiny, whether to heaven or hell, is pronounced.[55] Because the body is dead and in the grave, this judgment affects only the soul of the deceased. Later, at the Second Coming of Christ,[56] the dead will be raised and sentence on all nations and on every person will be pronounced. Then all the saved will rejoice in a new creation, the "new heaven and new earth."[57] The afterlife is marked, as it were, by two phases. Philosophy tells us that the soul is immortal,[58] and the Catholic Church has affirmed this.[59] In the next chapter we will reflect on what happens to the souls of the deceased from the moment of death until the Second Coming.

Death is classically described as the separation of the soul

---

55. *Catechism of the Catholic Church* (*CCC*) (Vatican City: Libreria Editrice Vaticana, 1993), 1021.

56. Ibid., 1038–41.

57. Rv 21:1.

58. *ST* Ia, q. 75, a. 6.

59. *CCC*, 366.

from the body. In death the body ceases to function, the ears cannot hear, the eyes no longer see, and the brain shuts down. In short order the body begins to corrupt, first as rigor mortis sets in and then, unless the mortician intervenes with his preservatives, the flesh decays. Soon nothing is left of the person except his soul, which survives the body's death until the Final Resurrection, when it will be reunited with the body. This means that death is a very real and very serious matter. The person who has died has no more bodily life. He has no bodily activity, no perception, no sensation, not even thought.

Our popular and cultural expressions, well-intentioned and hopeful as they may be, mislead us. When Clarence (the fictional angel in Frank Capra's 1946 film *It's a Wonderful Life*) died in the nineteenth century, he had no chance to read Mark Twain's latest novel, and Twain, for his part, would have had no chance to write novels in heaven. Both novelist and fan were dead. When Grandmother's pain ends in a peaceful death, she has not "gone to a better place," not literally. She has died. She cannot bake cookies or reminisce about her girlhood days on the farm. She cannot look down from heaven to watch her grandchildren play. All that remains of her is her soul (and this is important, as we shall see shortly). The reason for this is that she no longer has her brain or the rest of her body. Without the brain there is no thinking or feeling or imagining. Without the body, there is no *doing*. To die really is to lose one's life.

However, the soul does survive the body's death. In this life on earth the soul governs the body and uses the body to do its work. We cannot imagine what the soul by itself is like, because all our imagining is in terms of bodily images. However, the soul does have two powers that transcend the material order: intellect, which is the power to understand truth, and will, the power to love the good. Because they have formed the person's soul, these two capacities survive the death of the person. We must look more closely at these two characteristics of the soul, which are essential for understanding its state after this life.

Intellect or Understanding   Intellect or understanding is precisely a formation of the soul. By his understanding, the intellectual being conforms himself to the essences of the things that he understands. The chemist is so adept in the laboratory because he has conformed his soul to the chemical natures of things; he is, in a sense, living chemistry. Indeed, we speak of the process of education as *formation* of the mind or intelligence. This intellectual formation cannot, moreover, be reduced to the acquisition of facts. Without his brain, the deceased can remember nothing. Indeed, insult to the brain, such as that of Alzheimer's syndrome, can destroy much of the memory so that many facts previously known go lost to that person. Rather, understanding, or intellect, is the capacity of the soul by means of ideas to grasp the unity among things. Even if the brain may be damaged, the intellect remains, albeit without a responsive organ through which to manifest itself. The power of intellect is perhaps most manifest in the sciences, but it is not only in this realm. The creation of beauty in the arts, which consists in the imposition of form onto material elements, is a work of intellect. More important is the understanding of human beings by which we are able to manage domestic life and friendships and to govern cities and states. This intellectual formation, which is the basis of the person's knowledge and activity, survives the loss of the body by which it acted in the world.

Love   Love, by which the soul is directed toward the good, is the act of the will, and in a way complementary to intellect it forms the soul. Love, according to St. Thomas Aquinas, seeks union with its beloved.[60] If this beloved is an object, the union

60. *ST* Ia-IIae, q. 28.

is by possession and consumption, while love of some ideal or spiritual reality, such as love of music or science, is effected by entering into that activity. One who loves a person seeks to be in that person's presence, but also and more importantly to enhance the beloved's own good, to contribute to and will that good. What is most important to our present purpose is that love—any love, whether trivial or profound—forms the life of the lover. "Every agent acts for an end, as stated above (*ST* q. 1, a. 2). Now the end is the good desired and loved by each one. Wherefore it is evident that every agent, whatever it be, does every action from love of some kind."[61]

Even if someone may love material or temporal things, love is necessarily a spiritual power because it directs the entire soul, the entire being of the lover. The will—and therefore what one loves—is not predetermined by nature to some one kind of thing. Even if one might love himself and direct his life toward his own comfort, pleasure, and survival, he could also direct himself toward some ideal contrary to these. He may love his nation and strive at great risk to attain its independence and rightful sovereignty. He may love his spouse and children. He may love God and direct himself according to what he understands to be God's will. It is a serious error to reduce human love to nothing more than some nexus of physical desires, to evolutionarily determined wants.[62] To seek union with the object of one's love is to measure oneself by that object and in some way to conform oneself to it. The lover wants to conform himself and his life to the beloved's beauty that he so desires. The loving soul in some way imitates the beloved. Even if love be frustrated or beyond the power of the lover to fulfill, the lover is transformed by his love. His love forms his soul. This

61. *ST* Ia-IIae, q. 28, a. 6.
62. Reimers, *Soul of the Person*, 67–68, 214.

is particularly the case with the two opposed loves to which St. Augustine refers: the love of God even to contempt of self and the love of self even to the contempt for God.[63]

Therefore, all that the dead person has of himself is the truth he has understood and his love for the goods he has desired—that is, his personal integration in truth and virtue. And these can make all the difference, for they are spiritual goods. The human person is a spiritual being—even in this life with our bodies we are spiritual beings—and that part of him that is spiritual lives on. Although a disembodied spirit, like the soul after death, cannot interact with physical things, it can know and relate to other spirits. In particular, the soul is able to encounter God.

On Plato and Other Good Pagans

Before we move on, let us look briefly at the situation of the good persons who died without knowing Christ. To some extent, every human being (excepting Jesus and his mother Mary) has has fallen into sin. Nobody has lived in such moral perfection that his every thought and act was directed to the authentically true, the beautiful, and the good. And so it follows that no one has entered death in such a way that his soul can rest in perfect peace. What can we say about them? Dismas was welcomed by Christ himself into paradise. What about the many others who may have died that day or in the ages before?

Rather than entering in depth into the theological controversies about whether and how those who have not heard the gospel can be saved, I propose here simply to look at the souls of those who have died without direct contact with divine revelation in order to say something intelligent about their status.

63. Augustine of Hippo, *City of God*, Book XIV, chap. 28.

Two important associates of Plato (428–327 B.C.) illustrate this problem well. Socrates, Plato's teacher and inspiration, lived an austere life of searching for true wisdom, having accepted the responsibility from God, as he understood him, to encourage his Athenian neighbors to better themselves, to care for their souls rather than their pocketbooks.[64] Indeed, Socrates himself believed that the only things a person can take into the afterlife are the wisdom and virtue his soul had acquired in this life. He believed in the God or in gods as beings better than himself. In fact, he understood that his most serious moral responsibility was that to the God who had commissioned him.[65] Such was his character that at his death, his friends described him as "of all those whom we knew in our time, the bravest and also the wisest and most upright man."[66] Socrates seems to have been as good as we might hope for a pagan to be. Certainly, someone who had lived a good life, like Socrates striving to be virtuous, wise, and just, should be better off in death than a tyrant who indulges his appetites and vents his wrath on anyone who opposes him.

What is truly important about Socrates is not simply his morality, his striving for virtue and wisdom, but *his religion*. For him God, or "the God," was not a Kantian ideal, but rather a real being who commissioned him and to whom he was personally responsible.[67] The god Apollo had communicated to him, at Delphi through the unwitting Chaerephon, that there was no man wiser than Socrates and that he was to share this wisdom with his fellows. What we see here is not so much the reasoning of the philosopher as the reflections of one who has heard the prophetic voice addressed personally to him. In *Euthyphro* Socrates questions how one can know the will of the God or the gods, and in doing so he implies that such knowl-

64. Plato, *Apology* 30a–e.   65. Ibid., 21.
66. Plato, *Phaedo* 188c.   67. Plato, *Apology* 21a–23c; 28d–e.

edge must be universal and accessible to any rational inquirer.[68] In his *Apology*, however, Socrates speaks, on the basis of a revelation through a seer, as a believer who knows what the God asks of him. He is behaving *religiously* and not only *morally*. *Every Athenian* ought to care for his soul, pursuing virtue and wisdom, but *only Socrates* is charged with stirring the city from its moral laziness as a gadfly stirs up a great horse.[69] We may say that without knowing the Lord God of the Hebrews, Socrates believed himself to have heard the voice of God. Who was this god? He was not exactly one of the Olympian gods, concerning whose mythical accounts Socrates was decidedly skeptical, but of them, it appears that Apollo most closely resembled the God as Socrates conceived him.

The other associate of Plato was Aristotle, certainly the best of Plato's students. Unlike Socrates, Aristotle did not see himself as commissioned by God, and indeed, his intellectual concerns were primarily this-worldly. His philosophical project was intellectual rather than moral. In comparison to his famous teacher, Aristotle was a decidedly secular thinker. Nevertheless, he clearly undergirds his thinking with a metaphysical vision that is ultimately religious. This is clear, in the first place, from his *Metaphysics*, which begins by raising the question of the nature of "first philosophy," the science of being as such (being *qua* being). He asks whether this philosophy might be also a *theology*.[70] Aristotle thought yes. The climax of his inquiries comes in Book XII of that work. On the basis of his analyses of the first principles of the world, Aristotle concludes that there must be a being that, with respect to all other things, is their First Cause or ultimate principle of order and that is itself dependent on no other being.

68. Plato, *Euthyphro* 7a.
69. Plato, *Apology* 31a.
70. Aristotle, *Metaphysics*, Book I, chap. 2.

And God is in a better state. And life also belongs to God; for the actuality of thought is life, and God is that actuality; and God's self-dependent actuality is life most good and eternal. We say therefore that God is a living being, eternal, most good, so that life and duration continuous and eternal belong to God; for this is God.[71]

St. Thomas Aquinas will later use Aristotle's arguments in his own proofs for the existence of God.

Even though this God of Aristotle's is distant and hard to know, an impersonal being with no concern for human beings and their activities, its existence is still pertinent to the lives of human beings. Aristotle's *Nicomachean Ethics* presents a detailed analysis of the elements and structure of the good life, the happy and fulfilled life, which is the life of virtue in a well-ordered polis. His argument seems to come down to the acquisition of the moral virtues of prudence, justice, moderation, and courage, along with the intellectual virtues, all lived out in a good community of virtuous human beings. In the tenth and final book of his *Nicomachean Ethics*, however, Aristotle introduces a new element, contemplation, which he calls the capstone of virtuous living. The greatest pleasure of human existence lies not in sense experience or in the successful engagement in noble political activities, but in the intellectual contemplation of the highest truths. The reason for this is that such activity is the most divine.

If reason is divine, then in comparison with man, the life according to it is divine in comparison with human life. But we must not follow those who advise us, being men, to think of human things, and, being mortal, of mortal things, but must, as far as we can, make ourselves immortal, and strain every nerve to live in accordance with the best thing in us.[72]

71. Ibid., Book XII, chap. 7.
72. Aristotle, *Nicomachean Ethics*, Book X, chap. 7.

Furthermore, "the activity of God, which surpasses all others in blessedness, must be contemplative; and of human activities, therefore, that which is most akin to this must be most of the nature of happiness." Aristotle concludes:

For if the gods have any care for human affairs, ... it would be reasonable both that they should delight in that which was best and most akin to them (i.e., reason) and that they should reward those who love and honor this most, as caring for the things that are dear to them and acting both rightly and nobly.[73]

Therefore not only did Aristotle come to some knowledge of God, that God exists and indeed in unparalleled perfection, but, like Socrates, he recognized that the human being has certain responsibilities toward God. The best life, the life worth pursuing, can only be that which imitates the activity of the divine, in which the highest part of the soul attends to its highest object. Socrates, Plato, and Aristotle can be said to have found God, albeit "from a distance," not only as a theoretical first principle but as the fundamental moral principle to whom they saw themselves responsible.

Let us pause for a moment to consider this. In our day, belief in the existence of God is generally seen, especially among the better educated and our cultural leaders, as a matter of "faith" (construed generally as a kind of religiously motivated affirmation of things that cannot be known by reason) and not as a matter of truth, of objective reality. That God exists is taken to be a religious claim by those for whom such a claim is meaningful but not a fact that can be known by reason—that is rationally justifiable. Atheism, or at least agnosticism, is presumed to be the "default" setting of the human mind. The claim that God exists is not objectively verifiable. Socrates, Plato, and Aristotle,

---

73. Ibid., Book X, chap. 8.

however, stand as the originators of Western philosophy, thinkers whose works continue to be studied, debated, and interpreted anew. Socrates is virtually the living icon of philosophical wisdom. Dante referred to Aristotle as *"maestro di color chi sanno"*—master of the men who know.[74] Like Thomas Aquinas, he does not need even to call the philosopher by name. To this day, Aristotle's thought is studied, debated, rejected by some, accepted by others, but never relegated to irrelevance. And Aristotle maintained that God exists.

This belief in God by these Greek ancients cannot be ascribed to superstition or pre-scientific mythmaking, because it was precisely these thinkers who began to lay the foundations for rational, nonmythical understandings of the world and the divine. For his part, Socrates incisively criticized the mythical conceptions of the god as related in the Olympian myths by applying rational argument to determine what their nature must be.[75] Although Socrates indubitably believed in God, his analysis of piety in *Euthyphro* decisively undermined the simplistic conception of gods as simply immortal superhuman beings with the same moral shortcomings as are found among humans. The gods of ancient Greece, like those of polytheistic cultures in general, were not perfect, all-powerful, spiritual beings, as we conceive God, but were superhuman and supernatural beings who mysteriously controlled various natural forces and phenomena. Generally they were not concerned with morality, either their own or that of the human beings under their power. What they wanted, according to pagan understanding, was worship and sacrifice, ceremonies in their honor and signs of submission. It was not important to know what kinds of being they were—not really—but it was vital to satisfy their requirements for worship. To undertake a sea voyage without propi-

74. Dante Alighieri, *Inferno*, Canto IV, 131.
75. An important theme in both *Euthyphro* 6b–d and *Republic* 389a–91e.

tiating Poseidon was to invite shipwreck. Ontologically considered, they were the products of human imagination, formed by desires and fears. Plato and his teacher Socrates knew that whatever gods (or the God) might be, they could not be beings such as those described in the myths. They had to be morally and ontologically superior to human beings and not simply the creations of human imagination.

And if Socrates (and Plato) undermined the mythical conceptions of the divine, Aristotle's metaphysical analyses provided the conceptual underpinnings by which the nature of divine beings could in some way be explored. Aristotle does not even begin with an inquiry into the divine but with an investigation of the world and why it is as it is. Unlike modern thinkers, however, he asks not only about the material and efficient factors governing physical interactions, but also about formal and final causes—that is, about the meaning and the good of things. To account for efficient and material causality he introduces the complementary notions of potency (or potentiality) and act, which must finally become metaphysical principles. Although consideration of form and finality will lead him eventually to conclude that a First Cause must exist, he does not introduce these notions for the sake of undergirding a belief in God. Quite the opposite. He begins with those features of reality that can be known and is led eventually to affirm that there must be a First Cause in virtue of which the meaning and finality, as well as the operation of the world, can be explained. These are not religious concepts; indeed, they would have been useless to an ancient priest, much less a worshiper. Rather they are intellectual tools developed to explain reality as it could be known. By using them, Aristotle is able to affirm the existence of God as First Cause.

Let us contrast these ancient thinkers with our modern scientific materialism dominant in contemporary post-Enlightenment thought. Although they were untouched by the Jewish faith and its claims of revelation, and although they had worked more than three centuries before the advent of Christian theology, the traditions of Plato and Aristotle are curiously amenable to Christian thought and problematic for contemporary philosophical and scientific materialism. Far from being unbiased and objective, modern and contemporary thought have a bad conscience, which results from deliberate blindness. I propose that the cause for this blindness is that the post-Enlightenment eclipse of God has resulted in the disintegration of the human. Aristotle was confident that his humanity was not an obstacle to knowing the truth; that the principles he discovered—the four causes, potency and act, substance and accident—could enable us to know how things really are, and that through disciplined thought human beings could attain to the truth. From Descartes's universal doubt to contemporary puzzles over consciousness, modern philosophy has mistrusted the human capacity to understand reality. Because of the alleged presuppositions of our sciences, human freedom stands as a kind of antinomy of reason, an evident truth that stands in direct contradiction to other evident truths.[76] If the various sciences can account for the organic mechanisms by which our bodies are governed, including the complex bioelectrical networks of the brain, then consciousness itself becomes a veritable surd. Hence it is misleading to import human conceptions into metaphysics. That is, the careful metaphysician must beware of anthropomorphizing reality. From our human experience of working for a purpose one cannot infer that purposeful action exists in the world outside the peculiar realm of human consciousness. As we attempt to account for causality in the natural order, we must take pains not to model it, as Aristotle seems to have done, on that of the human carpenter who joins two

76. Peter van Inwagen, *The Problem of Evil: The Gifford Lectures Delivered in the University of St. Andrews in 2003* (Oxford: Clarendon Press, 2006), 170.

pieces of wood. In other words, the inner, ontological structure of the real world cannot be taken from the structures recognized by the conscious mind. Even from a phenomenological point of view, all that can be affirmed is the structure of the world-for-man, and not the world in itself. If we may say that through God's image in man Aristotle was able to glimpse something of God, the modern mind that does not want to acknowledge God has blinded itself to the human. Paradoxically, then, our trio of ancient Athenians were, by their openness to truth, more open to God than are contemporary atheists.

If this is so, then what could be the state postmortem of the soul of a Socrates or an Aristotle? It is an intriguing question, because they accomplished what St. Paul said they should have been able to do. "For what can be known about God is plain to them, because God has shown it to them. Ever since the creation of the world his invisible nature, his eternal power and deity, has been clearly perceived in the things that have been made."[77] If we ask what the status of the naturally good man is—the soul that never knew Christ but genuinely sought after truth and goodness—we ask a false problem. It is false because, in a way, no one has been completely ignorant of Christ—not Socrates, nor Gautama the Buddha, nor Emperor Moctezuma of the Aztecs. We know this because the Person of Christ is the Second Person of the Blessed Trinity: "all things were made through him, and without him was not anything made that was made."[78] The Person is the Word that the Creator eternally speaks and through which he created the world. This means that the world itself manifests something of the Word. "He [the Word] was in the world, and the world was made through him, yet the world knew him not."[79] It follows therefore that whoever looks at this world sees the intelligible effects of the

---

77. Rom 1:19–20.   78. Jn 1:3.
79. Ibid., 1:10.

Word of God. Everyone who experiences the goodness of creation has experienced the goodness of the Creator. This creation is the handiwork of a wise and loving God, who made it to be "very good" and a gift to us.[80] Even if we can glimpse him only dimly and distantly through his creation, we do know something of the Word in the wisdom written into its effects that we see around us. There is no cold, impersonal, brute reality. Aquinas writes:

For as a work of art manifests the art of the artisan, so the whole world is nothing else than a certain representation of the divine wisdom conceived within the mind of the Father, "He poured her (wisdom) out upon all his works," as is said in Sirach (1:10).[81]

Concerning this reality, John Paul II writes:

In this witness to the absoluteness of the moral good Christians are not alone: they are supported by the moral sense present in peoples and by the great religious and sapiential traditions of East and West, from which the interior and mysterious workings of God's Spirit are not absent.... The voice of conscience has always clearly recalled that there are truths and moral values for which one must be prepared to give up one's life. In an individual's words and above all in the sacrifice of his life for a moral value, the Church sees a single testimony to that truth which, already present in creation, shines forth in its fullness on the face of Christ.[82]

In this sense and to this extent, good ancient Greeks, among others, knew and could respond to Christ. The catch is, of course, to recognize the Word through his handiwork and respond appropriately. For the best of human minds lacking grace and revelation, the first principles of existence and moral-

80. Gn 1:31.
81. Aquinas, *Commentary on the Gospel of St. John*, Book I, lect. 5, 136.
82. John Paul II, *Veritatis splendor*, §94.

ity can be glimpsed only as hypotheses. Socrates knew that the God must be virtuous and wise, like Apollo in the Olympian myths, but he had no direct access to God's wisdom. Aristotle's First Cause, "Thought Thinking Itself," is not conceived as a personal being who loves his creatures. Aristotle had not even a hint that God is a Trinity of Persons. These thinkers knew that God exists, but not who God is. And here we encounter two serious problems for the wise pagan mind. First, Satan, too, knew both that God exists and that he rules creation, but he turned from knowing God himself. Satan's knowledge is broader, deeper, and more extensive by far than Aristotle's, and yet he turned to the gravest error of refusing the wisdom that comes from God—the wisdom that God *is*. Second, none of the wisest pagan minds could find a way to salvation from evil. Plato's Socrates could see his way clear to a eugenics program for breeding guardians, whose success was to be assured by exposing babies who were unfit to the elements.[83] Aristotle could not quite make up his mind whether some people were naturally slaves.[84] Most important, in neither Socrates (nor Plato) nor Aristotle do we find a robust presentation of the importance of love, although the end of the *Phaedo*, as well as the opening of *The Republic*, shows Socrates as a man capable of close friendship, and Aristotle's account of friendship in Book IX of the *Nicomachean Ethics* offers a glimpse of what true love must be like. On the other hand, Plato's *Republic* makes clear that the only way one can be saved from evil is either to embrace a philosophical life of study and contemplation of the Form of the Good *or* to live obediently in a regime ruled by a Philosopher-King. And after arguing for the nature and importance of moral virtue, Aristotle famously notes, "It makes no

83. Plato, *Republic*, 460b–c, 461c.
84. Aristotle, *Politics*, Book I, chap. 13, 1260a4–23.

small difference, then, whether we form habits of one kind or of another from our very youth; it makes a very great difference, or rather all the difference."[85] If one's parents reared him poorly, a man is almost certainly morally a lost cause.

The intelligence of Socrates and Aristotle does not suffice to save either them or their pupils from evil. Their knowledge of the God is ultimately negative; they can know *of God*, but they cannot know *God*. Here let us add a comment on a religious figure, the Buddha, whose situation is similar in this respect. Confronted in his youth with the reality of suffering, he undertook a quest in search of enlightenment, a quest that ended under the lotus tree, where he realized that the source of all suffering is attachment. Salvation, if one may use the word (a Buddhist would not), can consist only in the complete detachment from all desires.

Satan was offered happiness and turned away from it. He would not ask God to grant him what he most desired. This was his sin. He refused to receive God's gift and was therefore condemned to replicate it himself. Intelligence did not suffice to save him. Nor can intelligence alone save the good pagan. Salvation requires a response to the God who saves. "And without faith it is impossible to please him. For whoever would draw near to God must believe that he exists and that he rewards those who seek him."[86] The faith of the pagan must therefore lead to a response to God's goodness manifest in the creation. Everything is gift.[87] Whoever receives that gift with gratitude has already begun to respond to the Word of God.

Our philosophical reflections cannot answer the question of how and on what terms God might grant salvation to those un-

---

85. Aristotle, *Nicomachean Ethics*, Book II, chap. 1, 1103b25.
86. Heb 11:6.
87. *ST* Ia, q. 20, a. 2; q. 45, a. 6; John Paul II, *Man and Woman He Created Them*, 180 (13:3–4).

acquainted with his revelation. We cannot say what a Socrates or a Buddha—both were good men—experienced at the moment of death. Surely they became aware of the spiritual Presence that lies beyond our natural human powers. To see that Presence—to know him as Dismas did—is a gift from the One who was present. It is grace. But we may hope that those who had sought for whatever was true and good will recognize in him the One they had been seeking without knowing. Even those who see only the traces of the Word in creation can respond to their Author, however imperfectly. The Letter to the Hebrews teaches that "anyone who comes to him must believe that he exists and that he rewards those who try to find him." Salvation, the gift of the eternal vision of God, is a reward that God grants to those whom he chooses. But we can know something about such a soul, and what we can say has been said by Dante in his account of hell's First Circle.

> Here, for as much as hearing could discover,
> there was no outcry louder than the sighs
> that caused the everlasting air to tremble.
> . . .
> They did not sin; and yet though they have merits,
> that's not enough, because they lacked baptism.
> the portal of the faith that you embrace.
> . . .
> For these defects, and for no other evil
> we now are lost and punished just with this:
> we have no hope and yet we live in longing.[88]

Even if it should be that good pagans (and unbaptized babies) may be saved, Dante's image of the first circle is helpful to our present reflections. The great souls of Aristotle, Buddha, and others "have no hope" of intimate communion with God,

88. Dante Alighieri, *Inferno*, Canto IV, 25–27, 34–36, 40–42.

and so they are "living in longing." They see and delight in the beauties of the creation but without enjoying the fullness of beauty, whose existence is intimated by them. Having pursued in truth the limited goods of this life, they realize that the perfect fullness of good lies beyond their reach. And so although they live without the pain of punishment, they sigh for that which lies eternally beyond them. Such must be the state of the soul that in good conscience seeks truth, goodness, and beauty, but without the graced knowledge of God.

What can we make of this? The notion of a postmortem state of the good soul, one that has centered on truth and goodness, on wisdom and virtue, is a theoretical abstraction. What the soul takes with it when separated from the body are only its love and understanding, by which it has been formed. Dante's souls in the first circle of the *Inferno* reflect only this state. However, this entire analysis prescinds from the operation of God's mercy. God's self-communication to any human being is personal, intensely so, and depends ultimately on the free action of the divine will.

CHAPTER 3

Judgment and the Mystery of Evil

On the first page of his *Confessions* St. Augustine wrote, "You have made us for yourself, and our heart is restless until it rests in you."[1] Because God has created us for himself, the first thing that happens after a human being dies is that he encounters God's judgment. The nature of this encounter—whether it is to be happy or dreadful—depends on the person himself, on his soul's relationship with the complete truth and perfect good. It is this that he brings to this encounter, an encounter that itself is a personal judgment on his life. It is a judgment that the soul itself makes as it either embraces or shrinks in horror from the vision of God.

1. Augustine, *Confessions*, Book I, chap. 1.

The Experience of the Blessed

Let us consider first what we can know of the experience of the blessed and take the example of St. Peter. After a tumultuous life that started as an apprentice fisherman, he found himself called to be a fisher of men, alternately saying exactly the right thing[2] and then exactly the wrong thing,[3] heroically standing up for Jesus and then denying him, and finally charged with feeding his Lord's flock.[4] After all this he is condemned by Nero to be crucified in Rome, far from Galilee. And so, like his Savior, he dies on a Roman cross. What then? The weathered fisherman's hands are no longer there, nor are the feet that walked in Palestine and Rome. In a real sense the man Peter is no more. Nevertheless, the One he has come to know is there before him, and—oddly enough—without his bodily eyes he can see him more clearly than ever before. The beauty he had known, loved, and served was present to him with an immediacy that Peter had never before experienced. Having lost everything (and, really, everything was gone; he was dead) he had gained everything in the simple gaze on the God whom he had allowed to take over his life. He had gained eternal happiness.

Furthermore, after Peter's death a successor, Linus, had to be named and after him another, Cletus, and through history down to Benedict XVI, Francis, and beyond. Although Peter no longer had eyes, as he gazed on the Presence that embraced him, God allowed him a keen understanding of the challenges and hardships that confronted his successors. And knowing what challenges Linus faced (and Cletus and the others) and having loved the church that he had led, Peter turned in prayer to the God in whom he could have perfect confidence and began to intercede for his successors. In this way Peter united

2. Mt 16:17.   3. Ibid., 16:22.
4. Jn 21:15–19.

his love for the church more perfectly and completely with Christ's love. In the embrace of Divine contemplation he could make his prayer for the church completely one with Christ's.

And there was something else: shortly after Peter entered into the Divine Presence, Paul was executed. In a way that we who are living in the body can understand only with difficulty, he became aware of St. Paul's presence contemplating the Divine Essence. Peter recognized in his spirit the unmistakable presence of Paul of Tarsus, whom he had known, loved, and respected in his life. In this spiritual encounter of these two souls within the Divine Embrace, their friendship and love were perfected. During his life, Peter might never have felt completely comfortable with Paul. When Paul was around, the fisherman was probably keenly aware of who was the smartest man in the room. If Peter could be impetuous, Paul was often abrasive.[5] It took nerve for Peter to meet with this Pharisee who had earned a fearsome reputation for persecuting Christians.[6] Paul, who had not been one of the Twelve, even had the boldness to rebuke Peter in public![7] Working together with Paul was always a challenge to Peter. And now, in the presence of God, their friendship was pure. Peter and Paul completely understood, appreciated, and loved each other.

In other words, contemplating the face of God, Peter became aware of the saints who were with him and of the condition and needs of his fellow Christians still struggling in their earthly lives. Death destroyed the bodily connections with those in this world, but it did not destroy the bonds of love. In fact, those bonds are now purified and perfected.

Not everyone dies with the perfect love of God of St. Peter or St. Paul ... or of a St. Perpetua or St. Teresa, of a Maximilian Kolbe or Kateri Tekakwitha. The soul of such a person,

5. See Gal 5:12.   6. Acts 8:1, 9:1–2, 13–14, 22: 4–5.
7. Gal 1:11–14.

who has set his or her love entirely on God, rejoices to leave everything else behind and to run to God. But many, probably most of those who die loving God, go to him with attachments to this world—maybe an excessive fondness for wine, an attachment to gossip, a touchiness about personal reputation, a temper that is still hard to control. And in death they lose everything they have been attached to. This is an occasion of real suffering. If John Paul II is right that suffering is always the experience of some evil,[8] then death must be very painful to someone still attached to things of this world. Even though they are entering into the presence of the God who loves them more than they could ever imagine, losing old loves still hurts. In a way, it is a spiritual equivalent to tearing off a bandage that has been stuck too long to the skin. The enjoyment of God requires letting go of everything else, and that hurts. This is purgatory.

The Wicked Soul's Experience

Then there are those who have not loved God, who have set themselves against him and rejected his goodness. In his *Republic* the pagan philosopher Plato is asked to explain why we should not envy the life of a tyrant, enjoying fabulous wealth, along with the absolute power always to have our own way. Plato vividly describes the way tyrants really live:

Now in private life, before a tyrannical man attains power, isn't he this sort of person—one who associates primarily with flatterers who are ready to obey him in everything? Or if he himself happens to need anything from other people, isn't he willing to fawn on them and make every gesture of friendship . . . ? But once he gets what he wants, don't they become strangers again? So someone with a tyrannical na-

8. John Paul II, Apostolic Letter *Salvifici doloris* (Vatican City: Libreria Editrice Vaticana, 1984), §7.

ture lives his whole life without being friends with anyone, always a master to one man or a slave to another and never getting a taste of either freedom or true friendship. . . . His waking life becomes like the nightmare we described earlier.[9]

Of course, not everyone can be a true tyrant, ruling with absolute power over thousands or even millions of people, enjoying fabulous wealth and the complete obedience of their subjects. But Plato was not talking only about real tyrants. He was talking about those who have a tyrannical soul, those who love themselves first, who want to satisfy themselves above everything else. His keen psychological point is that the unruly desires within them—their concupiscence—rule their lives. Then the tyrannical soul will be least likely to do what it wants and, forcibly driven by the stings of lust, will be full of disorder and regret.[10] This soul is *not* happy, even if it has the power to take what it wants, because its concupiscence always demands more.

St. John the Apostle enhances this understanding of concupiscence:

If anyone loves the world, love for the Father is not in him. For all that is in the world, the lust of the flesh, the lust of the eyes and the pride of life, is not of the Father but is of the world.[11]

The person who has loved God, wanted *him* more than anything else, and has tried to find him and cling to him—"On my bed, at night, I sought him whom my heart loves. . . . I will seek him whom my heart loves"[12]—this person will recognize the one whom his heart loves. Of course, this soul may be painfully aware of its own inadequacy, of its often half-hearted love. It

---

9. Plato, *Republic*, Book IX, 575e–76b.
10. Ibid., Book IX, 577d.   11. 1 Jn 2:15–16.
12. Sg 3:1–2.

may know a deep shame for its frequently lukewarm devotion. But it will long to be with the One it seeks.

But our concern here is with hell. The soul governed by the "lust of the flesh, the lust of the eyes and the pride of life"— Plato's tyrannical soul—is confronted with Something unthinkable, Something it does not know, because it has not let itself know him. It is faced with the King, Jesus Christ, the Son of God. But why is this so awful? If the Judge were simply very big and powerful, a dazzling display of glory and might—"a *blazing fire*, or a *gloom* turning to *total darkness*, or a *storm*; or *trumpeting thunder* or the *great voice speaking*"[13]—someone sufficiently strong might eventually be able to cope with seeing him. But God is not like this. He "dwells in unapproachable light," the one "whom no man has seen and no man is able to see."[14] The best way to describe this awful encounter is that the soul is before an overwhelming *Presence*, which appears to it as *nothingness*, an awful abyss of power and fullness that the soul has no part in. The God who is light now appears to the damned soul as utter darkness. Why is this?

St. Augustine says that the sinful soul has chosen to love self to the contempt of God.[15] But this love of self is an illusion. The "self" that one loves is not the true self, because if it were it would recognize that God had created it for himself. We may say, with Maritain, that the sinful self clings to that which is materially determined, to himself as an individual, to the neglect of that which is *personal*, which is capacity to love.[16] The self that is loved is the self of bodily desires. Its love is the threefold concupiscence: the "lust of the flesh, the lust of the eyes, and the pride of life." What the damned person loves are his plea-

13. Heb 12:18–19. 14. 1 Tm 6:16.

15. Augustine, *City of God* XIV.28.

16. Jacques Maritain, *The Person and the Common Good*, trans. John J. Fitzgerald (Notre Dame, Ind.: University of Notre Dame Press, 1966), 34–42, 43.

sure, his possessions, and the honors of his reputation. Dead, lacking the resources of the body, the damned soul is helpless, experiencing the ultimate frustration. It cannot get what has always satisfied it. What it has always most wanted—although it refused to admit this—is now present in his awful majesty but absolutely invisible.

Dante described this dramatically in the story of Francesca da Rimini, whose husband killed her and her adulterous lover, Paolo Malatesta, when he found them in each other's arms.[17] In Dante's *Inferno*, the two are condemned eternally to swirl in the winds of hell's second circle, visible to each other but unable to join their bodies, still drawn by the powerful desires that drove them to adultery but now unable to satisfy them. In this respect their hell is within themselves. They gave themselves to sensual satisfaction, and now their souls, which they had put to the service of the body's pleasure, exist in permanent frustration, unable to rise to any good higher than the pleasures of their sexual union—a union now impossible to those with no bodies. Dante poetically expresses the truth that God may have made the human being for himself, giving him a restless heart that cannot rest except in him. It is the person's responsibility, his task in life, to recognize this and respond to the One his heart is seeking and not to something else in God's place. The moment of judgment for the damned is a kind of experience of nothingness. But is this necessarily so bad as to constitute *hell*? We need to look more closely at suffering.

The Sufferings of the Damned

"Depart from me, you cursed, into the eternal fire prepared for the devil and his angels."[18] Not only do we need to understand

---

17. Dante Alighieri, "Inferno," in *The Divine Comedy*, ed. and trans. Allen Mandelbaum (New York: Bantam, 1982), 5:100–107.
18. Mt 25:41.

better the nature of this "eternal fire," but more fundamentally why it is such a terrible place. We know that hell is a place of punishment "prepared for the devil and his angels," but the question remains as to why God has set up punishment for those who are banned from his presence anyway. We may well ask, "Can he not just leave alone those who choose not to love him?" To grasp this we have to return to consideration of Satan and his psychology, his motivations.

Satan has a brilliant, powerful intellect, but he lacks wisdom. He had the chance to turn to God to ask him for wisdom, and he chose himself instead. Impressed by his own beauty and power, he could not conceive how much greater God is than he. In a way, he thought that on his own he could be a perfectly competent god. And what does God do? God creates and orders the universe. If Satan is to be a god, he needs to make and order a world. Lacking the power truly to create from nothing—only God has the power to draw being from non-being—he can nevertheless form the existing world to some extent. And while his powers to change the forms of material things remain limited, he can interact with spiritual beings, as we have said, influencing them by trying to teach them. So, the satanic plan is to form his own society, independent of and parallel to that which God has envisioned. This is evident from the first temptation, when the serpent insinuated that God was not to be trusted, that he would not give the best goods to human beings, and further that the woman and her husband could become as wise as God. He did not, interestingly enough, propose to them that they follow and imitate *him*. The inevitable effect of following the serpent's suggestion was to break the bond of love between the two human beings, between man and wife, and their recriminations are evident in the biblical text: "The woman whom thou gavest to be with me, she gave me the fruit of the tree and I ate."[19] Obedi-

19. Gn 3:12.

ence to Satan's suggestions and temptations has the direct effect of disrupting the love between Adam and Eve.

With this we can begin to grasp what is the "hell" of hell, why it is so terrible. Hell is a place separate from God where Satan reigns. It is the realm of power, manipulation, and anti-love. We may regard this "place" from two perspectives, the positive and the negative. Negatively hell is the state of separation from God and his goodness. Positively, it is a state of satanic abuse and enmity. Let us consider these in turn.

Separation from God

God is the source and cause of all good. St. Thomas teaches that whoever sees God, whoever enjoys the beatific vision of the divine essence, lacks nothing, for all good things are good in virtue of their participation in and reflection of the perfect goodness of God.[20] Whatever good the intellectual creature yearns for and enjoys is from God who is its perfect exemplar. Because everything that exists comes from God, the exemplar of all good, and because everything by its very existence is good, then everything in hell is good, at least insofar as it exists.[21] Strictly speaking, there is nothing in hell not to love and to delight in. Nevertheless the damned soul has no delight, even if it there encounters that which had delighted it in earthly life. Dante's lovers, Francesca da Rimini and Paolo Malatesta, find each other in hell, but the thrill is gone. They cannot please or mutually reassure each other by their presence. Similarly, the intellectual, eternally alone with the reflections of his own mind, can find no contentment in the complex beauty of his ideas. Having lost sight of the perfect good, the damned soul is unable to recognize or appreciate the good of *any* good.

---

20. *ST* Ia, q. 2, a. 3; Ia-IIae, q. 5, a. 4.
21. *ST* I, q. 5, a. 3; Thomas Aquinas, *De veritate*, q. 22.

Forms of Suffering

We can distinguish three basic forms of suffering, the most general kinds of suffering.[22] The distinctions among them are not always "clean," since we generally experience two or three as interwoven and simultaneous. They are: (1) suffering as feelings or *pain*; (2) suffering as frustration of the will or *failure*; and (3) suffering as meaninglessness or *despair*.

Pain When we think of suffering, our initial thought is ordinarily of *pain*. In a way, pain is paradigmatic of suffering, and the terms are often interchanged. Properly speaking, however, pain has to do with the body, in particular with certain stimulations of nerve endings. When something is wrong with the body—a tooth is decayed, the appendix is inflamed, or the muscles are overworked—one feels pain. And although we all hate pain and want it to go away, it is a good thing. Physicians know and depend on this, because ordinarily pain alerts us to a problem in the body. Those who cannot feel pain are at serious medical risk, because they are often unaware when something is seriously wrong with their bodies.

Ultimately pain is bodily, directly, and intimately related to the state of the physical organism, and as such is experienced almost primordially as an evil. As an experience of bodily disintegration, pain is a sign of vulnerability more than a kind of signal that a part or organ system has malfunctioned, needing care or repair. Experiencing that bodily integrity is compromised, the patient experiences fear. The animal whose leg is

22. This section is based on and also develops my previous articles, Adrian J. Reimers, "The Structure of Suffering," in *Cierpienie, Umieranie, Śmierć: Wyzwania i dylematy ludzkiego losu w kontekście sytuacji granicznich* [Suffering, Dying, Death: Challenges and Dilemmas of Human Destiny in the Context of Boundary Situations], ed. P. Dancak, M. Rembierz, and R. Sieroń (Stalowa Wola, Poland: KUL, 2013), 27–42, and Reimers, "The Significance of Suffering," *National Catholic Bioethics Quarterly* (Spring 2003): 53–58.

injured feels the pain but not the dread that it may never again run fast. The sick or injured animal simply adapts as best it can. The human person, on the other hand, realizes that life will have changed, that it may even end. In the experience of pain we find the definitive refutation of Hume's distinction between facts and values, because pain is never a brute fact but rather is itself the experience of a value (or rather disvalue) that influences his behavior. One pauses in his walk to remove the miniscule pebble from his shoe. Physical pain can so color and fill one's world that it becomes impossible to ignore. Even in the certain knowledge that in an hour the dentist will have repaired the tooth, one cannot in the meantime disregard the ache so as to address pressing chores. We are told that under torture most prisoners, even those unquestioningly loyal to the cause for which they are held and abused, will tell their tormentors *something*, simply to put an end to the pain. To be sure, although there are techniques, some quite sophisticated, to manage pain, and although one can learn heroically to live with it, pain significantly and often even decisively forms how the embodied person lives in and relates to the world and those around him.

If death is indeed the separation of soul from body, it follows that the moment of judgment does not involve pain, because the soul at that moment has no body through which to feel pain. Death puts an end to pain, and in fact those who suffer greatly sometimes welcome death precisely as a release from their pain. How often do we remark after someone has died, "At last his sufferings are over"? After death, the disembodied soul cannot directly feel physical pain. However, bodily pain, no matter how severe, is not the worst kind of suffering, and, as we shall see soon, the disembodied soul is not necessarily free from the sufferings linked to bodily pain.

Failure   We know that pain is not the worst kind of suffering for the simple reason that people will endure serious bodily discomfort to succeed in achieving important goals. Mountain climbers brave harsh winds and cold, as well as the dangers of injury and death, forcing themselves to overcome their fatigue and soreness to reach the summit. Athletes routinely endure discomfort and pain in training and competition. And when a person is successful, the pain becomes unimportant. Think of the victorious boxer, his battered and swollen face alight with his smile as the referee raises his gloved hand. Jesus remarks that when a mother has finally delivered her baby, in her joy she forgets her labor pains.[23]

Failure hurts, but in a way different than sheer pain. Think of the bitterness of defeat, the wish to go back and undo that one moment, that mistake that lost the game. Couples who want to have children suffer from their failure to conceive. They are healthy and strong, enduring no pains, no illnesses—but they suffer nonetheless. The wife's menstruation becomes a monthly reminder that they have again failed. The student who has been denied admission to her chosen university, the entrepreneur whose business has failed, the candidate who lost the election ... all these would gladly trade the bitterness of defeat for a toothache or a broken leg. We humans are purposeful, goal-directed beings, and failure is hard for us to accept. In this context, of course, physical pain can also become more painful because of the compromise of the body and its capabilities. The pain of a jarring tackle in a football game is momentary, but a torn ACL in the knee brings immediate fear. Damage to the body and its capacities threatens future plans and hopes for the realization of certain values.

Failure is a more *personal* suffering than physical pain. That

23. Jn 16:21.

is, failure strikes more closely to the core of one's personhood because by his achievements the person distinguishes himself and leaves his mark on the world. Because the acting person is master of his acts, which arise as he exercises his mental and physical capacities, his failures belong immediately to him. The burn or toothache may have happened to anyone, but my failure to win or achieve the goal I wanted is *my* failure. Even if some other person or factor may be to blame, it is my failure.

Seen from a different angle, the insult represented by physical pain is physical because it arises from the compromise of the body, the physical organism. The insult represented by failure is also to the spirit. Reality—perhaps even by the agency of some other person—has opposed one's will. Therefore failure can and often does give rise to anger or resentment against that or him who opposed the agent's will. If what he undertakes is right, good, and just, then the failure of his enterprise can be regarded as an injustice, an offense to be remedied. *Pain* gives rise to the search for a cure, for relief, but *failure* provokes rumination or even obsession with plans to set right the wrong. Failure has the power to torment the person who has failed.

Despair   Despair is spiritual suffering that leads to death; it is Kierkegaard's "sickness unto death."[24] It is the pain of having nothing to live for, no purpose in life. Despair *can* result from physical suffering when someone cannot cope with and see his way through unremitting physical agony. On the other hand, we know that people can suffer great pain and remain hopeful. Despair *can* result from repeated failures: "No matter what I do, nothing works." As any motivational speaker will say, there is a great difference between failing and seeing oneself as

24. Søren Kierkegaard, *Sickness unto Death* (Princeton: Princeton University Press, 1983).

a failure. There are many who have had their dreams and plans thwarted who continue to live joy-filled, hopeful lives.

To despair is to lose hope for the good. Of course, it is reasonable to abandon hope for some limited goods that one might desire. The teenage boy who realizes that he will never be six feet tall and who cannot dribble a ball must give up his dream of being a basketball star, a good he can safely (and wisely) despair of attaining, his disappointment notwithstanding. Indeed, the process of maturing requires one to give up attractive dreams of childhood and adolescence in favor of more realistic and fulfilling adult goals. That being said, to lose the hope of attaining some highly valued goal can be devastating to the human spirit. Our loves and the hopes they engender give form to our lives; indeed, the project of life may be said to consist in the pursuit of one's loves. These loves may be transformed as specific plans meet defeats and disappointments. The pain of despair comes with the realization that one may never attain what he loves, what he most desires. The ultimate despair is to abandon *all* hope of realizing the good. It is to lose hope that one can ever attain to genuine and meaningful good, that one's own life can be good, that the good is real. With this the spirit dies.

To give up on the good is to give up on love. If there is no good for me, then I am not loved. St. John Paul the Great wrote, "Only love creates the good."[25] Despair is therefore a loss of love. The logic is inexorable. If indeed it is love that creates the good, and if I am cut off from the good, then it can only be that no one loves me. To despair is to find oneself cut off from love, indeed, unworthy of love. This does not mean that the desperate person is consumed by hatred (although in some cases he is), but only that he sees himself as unloved and hence unlov-

25. John Paul II, *Man and Woman He Created Them,* 147 (5:3).

able. The soul in despair is beyond the reach of the good, either to experience it or to attain it. This kind of suffering—that of despair—can be linked with pain and defeat, although the link is not necessary. Unremitting severe pain can suggest that life can offer nothing but evil, that the pain will never cease and will henceforth constitute the only meaning in one's life. It is this reasoning that makes suicide seem attractive to one in great pain. Repeated failure and defeat can also prompt despair, as one comes to believe that he can never achieve anything good.

Truly to despair is to stop loving. If I can do nothing that is really good, if all that I do is worthless or bad, then I do no good to myself or anyone. A person in true despair ceases to love and may well turn instead to indulgence—drugs or alcohol or sex— or to mindless activity and a whirl of amusements to take his mind off his despair. So we hear of people who have adequate wealth, decent health, and a circle of friendly acquaintances but who have to drink or party constantly, because when the music stops or the lights go out, the inner pain cannot be borne. The ultimate giving up on love is suicide, the final act of despair.

The person in despair has also implicitly given up on the love of others. Someone who knows that he is loved does not despair. The reason for this is clear. Love says, "You are important to me." This last form of suffering—the suffering of despair—is the suffering of the soul that has separated itself from God, its true good. There is no drink, no distraction, no sexual frolic, nor is there a game, a project, a hobby or achievement— nothing to take away its despairing pain.

We can better understand the damned soul's despair if we look at the seven deadly sins, which are the keys to despair. Although not in themselves sins or evil acts that a person commits, as attitudes of spirit these—*pride*, *covetousness*, *lust*, *anger*, *gluttony*, *envy*, and *sloth*—empty the soul and plunge it into despair. They are called "capital sins" because all other sins find their roots in them. Looking at them in turn, we can see how the damned soul actually despairs of any good.

Pride Understood as a capital sin, pride is identical with vainglory, which is simply to glory in vain things. It is right and good to seek our true glory according to our dignity as sons and daughters of God. We are indeed destined to eternal communion with God.[26] Vainglory is to seek our glory in something that is not God, in ourselves and what we can do ourselves. St. Thomas distinguishes three ways in which glory can be in vain: first when one glories falsely, second when he glories in a passing, temporal glory, and third "when man's glory is not ordered to its proper end."[27] In other words, the vainglorious soul takes pride in what is not its true glory. This was precisely Satan's sin when he turned from the offered joy of seeing God face-to-face, choosing instead to glory in his own brilliance and beauty. Satan chose for himself the prerogatives of God.

Everyone, even the professed atheist, believes in God. If "God" means "the supreme being," and if God is the touchstone of all truth, beauty, meaning, and goodness—the author and foundation of all reality—then everyone believes that a god exists. God is the most important being there is, the central reality in terms of which anything else is real, true, and good. The big question is not whether a god exists, but rather what that being is that really is God. Josef Stalin believed and acted as though he were God. He decided all the important questions for the Soviet Union that he ruled—who should live and who should die, what is true and what is false, what is good and what evil, what was the meaning of everyone's life. Speaking of the Stalinist system, Václav Havel wrote, "The principle

26. Second Vatican Council, *Gaudium et spes*, §19.

27. Aquinas, *On Evil*, q. 9, a. 1, trans. John A. Oesterle and Jean T. Oesterle (Notre Dame, Ind.: University of Notre Dame Press, 1995).

involved here is that the center of power is identical with the center of truth."[28] Anyone who challenged Stalin's "divinity" was punished. In virtue of his immense power, by which he was able to realize his vision of an empire ruled entirely by his own will, Stalin's case was distinctive. But to be vainglorious, to live as though one is a god, it is not necessary to have Stalin's power. If God is the ultimate touchstone of truth and reality and if only that which satisfies my desires and my perception of my worth is of real importance and validity, then I have arrogated to myself the status of divinity. There is a glory that comes from God, as Aquinas observes in the text cited previously, but if that is not the glory that a person seeks, then he must perforce seek a glory that comes from elsewhere. His value arises from within himself. In a way, vainglory seeks God's prerogatives.

St. Peter exhorts us, "Be subject to the elders. Clothe yourselves, all of you, with humility toward one another," for "God opposes the proud, but gives grace to the humble. Humble yourselves therefore under the mighty hand of God, that in due time he may exalt you."[29] The proud are those who are too good in their own eyes to do the two things St. Peter calls us to: first to serve other human beings, and second to bow down before the power of God. The proud are above serving the least of Christ's brethren. And they are above submitting themselves in obedience to God. Of course, no one (or not too many people, at least) will say explicitly, "I refuse to obey God!," but many may well find it beneath them to accept any significant claim to divine authority over their lives.

When the vainglorious person dies, he leaves this life boasting of a glory that his soul cannot sustain in the next life. In this life it has set itself against God, treating him as a threat to

28. Havel, "Power of the Powerless," 25.
29. 1 Pt 5:5–6.

its own sovereignty, but at the moment of death the proud soul is powerless, alone, and horribly aware that its arrogance was based on a lie. Only God is God, and the only lasting glory is his. He will gladly share it with the soul that turns to him, but the vainglorious person has trusted in a lie. He has believed that he can decide for himself what glory is. And instead of God, before whom it refused to bow in this life, it finds itself oppressed, ridiculed, and humiliated by another spirit—Satan, who in his pride said, "I will not serve."

Envy   Closely related to pride, envy is a distinctively spiritual sin; it arises from the spirit. Envy provides no direct pleasure, no satisfaction. Anger can rejoice in its vindication. Lust can revel in its pleasures. But envy merely gnaws and resents. It is a truly pointless sin. The devil, who is a pure spirit, envies.

Theologians tell us that envy is the sorrow over another person's good, because another's good is perceived as somehow opposed to one's own.[30] The envious soul resents that someone else should receive a good that it does not. The strange thing about envy is that the other's good is not necessarily something that envy really desires. Indeed, sorrow over another's good is particularly perverse precisely because it opposes the good of another simply because he is another. Unlike covetousness, which desires the other's good for oneself, envy simply resents that another has that good, whether I want it or not. As with anger, envy justifies itself by appealing to "the principle of the thing." So if the receptionist receives an "outstanding employee" award—a prize that management is not entitled to—the envious assistant vice-president will console himself that the award is only for "nobodies," for those whose contributions are minimal, and he maneuvers to see to it that *his own*

---

30. Aquinas, *On Evil,* q. 10, a. 1.

(presumably more substantial) achievements are given their due acknowledgment, even while the receptionist is being honored. Envy is an equal-opportunity vice. The envious soul can resent those who are more talented, gifted, and fortunate or those who are less so. The poor man can envy the rich, but the rich can resent the special provisions made for the poor, not because they cost him money, but because he is more deserving of special consideration.

Because envy is sorrow for another person's good, it is especially pernicious. It is sorrow for the *good*. An envious soul has a hard time loving other persons, because to love is to will the good of the beloved.[31] Love will never begrudge honors and benefits to its beloved. Furthermore, it is typical of envy not to notice the good that has come its way. That is to say, the envious soul is often so preoccupied with the small gifts that someone else has received that it ignores the great gifts that he has received himself. The professor with his advanced degree and professional plaudits resents the award ceremony for the student and insinuates his own preeminence into the public celebration. No matter what the envious soul may have, it is not satisfied if someone else should seem to have more. In death the envious soul is especially alone, having and wanting no one to turn to, no one to wish well to, and no one to acknowledge its presumed preeminence.

Covetousness Covetousness is simply the inordinate desire for material possessions, the preoccupation with having "things." Because we need material things to get through life, it is very easy to see our lives in terms of them. It is enough to think of the concerns of any young family, for whom it is necessary to provide a home and its furnishings, clothing for the children,

---

31. Aquinas, *Commentary on the Gospel of St. John*, ed. James A. Weisheipl, OP; trans. Fabian R. Larcher, OP, and James A. Weisheipl, OP (Toronto: Pontifical Institute of Medieval Studies), chap 5, §§ 753, 1238, 1643; *ST* Ia, q. 20, a. 2.

food, and medical care, as well as toys for the children and recreational resources. For the ordinary family there never seems to be enough money. There always remain needs to be met. Or we may consider the worries of any business owner or manager, who faces constant pressures to meet expenses and balance the budget. The demands of meeting our financial and material needs has the effect of fostering habits of seeing the world in material terms and relating to it materialistically. The mind and character can be subtly formed by material things, so that it becomes a practical reality that a person's life consists in these things.

Pope John Paul II warned repeatedly against the dangers of consumerism, maintaining that the measure of a human person is not what he has but who he is.[32] The consumerist mentality constitutes a serious temptation, because one may come to measure his worth by what he has. Contemporary shopping malls are not primarily for conveniently purchasing life's necessities, but for entertainment as shopping increasingly becomes a recreational activity. But, argues St. John Paul II, it is not *what a person has* but *who he is* that makes someone important because a person is primarily a *who* and not a *what*. And who is this person? The answer is not homeowner or Lexus-owner or business manager. It is "father" or "mother," "son" or "friend," "daughter," "Christian," "peacemaker," "servant of the suffering." Only this "*who*" will remain as she departs this life and her heirs fight over the Lexus.

In his *Republic*, Plato describes the oligarchic soul, whose desire for wealth supersedes his desire for wisdom: "He makes the rational and spirited parts sit on the ground beneath appetite, one on either side, reducing them to slaves. He won't allow the first to reason about or examine anything except how

---

32. John Paul II, Encyclical *Evangelium vitae* (Vatican City: Libreria Editrice Vaticana, 1995), §23; Encyclical *Centesimus annus* (Vatican City: Libreria Editrice Vaticana, 1992), §19, 36, 41; *Man and Woman He Created Them*, 661 (133:3).

a little money can be made into great wealth."[33] The covetous soul has trained itself, formed itself, to understand only the laws of acquisition. Its mindset is perpetually ordered toward "how a little money can be made into great wealth." This mental formation is such that such a mind has lost its capacity to understand anything else than the laws of commerce, the principles of acquisition, and retention of wealth. Even though in this regard it may be very clever and even creative, this mind can no longer grasp how an activity can be prosecuted intelligibly without reference to the acquisition of profit.

In our discussion thus far here we have not distinguished well between natural wealth, which consists in usable things, and artificial wealth, or money. Certainly one can covet a neighbor's possessions, his house or car or gold watch. However, money introduces a new dynamic, one noticed by Aristotle,[34] Aquinas,[35] and John Locke.[36] Whereas there is a natural limit to the acquisition and use of natural wealth—one can accumulate only so many apples to consume, for the excess will decay, and in general one can actually enjoy the possession of only a finite number of things—the acquisition of money is potentially infinite. Furthermore, money can be exchanged for any other thing. As his neighbor's luxury car ages and begins to rust, the man with money sits secure knowing that at any time he can purchase a newer and better car. Money in one's treasury stands as a hedge against future want. Even if drought and famine strike, the rich man can buy what he needs. His money is a sort of real power by which he can acquire what he wants, control others, and secure himself against future needs. And because money is potentially infinite,

33. Plato, *Republic*, Book VIII, 553c–d.

34. Aristotle, *Politics* I.9.1257b 39–41, trans. C. D. C. Reeve (Indianapolis: Hackett, 1998).

35. *ST* Ia-IIae, q. 2, a. 1.

36. John Locke, *Second Treatise of Government* (Indianapolis: Hackett, 1980), §§47–50, 28–30.

then there is no limit to the amount he might acquire. In this way, money, as the solution to all problems and the guarantee against future misfortune, takes on the character of an *idol*, which must be served by constant vigilance and activity. The laws of finance and acquisition become the laws of the miserly life. In this way, money truly can take the position of the divine. Money, by its nature, tends toward idolatry.

In death the covetous soul has nothing left. It is lost, confused, almost terrified because there is nothing for it to measure itself by. Its mental principles for understanding reality are disconnected from its new reality. And it is cut off from the Creator and giver of every good gift.[37]

Lust   To understand the power of lust we must consider its nature more closely. After noting that "pleasure is one of the conditions of happiness," Aquinas continues, "Now sexual pleasure, which is the end or object of lust, is the most intense of physical pleasures."[38] Therefore, lust is "a disorder in the desires for venereal pleasures according to excess."[39] This disorder can arise either because the act itself is disordered, as in the case of fornication, or because the desire itself is disordered, which can even occur in a man's otherwise lawful union with his wife. St. John Paul II speaks of the latter as he argues that a husband can "commit adultery in his heart" even with his own wife if in their marital relations he regards her only as an object for the satisfaction of his sexual drive.[40] Lust expects the greatest imaginable pleasure from sexual activity, and even in the context of conjugal relations, lust craves satisfaction and, if given rein, can come to ignore love. In the final analysis, lust is selfish and cares nothing about the *person* whose body satisfies it.

37. See Jas 1:17.   38. Aquinas, *On Evil*, q. 15, a.4.
39. Ibid., q. 15, a. 1
40. John Paul II, *Man and Woman He Created Them*, 299 (43:3).

The scriptures provide an excellent illustration of lust's effects.[41] "Now Absalom, David's son, had a beautiful sister, whose name was Tamar; and after a time Amnon, David's son, loved her." Amnon wanted her but it seemed impossible for him to have her. With the help of a disreputable cousin, he found a way to be alone with her and to take her. Let us look at the scriptural text itself:

But he would not listen to her; he overpowered her; and being stronger than she, he forced her, and lay with her. Then Amnon hated her with very great hatred; so that the hatred with which he hated her was greater than the love with which he had loved her. And Amnon said to her, "Arise, be gone." ... He called the young man who served him and said, "Put this woman out of my presence, and bolt the door after her."[42]

It is a brutal story, but psychologically accurate and true, not only of Amnon and Tamar, but of the dynamic of lust in every age. Having used her to satisfy himself and his sexual craving, he found her—in spite of her innocence and decency—disgusting. He cared nothing for her, only for her body as a source of delight for himself. Lust works against love. Even when a genuine affection and friendship may also be present, lust strives to take over. The relationship in which lust has power falls increasingly under its sway. More and more it becomes a matter of satisfying sensual desire and less and less about friendship and the flowering of authentic love.

The soul dominated by lust has lost everything at death. There are no bodies to enjoy, and without its own body the lustful soul is aimlessly and incessantly restless. The lustful soul without its body is in exactly the state of Dante's Francesca and Paolo.

41. 2 Sm 13:1–19.
42. Ibid., 13:14–17.

Love, that can quickly seize the gentle heart,
took hold of him because of the fair body
taken from me—how that was done still wounds me.
Love, that releases no beloved from loving,
took hold of me so strongly through his beauty
that, as you see, it has not left me yet.

. . .

There is no greater sorrow
than thinking back upon a happy time
in misery—and this your teacher knows.[43]

Gluttony Like lust, gluttony focuses on pleasure, on self-satisfaction. Gluttony, however, looks inward to fill itself up, while lust looks outward to find the body to touch and enjoy. The cravings of the belly are, as it were, more available than venereal pleasures, for their object is but a thing and not a possibly uncooperative person, but they are less intense. To fill up the gluttonous desire, all that is required is something pleasant to eat. The gluttonous soul wants constantly to devour, to consume. Gluttony is always thinking of the next meal or drink. Intake is almost always on its mind. The alcoholic (for alcoholism is a form of gluttony) structures his life around the availability of alcohol. His life is full of strategies, so that he is never too far from the next drink. It is similar with the glutton for food. The next meal, what to eat next, is an ongoing preoccupation. The glutton must be satiated, full, and over-satisfied.

Gluttony wars against spiritual pursuits, which is why the great spiritual masters have always encouraged fasting. Even though God has made us for himself and our hearts are restless until they rest in him, we can easily mask this restlessness by

---

43. Dante, *Inferno*, Canto V, 100–105, 121–23. The "teacher" is Virgil, Dante's guide through hell.

feeding our appetites for food and drink. Because satiety makes one lethargic, the over-satiated person cannot easily see that he is hungry for God. Indeed, after a big meal it is natural to fall asleep. And this lethargy cripples the energy for spiritual pursuits—whether intellectual studies in search of the true or growth in virtue to attain the good. The gluttonous soul focuses primarily on what satisfies the body, not what satisfies itself. Like the lustful, the gluttonous soul finds itself completely frustrated in death. Without the body's appetites to look out and provide for, without having a body to take satisfaction into itself, the soul is lost, directionless, anxious.

Anger   As a reasonable response to evil or to threats, anger is appropriate. Physical assault arouses anger. Having learned of grave injustice, one *should* experience anger. Because it is contrary to a perceived evil and stands against it, anger is also emotionally rewarding. An offended person, someone who experiences evil, has the *right* to be angry. Therefore the attitude of anger becomes resentful, looking for a fight. Anger wants to teach someone a lesson and is disappointed if the alleged offender turns out to be innocent after all. We may recall St. Paul's admonition that love "does not take offense, and is not resentful. Love takes no pleasure in other people's sins."[44] We can best see the dangerous attraction of anger if we look at the "righteousness" of an angry person. In a way, anger always believes itself justified.

In one way, anger really is always justified. Because time is irreversible and history inalterable, nothing can, *strictly speaking*, undo an offense or injury. Even if the offender tries to make amends, the offense itself has been given and cannot be revoked. Nothing can make right the injury. Because time is unidirec-

44. 1 Cor 13:5–6.

tional—what is done really is done—evil is a kind of absolute. Restitution, repair, and apologies can offer compensation, but they cannot undo the damage. The only way a wrong can be set right is if the offended person accepts it as having been set right. On the level of experience, there is no satisfaction until the injured party is satisfied.

Anger gives a person the *right to exercise power against another*. To be angry is to hold the power of justification, of absolution over another person. The offended one is entitled to satisfaction, entitled to tell the story of his offense to all who will listen. Justice has been violated, and anger is its vindicator. The angry soul seeks to assert itself and to exercise its power. But after death it has no more power. Against whom can it assert itself? Rendered powerless by death, how can it assert its presumed authority? In hell's lonely solipsism no one is impressed with the force, fury, and righteousness of an angry soul's wrath.

Sloth   Like envy, sloth is a kind of sorrow. Although we usually think of sloth in terms of laziness, laziness is not a necessary consequence of sloth, which is of its essence sorrow over spiritual growth and good. The slothful person may well be lazy, of course, because every form of laziness hates to put forth effort to accomplish something good. On the other hand, a very energetic and busy person—someone who is always at work accomplishing something—may also be slothful. It is easy to bury oneself in activity in order to avoid dealing with what is really important. As such, sloth may be (and often is) evident in the workplace, as, for instance, when the slothful manager is too busy supervising the accounting department (which is functioning well) to attend a disagreeable, but urgent, meeting with the dissatisfied customer. Sloth, as sorrow over the good, neglects the effort to accomplish the true good. By nature the human being desires the good, indeed, the highest and ultimate good, and this is why we cannot help seeking goodness. However, the highest good is demanding, because it is not simply a good to be acquired and possessed, but rather a good to be lived, one to which one gives himself. The perfect good, says St. Thomas, is an activity (*operatio*), ultimately the activity of contemplating God himself.[45] The pursuit of this good requires a transformation of one's life, a redirection of his will, a reformation of his loves. Because this demands fundamental changes to one's life and sense of self, it is easy to disguise this yearning for the highest good by turning to many essentially joyless activities—it could even be a frenzy of ordinarily worthwhile activities—that mask the failure to pursue the one essential thing. The need for distraction or for change of scenery or situation is a symptom of sloth.[46] Or sloth may choose inactivity, despairing that, in one's own case at least, the good is not attainable. With this comes not simply laziness, but also depression. If the true good is out of reach, it is bootless (futile) even to try.

Properly speaking, sloth (*acedia*) has to do with neglecting our relationship with God, and this is very strange. To grow in the love of God, one must pray, meditate, read the scriptures, and attend sacred liturgy. All these things are fairly relaxing. "Be still, and know that I am God."[47] The need to care for the spiritual life is practically a license for rest and relaxation. Indeed, God *commanded* the Israelites to keep holy the Sabbath. To pray and draw close to God is not a demanding, strenuous task, and yet many of us would rather clean out the basement or paint the garage than to spend significant time in prayer. More typically, of course, we will spend time in distractions—watching television, playing games (especially computer and video games), or shopping.

---

45. *ST* Ia-IIae, q. 3, aa. 2 and 8.
46. Jean-Charles Nault, OSB, *The Noonday Devil: Acedia, the Unnamed Evil of Our Times* (San Francisco: Ignatius, 2015), 30–32, 113–16.
47. Ps 46:10.

Sloth has its roots in fear. The spiritual life is about facing oneself and facing God. This is a great mystery, but it is also our common experience. We may recall Auden's "faces along the bar": if the music stops, if the lights go out, then I must face the questions.[48] Am I good? Do I know what good is? Do I care? What do I really love? Myself? Those near me? God? By trying to solve immediate, everyday problems (which, indeed, may well need to be addressed), it is possible to avoid facing oneself and what love one owes to God.

In death the slothful soul is in dire straits. Having in life buried itself in distractions in order to avoid facing its need for God, it finds itself alone and terrified with none to console it but he from whom it had fled, the one from whom he—alas!— had turned. In the boredom of its eternal solipsism, with none for company but itself, it becomes almost frenzied in its craving for a focus, for a meaningful activity.

The Damned Soul's Company

In death the sinful soul—the soul of him who has loved self to the contempt of God—is not alone, not completely. There is the Awful Presence, God himself, which this soul cannot see and, in any case, could not abide seeing. But there is another spirit there. Indeed, there is a host of spirits. Recall how the history of sin began. The Serpent in the Garden suggested to the woman that she eat the fruit. She saw that it was "good to eat and pleasing to the eye, and that it was desirable for the knowledge that it could give,"[49] and so, at the Serpent's urging, she opened herself to the threefold concupiscence: the lust of the eyes, the lust of the flesh, and the pride of life. The demon's task is much easier with us who are Eve's children, because original sin has made us already susceptible to concupiscence. But Satan is not one to leave us to

48. See note 3 in the Prologue.
49. Gn 3:6.

our own devices. He and his minions are happy to encourage our yielding to sin. And particularly important is that moment when the sin is mortal, when to the many little compromises with lust or greed or pride is added the decisive action. This may be the choice to spend the night with someone else's spouse, or it may be to tell the slanderous lie or to falsify the expense account and defraud the company. This sin is an act contrary to God's love. It is a choice for self-love, which cannot be reconciled with love for God and neighbor. The damned soul is in this state because, at the urging of the evil one, it turned to its own satisfaction and never saw fit to plead for God's mercy. Now for company it has only the Tempter, whose mocking presence it already feels.

The sinful soul, which has definitively turned to love of self and contempt of God, faces death in darkness, futility, terror, and despair. In its vainglory, anger, and envious vanity, it had exalted itself above others and now finds itself alone with no rights, no power, no prerogatives. Having given reign to lust, gluttony, and greed, it is without the body to seize and enjoy property and pleasure, but lives instead in frustrated futility. If these capital sins have formed the soul, then, after the loss of the body and its distractions, that soul finds itself in darkness, loneliness, confusion, frustration, and despair, with no company but that of the demons who gloat over its fall.

An old joke has it that even hell cannot be so bad, because there the sinner will meet with his friends, with whom he had enjoyed the good times that merited his damnation. The joke is cute and clever, but it is cruelly false. Hell is lonely and unfriendly.

The Soul of Dismas

It was the worst day of his miserable life. Finally, after the soldiers smashed their clubs against his legs, there followed a few moments of excruciating pain, and it was over. Dismas was dead. Having lost everything, he was unconscious, but in the unconsciousness of death he became aware of a Presence. Even though he had met this Person only once—and that just three hours prior—he unmistakably recognized the One who had said, "Indeed, I promise you, today you will be with me in paradise." In this presence, he felt his shame welling up, not a redness of face—he had no face to blush, no blood to fill his capillaries—but a spiritual shame, the shame of one who had spent most of his life in theft, betrayal, self-aggrandizement, self-indulgence, and deceit. It was all there with the keen awareness that this One had every right to cast him from his sight. But instead of being rejected, he was embraced. The spiritual tears of shame were wiped away. In one instant, on the spur of the moment, he had turned to Jesus in mercy and then in faith. Now that same Person welcomed him into his friendship.

"You made us for yourself,"[50] wrote St. Augustine. Dismas, too, was made for God. He had not been a very good man. It was Roman power and justice and not his own repentance that ended his life of crime. Jesus died the same death as Dismas, punished for crimes against Rome, and in doing so he transformed the soul of Dismas into a reflection of his own. He had redirected Dismas, in a way, redeeming all that was good but misdirected. And Dismas experienced the consolation God has for those who love him. Expecting darkness—knowing that for his sins he deserved darkness—the criminal found light. His life and his whole being finally made sense. He was embraced by the light that loved him. Having taken those two steps, first of mercy—"Have you no fear of God.... This man has done nothing wrong"—and then of faith—"Jesus, remember me"— he was saved from all his sins. He was genuinely happy.

50. Augustine, *Confessions*, Book I, chap. 1.

CHAPTER 4

Resurrection and Final Judgment

When they wanted to entrap Jesus, the Sadducees challenged his teaching of the resurrection of the dead.[1] Jesus did not console Martha by telling her that her brother's soul "has gone to a better place," but by challenging her to believe that he was indeed the resurrection and the life,[2] and Jesus proved his claim by raising Lazarus from death. Jesus promises expressly,

I tell you most solemnly, the hour will come—in fact it is here already—when the dead will hear the voice of the Son of God, and all who hear it will live. . . .

Do not be surprised at this, for the hour is coming when the dead

---

1. Mt 22:23–32.
2. Jn 11:24–27.

will leave their graves at the sound of his voice: those who did good will rise again to life; and those who did evil, to condemnation." (Jn 5:25, 28–29)

And in St. Paul's letters, we find repeatedly the promise of resurrection. When the Thessalonians needed to console each other for the deaths of their loved ones, St. Paul told them not to grieve like those who have no hope. "We believe that Jesus died and rose again, and that it will be the same for those who have died in Jesus: God will bring them with him" (1 Thes 4:11–18). This is especially clear in 1 Corinthians 15, where Paul gives an extended explanation of the resurrection and its importance, concluding with these words:

When this perishable nature has put on imperishability, and when this mortal nature has put on immortality, then the words of scripture will come true: Death is swallowed up in victory. Death, where is your victory? Death, where is your sting?" (1 Cor 15:54–55)

Although we philosophers focus on the immortality of the soul, the New Testament teaching on the afterlife almost always speaks of the life of the resurrection—a return to bodily life, albeit under conditions different from those of this present earthly life. Even if when the person dies something of him—his rational soul—lives on, this is not the central hope in the gospel. Christ has conquered death and promises to share that victory with humans. Because Christ was raised from the dead, all will be raised. The final resurrection depends entirely on Christ and his resurrection. This is the destiny of every human being. Therefore, there is not a kind of natural heaven for the souls of good people who were not religious, a state akin to what Socrates hoped for. What will happen is that Christ will come again and all the dead will be raised in their bodies. Then all will come before the King for judgment.

Time and Eternity

Before turning our attention to the Last Judgment, we need to reflect on the resurrected body's condition, which poses some peculiar and difficult conceptual problems. Bodies exist in space and time, reacting to and interacting with other bodies. The separated soul, however, can be considered outside the categories of space and time. We can think of the soul as existing in a kind of quasi-eternity with only a vague awareness (if any) of the passing of time. The life of the resurrection, on the other hand, poses very directly the question of space and time. If the bodies of the just will be in heaven or in the heavenly Jerusalem, where is this in relation to our present earth? If Jesus ascended into heaven and his Mother was assumed bodily into heaven, we may ask where this is in relation to the earth or Mars. Equally troubling is the question of the perpetuity of the resurrected life. Even if nobody wants to die, the prospect of billions—trillions—of days of future life, to be followed by billions more, is disconcerting. What does one do for so long a time? If the Virgin Mary is the only human being besides Christ bodily to have entered into glory, then what does she do all day? Her visits to Guadalupe, Lourdes, and Fatima would provide precious little diversion for a life without other people to be with and to talk with. More soberly, perhaps, Benedict XVI writes, "do we really want this—to live eternally? . . . To continue living forever —endlessly—appears more like a curse than a gift."[3] Benedict answers his own question by looking at what it is that we really want:

To imagine ourselves outside the temporality that imprisons us and in some way to sense that eternity is not an unending succession of

---

3. Benedict XVI, Encyclical *Spe salvi* (Vatican City: Libreria Editrice Vaticana, 2007), §10.

days in the calendar, but something more like the supreme moment of satisfaction, in which totality embraces us and we embrace totality—this we can only attempt. It would be like plunging into the ocean of infinite love, a moment in which time—the before and after—no longer exists.[4]

Because we live in time, we are ordinarily blind to the eternal. Whatever we imagine is perforce temporal, because our imaginings are constructed from our sense experiences. However, there is more to us than our bodies and the mental events that the brain gives rise to. Even in this life we live in relation to the eternal. This is evident from our intellectual ability to transcend space and time. My own "personal world" began shortly before the Japanese surrender in World War II, an event of which I have no direct memory. And yet like you, my reader, I read about and discuss the events of that war, its causes, and the alliances it gave rise to. Even though he died long ago, we are intrigued to learn that the remains of England's Richard III have been found and properly buried. It is at least of some interest that scientists have determined that the Big Bang occurred 13.8 billion years ago and not 13 billion, as had previously been thought. Our capacity to think "outside of time," *sub specie aeternitatis*, evidences that the human intellect has an eternal character—that is it related to eternity. Karol Wojtyła writes, "The values by which a person as such lives are by nature transtemporal, and even atemporal.... One can say, therefore, that the very content of the person's life points to the eternity of the person."[5] Most important is that the human will desires and reaches for the eternal, unchanging good that is God himself. This is Pope Benedict's point: that in desiring the fullness of good, we desire eternity. The truth about the human person is, therefore, that we are creatures not

4. Ibid., §12.
5. Wojtyła, "Thomistic Personalism," 175.

only of time but also of eternity. And so we see the cynicism of Elbert Hubbard's mot that life is just "one damn thing after another." Even human conjugal love, lived with all the changes entailed by a life shared over the course of years, reflects eternity. What is important—any couple who has experienced several decades of conjugal love can attest to this—are not the continuity and duration, but the heart of that love, which is timeless. This timelessness lies at the heart of the requirement that marriage, founded as it is on an unconditional vow of fidelity, be indissoluble. In time everything changes; change is what time is about. The marriage vow defies the demands of time in this way: that nothing that occurs during the lives of the spouses can warrant dissolution of the vow. Only death, which destroys the body of one partner in this essentially bodily union, can dissolve the union. If love is real, then eternity lies at its core. If this is so, then the life of the resurrection must be one in which the experience of the eternal will not only be direct, an effect of the immediate vision of the divine essence, but will be predominate in relation to sense experience.

Space and the Resurrected Body

The question of the body's relationship with space is perhaps even more puzzling and problematic. The apostles watched the resurrected Jesus ascend until a cloud took him from their sight.[6] The scriptures tell us that before his ascension, Jesus was able suddenly to appear to his disciples without entering through a door and subsequently disappear from the room.[7] That he was present physically and not as a ghost he proved by inviting them to touch him and then eating in their presence.[8] The gospel insists that Jesus's resurrection was a physi-

6. Acts 1:9. 7. Jn 20:19, 26; Lk 24:36.
8. Lk 24:37–44.

cal, bodily event. We might add further that when Mary, who was assumed bodily into heaven, appeared to Juan Diego, she arranged with her own hands the roses he had gathered in his *tilma*. In this way the testimonies from Marian apparitions are consistent with the accounts of Jesus's resurrected body. Thus we have a concept of bodiliness according to which the person concerned (Jesus or the Virgin Mary) is capable of appearing in a location and effecting things at that place—Jesus eats, Mary arranges flowers, and both speak and listen to others—but without traversing the intervening space from the place, wherever it might be, from whence they came.

To grasp this conception it is also helpful to consider one further and especially important factor. Catholics believe that in the sacrament of the Eucharist, Jesus Christ is bodily present.

> In the most blessed sacrament of the Eucharist "the body and blood, together with the soul and divinity, of our Lord Jesus Christ and, therefore *the whole Christ is truly, really, and substantially* contained....
>
> Christ is present, whole and entire in each of the species [bread and wine] and whole and entire in each of their parts, in such a way that the breaking of the bread does not divide Christ.[9]

If the Real Presence is what the church claims it to be, then this man, the resurrected Jesus of Nazareth, is bodily present, just as much as the priest and worshipers are present in the church. He touches and is touched by those who touch the host just as really as he was touched by Mary Magdalene and Thomas the Apostle.

The bodily presence of Christ in churches and tabernacles around the world is, of course, much different from the presence of one's friend sitting in the next room. No other person exists physically in such a way. On the other hand, the Eucha-

---

9. *Catechism of the Catholic Church*, 1374, 1377. Within, the text cites the Council of Trent (1551), DS 1651.

ristic presence of Jesus is not entirely foreign to human experience. Aware of the transience of our lives and of our relative insignificance, we want to leave mementos of our presence in the world. The human spirit rebels at the oft-cited metaphor of the hand in the water: no matter how great or powerful the hand, no matter what waves it may stir up, when it is withdrawn the water returns to its earlier state, leaving no evidence of its earlier presence. So, the lesson goes, when we leave this life, the world will go on as though we were never here in the first place. And so we try to leave monuments or mementos of ourselves to maintain our presence in the world after our deaths. While we live we use tools to extend our influence, activity, and power. With letters, email, telephones, and mass communications, human beings find ways to be where they cannot be. Soldiers serving overseas still talk with their children over Skype. How many love stories are built around a talisman that the lover gives to be his presence to the beloved while he must be gone? Of course, the physical traces of our presence fall far short of Christ's presence in the Eucharist. The presence of Abraham Lincoln in the memorial named for him does not compare with his presence at the Gettysburg cemetery in 1863, even if the visitors feel that they have come to know him there. The soldier in Afghanistan cannot hug his child through the computer. Nevertheless, the notion of somehow being present where one is not is an integral part of human experience.

Because we are rational and therefore spiritual beings, our existence cannot be strictly confined to the here and now. Even if the bodily frame is limited and determined, as it were, by the here and now, the spiritual relates to truth and the good. The person as a spiritual being extends himself, in a way, beyond space and time by his understanding and love. So, when I find myself perplexed and in need of help for thinking something through, I can turn to my long-deceased colleague Aristotle, whose writings are on my shelf. Granting that he cannot directly answer my follow-up questions by the sound of his voice, and granting that he had no idea of my being one of his future readers, his reflections on philosophy touch me and many like me. Similarly, Raphael has touched us with his vision of a community of scholars in his mural *School of Athens*. This is why it is possible for us to regard distant and deceased persons as our friends. The ordinary human being by his ordinary human powers can reasonably be said to exist when and where his body no longer is. It is a philosophical mistake, then, to say that the human being is only where the confines of his body are. Hence, the resurrected body, mysterious as its mode of existence may be, is not unintelligible. We see reflections of it even in this life.

The Last Judgment

When the Son of Man comes in his glory, and all the angels with him, then he will sit on his glorious throne. Before him will be gathered all the nations, and he will separate them one from another as a shepherd separates the sheep from the goats.[10]

The church teaches that there is also a judgment at the moment of death, a private judgment when the soul is alone before God. Some will enter into a deep and personal communion with him, and others will find themselves separated from him adrift in despair and confusion. The Last Judgment will be much different. This will be a real event, at which everyone who has ever lived will be present, and all will see Jesus Christ in the fullness of his glory as king and judge. Then every man or woman who has ever lived will appear in his or her full humanity before the King in his full humanity. The damned as well as the saved will see Jesus the King and hear his judgment.

10. Mt 25:32.

Michelangelo, fresco of the Last Judgment, altar wall of the Sistine Chapel

At that point Jesus will separate the "sheep" from the "goats," welcoming the blessed into their heavenly mansions and consigning the damned to the place prepared for the devil and his angels.

This is the definitive judgment—definitive in the sense that the whole being of the damned person begins to experience the repercussions of the judgment against him. The soul separated from the body in death may suffer the pain of confusion and despair as it is cut off from the One for Whom it was made. It had even begun to experience the torments of demonic mockery, but the full ramifications of its situation are probably not clear. In his marvelous—and very sobering—Last Judgment mural in the Sistine Chapel, Michelangelo portrays the moment in which Christ commands the "goats" to depart from him (see p. 121).[11] To his left we see devils grasping despairing sinners to drag them to hell. Their faces express confusion, disbelief, and fear. They were perhaps dimly aware of having turned from God, but they had never expected that it would turn out like this. Directly to the King's left we see an old man and a younger one who seem to be saying, "Lord, Lord, did we not prophesy in your name, and cast out demons in your name, and do many mighty works in your name?"[12] and to their faces Jesus replies, "I never knew you; *depart from me, you evildoers!*"[13] Below these two, separated from the other figures, is the famous woman in despair, her hand covering half her face, as two demons grasp her legs and body to drag her to the mouth of hell.

How could they be confused and in despair? If the judgment is just—and surely if anyone's judgments are just, God's

---

11. "Michelangelo, Giudizio Universale 02," by Michelangelo Buonarroti, Web Gallery of Art, October 1, 2005; licensed under Public Domain via Wikimedia Commons, http://commons.wikimedia.org/wiki/File:Michelangelo,_Giudizio _Universale_02.jpg#/media/File:Michelangelo,_Giudizio_Universale_02.jpg.

12. Mt 7: 22.

13. Ibid., 25:41.

are—then there is no way to argue with them. And it can be argued that no one goes to hell unwillingly—that God does not so much *send* people to hell as that he *allows* those who have chosen hell to go there. Nevertheless, because the sinner's power to reason is corrupted by his sin, the damned almost certainly feel themselves to be treated unfairly. All human reasoning is based on truths that are already known. All our judgments about true and false, good and evil are based on the thinker's first principles of truth and goodness. As Samwise struggles with the hardships of the journey to Mordor, Gollum's treachery, and Frodo's erratic behavior in Tolkien's *Lord of the Rings*, he is guided by the principles of friendship and loyalty: you never turn your back on a friend but remain faithful. Members of the Corleone family never speak about family business with outsiders.[14] We all learn and adopt principles of truth and goodness early in life. Generally we believe and accept what our parents teach us. We judge newly proposed truths on the basis of the truths that we have already accepted. If something conflicts with what a person knows to be true, then he does not believe it. This is why it is often hard for individuals and social groups to change. How does one accept that his father—or his nation's heroes—could be wrong?

The damned, by choosing self to the contempt of God, has made himself into his own highest good, and as a simple consequence of this he must conclude that whoever denies his goodness must be wrong. If his own goodness constitutes a first principle of his thinking, then he cannot recognize himself as deserving punishment. The reason one grows resentful when someone criticizes him for doing wrong is that it is easy—indeed, almost natural—to believe in one's own goodness. Therefore, a person who has chosen self over God is no longer

14. In Francis Ford Coppola's film *The Godfather* (1972).

capable of recognizing his own guilt and hence that he deserves punishment. Indeed, God should recognize his goodness. This is why St. Thomas Aquinas holds that the sinner has lost even the capacity to recognize his own sin and therefore has within himself no power to turn away from his sin.[15] This is why the damned are befuddled by the consequences of their choices. "Lord, when did we see thee hungry or thirsty or a stranger or naked or sick or in prison, and did not minister to thee?"[16] They feel themselves unfairly treated because they have blinded themselves to the truth about the good. The damned cannot recognize their punishment as just.

Judgment of the Nations

Before analyzing the individual's experience of this judgment, let us reflect on the judgment of the nations. Jesus promises that when he comes in glory, escorted by his angels, he will sit on his throne of glory, and "before him will be gathered all the nations."[17] The reference to "the nations" is significant. Under the Old Covenant God judged nations according to their obedience or disobedience to him, and when he punished, it was the entire nation that was chastised. Speaking of Babylon, Jeremiah writes:

> Therefore thus says the LORD:
> "Behold I will plead your cause and take vengeance for you.
> I will dry up her sea and make her fountain dry;
> and Babylon will become a heap of ruins,
> the haunt of jackals,
> a horror and a hissing
> without inhabitant."[18]

15. *ST* Ia-IIae, q. 88, a. 1.   16. Mt 25:44.
17. Ibid., 25:32.   18. Jer 51:36–37.

Because Babylon and its gods had offended the Lord, doing violence to Zion, he punished the entire nation by allowing Cyrus of Persia to conquer them and destroy their empire. Before this he had punished his own people, Judah and Israel, by allowing Assyria and Babylon to invade their land and take them captive, even to the point of allowing them to destroy Jerusalem. In the Old Testament, God punishes nations collectively. The God-fearing Babylonian (if there were any) suffered the pillaging by the Persians, just like his neighbors. When God punished his own people for their sins of idolatry, the faithful as well as the idol-worshippers had their homes destroyed and lands occupied by Israel's enemies.

When God judged and punished nations in Old Testament times, in one way or another it was because of their idolatry. Nations at that time identified themselves by their gods. We can see this in the book of Acts, when the many conversions to Christianity in Ephesus hurt the business of the silversmiths, who made their living supplying miniature shrines of Diana for the tourists.[19] The silversmiths managed to incite a riot with a crowd of townsfolk proudly shouting, "Great is Diana of the Ephesians!"[20] More ominous are the words of Sennacherib when he set out to attack Jerusalem, boasting that no gods of any of the nations had been able thus far to withstand the kings of Assyria and neither would the God of Israel.[21] The Assyrian gods were cruel and warlike, and in their name Sennacherib proposed to defeat the Lord, Israel's God. So when God judged the nations, he was judging their gods and showing that only he was truly God.

What has this to do with us? Billy Graham is supposed to have remarked once that if God does not punish the United States for its immorality, then he will owe Sodom and Gomor-

19. See Acts 19:23–41. 20. Ibid., 19:28, 34.
21. 2 Kings 18:34–35, 19:10–13.

rah an apology.[22] Will God judge the United States of America? Will he judge England or France or Russia—or perhaps the European Union? The Last Judgment scene in Matthew 25 states that "all the nations" will be gathered before him. Although it is clear from the text that individuals will be judged, the "you" to whom his judgment is addressed is in the plural. This is a judgment on nations. In the context of reflecting on the United States of America, it may be helpful to consider Ezekiel's prophecies against Tyre. Even if we cannot repeat them here in full, a few snatches will be worth considering. "O Tyre, you have said, 'I am perfect in beauty. Your borders are in the heart of the seas,'"[23] and the prophet writes of the beautiful products Tyre had won by its seafaring tradesmen.

At the sound of the cry of your pilots the countryside shakes, and down from their ships come all that handle the oar. The mariners and all the pilots of the sea wail aloud over you, and stand on the shore and cry bitterly.... "Who was ever destroyed like Tyre in the midst of the sea? When your wares came from the seas, you satisfied many peoples; with your abundant wealth and merchandise you enriched the kings of the earth."[24]

Tyre was a trading city in what is now Lebanon, situated on a small peninsula that reaches into the Mediterranean Sea. From that vantage point its merchants managed to do very well as a center for trade. Tyre did not persecute God's people but simply went about its business of getting rich. When Tyre fell, kings and merchants around the Mediterranean were dismayed. Tyre was not an enemy of God or his people. Rather, it did not care about God. They were seafarers who became rich by trad-

22. Billy Graham, "Billy Graham: 'My Heart Aches for America,'" *Billy Graham Evangelistic Association*, July 19, 2012, http://billygraham.org/story/billy-graham-my-heart-aches-for-america/; accessed November 29, 2015.
23. Ez 27:3–4.
24. Ibid., 27:28–30, 32–33.

ing with other nations around the Mediterranean. We might call Tyre's strategy a win-win proposition. Unlike the conquering Assyrians, when Tyre did well, everyone profited. In many respects, today's Western nations, especially the United States, resemble Tyre. Today the other nations of the world count on the United States as an anchor of prosperity and a trading partner with which they can become rich.

When God judged the nations, he did so for their idolatry, but in the scriptures we do not read about Tyre's idols. Historically, of course, Tyre had its gods, which were closely related to the Phoenician gods, but the principal interest of the scriptures is with the wealth of Tyre. Here, therefore, we must consider more closely the nature of idolatry. Every nation, every people has its god or gods, to whom it pays homage. A god is a higher being, an immortal and powerful being that enjoys a certain sovereignty over life or some sector of life and nature. As such a god is to be honored with appropriate worship and sacrifice. Failure to give the god his prerogatives will ordinarily result in failure or even disaster. The gods of the peoples are not so much interested in or concerned for moral behavior as they are for obedience and homage. In this respect we can speak intelligibly about the idolatry of money. Precisely in this context we must note the Lord's phrasing when he addresses the choice between God and mammon: "No servant can serve two masters; for he will either hate the one and love the other, or he will be devoted to the one and despise the other. You cannot serve God and mammon" (Lk 16:13). Jesus speaks quasi-personally of mammon as a master whom one can serve, love, or despise rather than God. In other words, mammon can be an idol.

What are the characteristics of this idol? Let us begin by noting that mammon is particularly evident in that artificial form of wealth that is money. As we have already remarked, in contrast to material things—land, apples, grain, gold watches, and houses—money is, in principle, infinite. Not only is the capacity for acquisition of money virtually infinite, but money is fungible for anything. With enough money one can buy whatever he wants, access the talents of others, and control sources of power. In principle, money can do anything. This is why Karl Marx credits money with the power to level social distinctions. In virtue of its money, argues Marx, the bourgeoisie

has stripped of its halo every occupation hitherto honoured and looked up to with reverent awe. It has converted the physician, the lawyer, the priest, the poet, the man of science, into its paid wage labourers. The bourgeoisie has torn away from the family its sentimental veil, and has reduced the family relation to a mere money relation.[25]

Mammon has its own laws, which must be respected and obeyed, under penalty of failure and even disaster. Every goal, every project, every plan of implementation must be measured in terms of the money required for its implementation. Within the logic of mammon, money becomes the measure of everything, converting the "physician, the lawyer, the priest, the poet, the man of science" into paid laborers, whose value is measured in terms of cost-benefit analyses.

Let us carefully note what is at stake here. Thrift is a virtue. Financial planning is important. Christ himself points to the foolishness of attempting a major construction project with insufficient resources.[26] The rule of mammon, however, goes beyond financial planning and management, turning these legitimate means into ends. Mammon insists that money determine what *can* be done and what *should* be done. If all the world is measured by money, then money must necessarily be the supreme good.

25. Karl Marx and Friedrich Engels, "Manifesto of the Communist Party," in *The Portable Karl Marx*, ed. Eugene Kamenka (New York: Penguin, 1983), 206.
26. Lk 15:28–29.

St. John Paul the Great repeatedly warned against the consumer culture, in which persons are valued not for who they are but for what they have.[27] For a nation to be a wealthy commercial power is not in itself bad, but the tokens of wealth can quickly become the supreme measure of human life. The wealthy of the ancient Mediterranean societies prided themselves on their cedar-paneled walls, with the wood shipped in from Lebanon, and on the luxurious cloths imported from Persia, just as today we pride ourselves on our fine electronics and elegant homes in the Italian villa style. More important— we can read this regularly in the news and hear it often from candidates for public office—in virtue of its wealth and power to determine the course of world affairs, the United States of America is "great," with a greatness of which its citizens ought to be proud and that they are obliged to help preserve. When we read about Tyre, we read about ourselves.

Here it is helpful to speak of "structures of sin": customs, traditions, practices, and laws that contravene God's intention and law.[28] To the extent that any individual person enters into those structures of sin, to that extent he sins personally. Because every sin is committed by an individual person, the culture or nation does not sin for him. Nevertheless, when one participates in and is formed by the sinful structures of nation or culture, then he falls under God's judgment because he incorporated that structure of sin into the pattern for his life. He makes that sin his own.

Caught up in our daily lives, we Americans readily lose sight of the extraordinarily privileged lives we live. If the entire world were one society, Americans would be atop the aristocracy. They are far wealthier than most of their contemporaries,

27. John Paul II, *Man and Woman He Created Them*, 662 (133:3); Encyclical *Centesimus annus*, §43; Encyclical *Sollicitudo rei socialis* (Vatican City: Libreria Editrice Vaticana, 1987), §28.

28. John Paul II, *Sollicitudo rei socialis*, §36.

better educated than most of the human race around the world or in the history of humanity, more comfortable, safer, and better cared for than almost all our neighbors outside Europe, Australia, and some parts of Asia. And even those Americans who are less well-off still enjoy the fruits of prosperity far more than most of the rest of humanity. God does not judge people for these advantages, but he will judge them for what they make of them. Characteristically, aristocrats come to think of themselves as *deserving* of their wealth and privilege. Although it is not a sin to be rich or to have inherited great wealth, it is wrong to believe that one *deserves* to have that status. In that respect we are like the nineteenth-century English aristocrats whom Dickens so scathingly portrayed. We are not entitled to live better off than the rest of humanity.

Mammon is not alone as an idol but finds its place in relation to other gods. It is true that if the Lord, the God of Abraham and Moses, the God revealed in Jesus Christ, is God, then there is and can only be but one God. Indeed, St. Thomas Aquinas shows with inexorable logic that God must be unique and unrivaled in his divinity.[29] Among idols, as we have indicated previously, no such exclusivity exists, even if one particular idol may inevitably assume primacy. Closely related to the idolatry of money (mammon) is the idolatry of the self, which in its subjectivity arrogates to itself the authority ultimately to determine what is true and good, indeed to determine what is real. The measure of truth is what the "I" thinks and wants to be true; that of goodness what it wants to be good. Another who should presume to deny the "I's" truth and goodness is not only a fool, but an enemy. Such a denial need not be absolute, however. It is generally acceptable to allow every other individual a similar divine prerogative, so that each person may af-

29. *ST* Ia, qq. 2, 3, 4, and 11.

firm himself the ultimate judge of truth and goodness for himself, so long as he does not deny another's prerogatives. This idol of self is not, however, a Nietzschean *Übermensch*, asserting his own will to power. He is, rather, the consumer, the utilitarian man, who judges his life and its meaning according to the acquiring of possessions and pleasant experiences. Life so conceived becomes a kind of commercial enterprise consisting of a perpetual series of cost-benefit analyses, balancing the possible future benefits of unpleasant "investments" of time, effort, and treasure, the object being to secure as pleasant a life as possible within the scope of one's own resources and opportunities.

If one has centered his life on the values of Tyre—that is, on the values of profit and acquisition—then when God judges those nations, that person will be judged with those nations. "As for the rich in this world, charge them not to be haughty, nor to set their hopes on uncertain riches, but on God who richly furnishes us with everything to enjoy."[30]

Threefold Concupiscence and Idolatry

The judgment against the nations will be for their idolatry, for their turning to other gods. One can, of course, argue that, strictly speaking, no modern nation is involved in idolatry. We Americans do not, like the ancient Canaanites, have altars to Baal erected on high places. Indeed, one might plausibly enough argue that the modern Western civilization has no gods, that we are peculiarly nonreligious. In such a context it is necessary for us to delve more deeply into the roots of idolatry, into its spiritual nature.

The key to understanding idolatry, the connective concept that links the sins of the nations with personal sin and that constitutes idolatry, is human concupiscence, from which the idols

30. 1 Tm 6:17.

gain their power to rule individual souls. John Paul II's analysis in his theology of the body of the "threefold concupiscence" from the First Letter of St. John is particularly relevant for our discussion here. St. John writes, "If anyone loves the world, love for the Father is not in him. For all that is in the world, the lust of the flesh and the lust of the eyes and the pride of life, is not of the Father but is of the world."[31] It is from the power of concupiscence that idols, including mammon, gain their power to rule human lives. The forms of concupiscence arise from natural desires—the desire for sexual union, for material possessions, and for the freedom to exercise one's own will. The desires arise, to be sure, from our "animal nature," but their working is more than animal. In this context John Paul II cites Paul Ricouer's identification of the three "masters of suspicion," Marx, Nietzsche, and Freud, and he correlates each of these with one of the three forms of concupiscence from 1 John 2:16[32]—Marx with the lust of the eyes, Freud with lust of the flesh, and Nietzsche with the pride of life. These are "not of the Father"; rather they are "of the world."

Why are Marx, Nietzsche, and Freud called "masters of suspicion"? The common factor in the thought of all three, according to John Paul II, is that they identify some form of concupiscence as that which is deepest in man and the primary source of his wants and behavior. John Paul II argues that in the face of concupiscence the human heart is called, but not accused; that notwithstanding its inclinations, the heart can respond to God's call and attain to its proper destiny. The master of suspicion, however, holds that the heart is determined by its concupiscent inclinations. If you are a bourgeois capitalist, according to Marx, you *will* pursue profit, even if you try to make yourself a friend to the workers. No matter how hard the superego tries to

31. 1 Jn 2:15–16.
32. John Paul II, *Man and Woman He Created Them*, 311 (46:3).

discipline and control the id, the sexual forces within the person will find their way either directly or unconsciously to govern his life. Similarly, in every free man Nietzsche finds an irrepressible will to power that demands expression.

For the "master of suspicion," each of these forms of concupiscence is more than simple desire. Let us consider sexual concupiscence or lust. As an animal appetite, it seems to be straightforward. Sexual desire arises and stirs the animal into action. The human being, experiencing this desire, may try to resist it for one reason or another, but the force still stirs within him. But the human being is not like the animal in this respect, for the animal is not subject to lust. The tomcat does not normally experience his sexual desires until a nearby female goes into heat, at which point, responding to her smell, he strives to mate with her. The experience of the young man, however, is quite different than this. Even if there is no specific woman nearby with whom he might mate, he is interested and desirous. His interest is triggered not only by the proximity of a desirable young female, but also by visual images, sounds and messages, smells, and even his own imagination. In fact, imagination plays an enormous role in human sexual concupiscence. Men and women (including adolescents) are attracted by pornography—albeit in different forms for each sex—movies, music, and television shows that reflect and feed their desires and give them form. It is plain that fantasy plays a major role in the development and operation of sexual concupiscence. The animal mates in response to desires triggered by the opportunity to mate. Some apes even mate for the sake of the comfort and physical pleasure that such contact affords. The imagination of the human being, however, feeds the natural desire and fosters it in a way that enhances and directs it. In this way sex seems to promise something much greater than physical satisfaction.

Sex promises happiness, and this gives it a power of transcendence, the power of an idol. Let us examine this closely. It is a commonplace that all human beings desire happiness. But after affirming this, there remains the question of what happiness is. Is it pleasure? Is it fame or honor among one's fellows? Is it success? Or is it something else?[33] Addressing this question, Thomas Aquinas argues that complete happiness can consist only in the uncreated good, which is God alone.[34] Anything less than God can yield only a participation in true happiness, a distant likeness of it. No matter what we may desire in this life, our desire will necessarily remain unfulfilled even if we attain those things that we explicitly desire.[35] As an immediate consequence, a corollary, if you will, happiness cannot consist in sexual pleasure, but that is not the main point here.

What is decisive for our argument is that happiness cannot be the satisfaction of any definite, limited desire. The tomcat whose desire to mate is triggered by the scent of a female in heat is satisfied by mating with her and expects no further satisfaction. The human will, which is the appetite for good in general,[36] cannot be so satisfied by one limited good at one point in time. What a human being conceives as his happiness must be something that endures, that will not pass away. If the tomcat should never again encounter a female in heat, he will be contented. The human being, however, will want the continuation or development of that singular satisfaction. It is sometimes noted that for the human being, sex is always more than sex, for what we expect from sex is a transcendent fulfillment of one's entire being. Here we may consider the Romantic extreme, as expressed by Wagner's Tristan, singing his praise to the love potion that drove Isolde into his embrace.

33. See Aristototle, *Nicomachean Ethics*, Book I, chap. 7, 1095a17.
34. *ST* Ia, q. 2, a. 8.
35. *ST* Ia-IIae q. 5, a. 3.
36. *ST* Ia, q. 80, aa. 1–2; Ia-IIae, q. 1, a. 2, ad 3.

Hail to the potion! Hail to the draught! Hail to its magic's sublime power! Through Death's portals wide and open it flowed towards me opening up the wondrous realm of Night where I had only been in dreams. From the image in my heart's sheltering cell it repelled day's deceiving beams, so that in darkness my eyes might serve to see it clearly.[37]

The magical power of the potion opened up "the wondrous realm of Night," when he and Isolde were able to consummate their love. The day, when the lovers are exposed to discovery and are in fact discovered to be situated within the larger world, renders such love impossible; the two are "in public." But in the night they may be alone in a world that includes only them, in a realm where "I had only been in dreams." Even granting that Wagner's portrayal of the love may be overdrawn, at least for contemporary sensibilities (although we might recall Ritchie Cordell's popular song from 1967, "I think we're alone now"),[38] the desires of a purely erotic love are generally shaped by fantasy. Sexual eroticism creates, as it were, its own private world, a realm in which desires require a perfect fulfillment. Such a fulfillment may involve more fantastic or dramatic setting and activity. We may think of the lovers in *Like Water for Chocolate*, whose eventual consummation of their forbidden desire ends as the flames from the candles consume them in their tent of love.[39] It is a kind of *Liebestod* in Spanish. Or this fulfillment may require a perpetual repetition of the original erotic encounter, but with different partners. This is Don Giovanni's strategy in Mozart's opera,[40] but also that of the modern sex addict who has to find a sexual partner every weekend. The

37. Richard Wagner, Libretti, *Tristan und Isolde*, act 2, scene 2 (1859; http://www.rwagner.net/libretti/tristan/e-tristan-a2s2.html).

38. Originally recorded by Tommy James and the Shondells.

39. *Like Water for Chocolate*, directed by Alfonso Arau (1992).

40. See Søren Kierkegaard's analysis, "The Immediate Erotic Stages or the Musical Erotic," in *Either/Or*, trans. David F. Swenson and Lillian Marvin Swenson (Garden City: Doubleday, 1959), 1: 43–134.

phenomenology of lust could be devoted in much greater detail than we have space for here, but the important point for us is that lust, sexual eroticism, shapes a world in which the "man of concupiscence" (to use John Paul II's term) lives. It is not the real world; sexual encounters cannot deliver the joy, the ecstasy, the fulfillment that the erotic imagination desires. However, it is a world in which real men and women live and according to whose principles many are subject.

This "world of lust" is ruled by a fantastic idol, whose "teaching" and ideals are represented in various media and social structures, which we may call structures of sin. They get their power from the willingness of human beings to subject themselves and their imaginations to these idols. What the idol offers is compelling, and it shapes the lives of those subject to it.

In *Man and Woman He Created Them*, John Paul II's principal concern is with the "lust of the flesh," which militates against the appropriate sexual expression of the gift of self in love. Mammon, or the "lust of the eyes," is the second form of concupiscence. Its operation is in the most important respects like that of the lust of the flesh. What mammon offers is not pleasure but security and control. The laws of acquisition and increase of money must be known and obeyed, because the future is uncertain. One's life can be ruined if the market fails, if medical or physical disaster strikes. On the other hand, money can insure the good life, because with enough money any dream can be realized. In effect, money is salvific; lacking it, one is subject to every evil. However, to the one who has it, money offers control, immense power, and enhanced status before others. Within the world of mammon, there are many values to be pursued—art, learning, sports, appreciation of nature—but all are subject to the rule of money. Before any value can be realized in this world, the financial implications and cost must be consulted. We may remind ourselves here of Plato's judgment about the rule of the acquisitive part of the soul, which "makes the rational and spirited parts sit on the ground beneath appetite, one on either side, reducing them to slaves."[41]

As noted previously, the ancient pagan myths allowed of many gods, so that a farmer, who normally concerns himself with appeasing the gods of fertility or the harvest, must sacrifice to the god of the sea before making a voyage. Idols are not in this respect jealous gods. So it is with the contemporary idols. A person can (and many people do) subject himself simultaneously to several such idols, believing himself to be independent of them all, to be master of his own life. His self-mastery may well be illusory, as his idolatry of self will increasingly demand his submission to the other idols. The idols of the nations, governed as they are by spiritual beings who can use them to teach, manipulate, and manage human concupiscence, do rule human persons. And at that last judgment, these will stand to be judged.

41. Plato, *Republic*, 553c–d.

CHAPTER 5

Mystery of Iniquity

One of the great errors of this present age is that we no longer believe in real evil. We refuse to believe that a human being is capable of true wickedness, that I or some person near me or like me might possibly be or become evil. One slogan has it, "There are no bad people, just bad incentives." However, ordinary nice Americans (and Spaniards and Brazilians, Nigerians and Vietnamese) *can* behave wickedly. We acknowledge some notorious villains—Hitler is always a good example—to be icons of evil, even in this day. His evil is seen to be so great as to be incomparable with the character of any other human being, so much so that the biographer who "humanizes" him may be accused of minimizing his evil. To compare any other leader's behavior or policies with those of Adolf Hitler is to fall into the crudest form of insult. In other words, although we may acknowledge Adolf Hitler to have been wicked, we generally see his evil as discontinuous with any other wrongdoing on the part of almost any other person. With the exception of *der Führer* and perhaps a handful of others, human beings are presumably not really capable of evil.

But this is too convenient. Hitler was only human—a very talented and charismatic human being, to be sure—and not the only wicked man in the twentieth century. Rather, a combination of his talent, charisma, and opportunities made his wickedness so effective and dangerous. But he was not alone in his wickedness. In recent years there have come to light happy photographs from the Nazi concentration camps—snapshots of guards, their wives, secretaries, staff drivers, and others enjoying picnics, outings, play with children, and Sunday church.[1] They were ordinary people. Did they hate Jews, Gypsies, and Poles? Probably not. They had work to do, lives to live, just as we all do. They were getting on. In recent years there have been unearthed similarly disturbing photographs of decent white folk watching lynchings in the American South. To bring this point home, Robert Bolt's play about St. Thomas More, *A Man for All Seasons*, ends on an especially annoying note. Having been condemned by vindictive and opportunistic men, More is led to his execution. As the ax falls with a loud "thunk," the stage goes suddenly dark, and the executioner proclaims, "Behold—the head—of a traitor." A few moments later, lights come up and "Common Man" steps onto the stage and brazenly addresses the audience: "I'm breathing. Are you breathing too? It's nice isn't it?"[2] Common Man goes on to congratulate the audience for having managed, like him, to stay alive. We *are* alive, sitting comfortably in the theater after the

1. "Laughing at Auschwitz: Leisure Photos of Camp Guards Shock Germans," *Speigel Online International*, http://www.spiegel.de/international/germany/laughing-at-auschwitz-leisure-photos-of-camp-guards-shock-germans-a-507175.htm; accessed September 21, 2007.

2. Robert Bolt, *A Man for All Seasons* (New York: Vintage, 1990), 162.

execution of the martyr. But we resent "Common Man's" implication that, like him, we are cowards who know how to keep out of trouble. Richard Rich, who perjured himself against More to advance his career, was wicked, but we want to think we are not. Wicked people lived in Hitler's Germany, Pol Pot's Cambodia, Stalin's USSR ... but not here, not in South Bend or Savannah or Sioux City.

The Cross and the *Mysterium iniquitatis*

The mystery of iniquity is most evident in the greatest crime ever committed—the condemnation and crucifixion of Christ, when human beings raised their hands against God Incarnate. If we enter imaginatively into the drama of the moment and sympathetically into the minds of the principal (and even the secondary) players, it becomes clear how much like us they were. Judas has long been a villain par excellence; Dante places him in the lowest part of hell, condemned to be perpetually chewed in the maw of the great serpent, Satan himself.[3] In our day, however, we try imagine what his motivations might have been. Maybe Judas misunderstood Jesus' goals and tried in his own way to help the cause, to provoke a crisis so that Jesus would take the situation properly in hand. Or perhaps he was legitimately frightened by the path that Jesus was taking, as he realized that his Lord was not soon going to triumph over his enemies and those of Israel. This is reasonable, because in fact everyone always acts for a reason that he finds persuasive. All persons act to achieve what they perceive to be good, do they not? Can we say that Judas was all that wicked? Nobody admires Pontius Pilate, the venal, ambitious, and somewhat unprincipled procurator. But was he *evil*? Objectively speaking,

3. Dante Alighieri, *Inferno*, Canto 34, 61–63.

he was in a hard situation. The Jews resented Roman authority, which means that they resented him. He needed the ongoing cooperation of the high priests and Sanhedrin to keep the peace. He had to deal with them on their own terms, at least to an extent, simply to meet the emperor's expectations. And the Jewish leaders *did* have to deal shrewdly with the Romans. Furthermore, they were the guardians of Jewish orthodoxy. Jesus' preaching came dangerously close to blasphemy; at times he seemed to be claiming equality with God. What else could they do? The soldiers with their nails and whips were under orders. (The crown of thorns and mockery may well have been excessive, but we must look at the situation through their eyes. They were probably Syrians, on hard duty in a disagreeable little country. Tormenting the condemned was for them simply a way to let off steam.) We continue on through the other personages. As Jesus' "Number two," Peter was in a dangerous situation. Cold, tired, and unprepared, he panicked and denied his Lord. How well would anyone else have done? Except for John, the other disciples ran away. If we try to empathize with them, to understand their situations and psychologies, we can make the same kinds of excuses for all these people that we make for ourselves. And they betrayed, denied, judged, and killed the Incarnate Word of God.

When we look at the crucifixion, at the crime of deicide, we do not find one master of evil attacking and overpowering Jesus, but rather very ordinary people committing very ordinary sins. Mel Gibson's film *Passion of the Christ* reignited the debate about whether the Jews (or their leaders) were at all responsible for the death of Christ, or whether it was solely the work of the Romans.[4] In fact, the villains (which Gibson himself acknowledges by having his own hand hold the first nail in

4. *The Passion of the Christ*, directed by Mel Gibson (2004).

the crucifixion scene) are all of us. Judas deliberately betrayed his Master and Friend. Peter denied him. Caiaphas embraced the principle that an innocent man can be sacrificed for the greater good. For expediency's sake, Pilate condemned a man he knew to be innocent. The other apostles and disciples knew that there was not much they could do, that the situation was dangerous, and so they abandoned their Lord. It is all very tawdry. And all had a share in this great wickedness.

Philosophical Analysis of the Mystery

Evil is a mystery because every explanation of it explains away the evil. To maintain that a certain person has freely chosen evil as such is incomprehensible. Every person does what he does for some good, to attain some goal that he has in mind. This is a common enough philosophical position, but it is also the perspective of the "ordinary man." When we ask why a miscreant has done what he did, we look for some good that, at least in his own eyes, accounts for his misdeeds. We ask why Jones abuses his wife and children, and we learn that Jones is the son of an abusive father. From childhood he has learned that intimidation and violence are the primary tools for coping with perceived disorder and frustration at home; that disrespect of the man—no matter what form it may take—cannot be tolerated. Such an explanation is only partially satisfying, however, because we realize also that many sons of abusive fathers do not themselves become abusers. The genetic explanation does not seem to account for all instances of the evil. But there is a further problem. If indeed *this* man's abusive behavior can be completely and adequately explained by his own history, then he is no longer wicked. His behavior becomes merely unfortunate. He is comparable to a perpetually mistreated dog that bites any stranger that approaches it. If the behavior that we call evil is adequately and completely accounted for in terms of external factors (to the miscreant's mind), then the miscreant cannot be called *free*, and his actions cannot properly be called evil or wicked. Such an explanation would certainly apply to St. Peter in his denial of Christ. In the calm of two days before, he could confidently affirm that he would even die for Jesus,[5] but in the confusion and chaos following Christ's arrest, the instinct for self-preservation kicked in and Peter denied that he even knew the man.

One possible explanation for evil is to appeal to ignorance. The miscreant simply does not know what is best for him; had he known better, he would have done otherwise. Jesus himself said, "Father, forgive them; for they know not what they do."[6] St. Paul seems implicitly even to give Pilate a pass: "None of the rulers of this age understood this; for if they had, they would not have crucified the Lord of Glory."[7] Pontius Pilate knew that Caesar was his king and therefore sought to please him. Had he known that Jesus was a more powerful king, the "Lord of glory," he would never have been so foolish as to condemn him. Pilate could thus claim ignorance for his excuse. The two accounts of evil, the genetic causality and ignorance, can work together. The scion of an antebellum plantation owner had learned from boyhood how to acquire and manage slaves, and he had learned from his parents and the pillars of Southern society that black people are not quite human; that they are appropriate beings for slavery and the harsh discipline that must be imposed on them. In light of these factors one may well argue that no blame can attach to his owning, selling, working, and beating his slaves.

To better grasp the roots of evil, we would do well to turn to the architect of evil in creation: to Satan himself. An angel, and hence an incorporeal being, Satan is not subject to causal influences of pleasure or fear as a human being is. Indeed, he

5. Lk 22:32.   6. Ibid., 23:34.
7. 1 Cor 2:8.

exists outside of time itself. Furthermore, he did not fall because of ignorance. To understand Satan's sin we can take into account only the will and its freedom. At the moment of his coming into existence—and let us be constantly aware that the use of this term "moment" must for us be analogical, for angels are not temporal beings—Satan and his angels were faced with the offer of God's love. If they would simply ask, to open themselves to receiving their happiness from God, a happiness consisting precisely in the direct vision of the divine essence, then they would see God face to face and by this be filled with ineffable joy. No created being, not even an angel, can by its own powers attain to this vision.[8] Even an angel can attain this happiness only as a result of God's gift, and to receive this gift, he must submit his will to God by asking for this gift.

Satan and his angels chose not to look to God for their happiness, their angelic fulfillment, but to themselves, a choice by which they condemned themselves. This choice was an eternal and irrevocable choice, and the reasons for this are directly pertinent to our current discussion of the mystery of evil. As an intellectual creature, the devil is a personal being desirous of knowledge and understanding. By his own natural powers he understands himself and all that falls naturally within his purview. His choice was for that fulfillment alone, rejecting what God had to offer him. As human thinkers we are tempted to imagine this as happening in time, as though upon his creation the angel "looked around," as it were, and, realizing somehow that God had proposed a kind of choice, thought a moment and responded to God with either "yes" or "no." If this were how it occurred, then it would be reasonable to ask whether the angel, having seen the consequences of his choice and repenting, might turn back to God. But such an image is wrong, because

8. *ST* Ia, q. 12, a. 4; Ia-Iae, q. 5, a. 5.

this event did not happen in time; there was no time-interval between the angel's creation and his decision. The decision of the will is super-temporal, above and without respect to time.

The will is the faculty by which the intellectual creature desires the good known by reason. For an angel, which has no sensory organs of cognition, the will is directed entirely by the intellect, which for its part is informed by what it understands. The understanding of the intellect informs, as a first principle, all the intellectual creature's knowledge and activity. For a classic and traditional human example, all the geometer's knowledge of figures in space is formed by the axioms and definitions of geometry, and his thinking about the physical world is formed and directed by these axioms and the geometric way of thinking. (Of course, as Ivan Karamazov famously complains, his "Euclidean mind" cannot grasp the deeper mysteries of suffering.)[9] It is not only knowledge that is at stake, however, for besides the first principles of knowledge (bases of understanding), the will is founded also on its own principle, which is the desire for the good. Will desires the ultimate good, the good without qualification, which is to be known by reason. That good is the perfect good of all creatures—of all creation itself—and is precisely God alone.

The will, the rational appetite, of an intellectual creature is for the good as knowable and known. Like a human being in this life, the angel at the instant of its creation does not see God. Because God is the perfect good, whoever sees him, who contains within himself the perfection of all good, cannot but love him. Then how can the intellectual creature love God if he does not yet see him? By his own intellectual light (and for humans by the exercise of their reason) the angel could know

9. Fyodor Dostoevsky, *The Brothers Karamazov*, ed. Mortimer J. Adler, trans. Constance Garnett, in *Great Books of the Western World* (Chicago: Encyclopedia Britannica, 1952), 52:125.

of God that he exists, that he is supremely powerful and knowing, that he is the Creator of all things. Furthermore, in his love for the angel, God revealed to him that by turning to God, the angel could enjoy his perfect goodness. The choice to be made is whether to entrust himself, his angelic beauty, and powerful angelic mind to God or to himself and his own wonderful powers, which he (the angel) knows directly. The Satanic choice was for self. He chose to find within himself the principles of truthful understanding and of the ultimate good. We must carefully note: this was not an irrational choice, not strictly speaking. Satan knew indeed that God is great, but without knowing God directly, face to face, he could question how great God might be. His choice was between trusting his own resources and surrendering himself to the almighty being who promised to love him. He chose himself. This was an immediate irrevocable choice for an angel. Having rejected the gift of God, the demons—including, of course, Satan himself—have no criteria for reevaluating and reconsidering their choice. Satan can, of course, recognize that after his choice, as a result of his turning away from God, his existence has somehow become bad, but he is incapable of understanding why. Having chosen himself as the highest truth and the criterion of all good, he lacks the intellectual resources to repent. If Satan suffers, he can attribute it only to God's vindictiveness.

Let us note one final point about Satan's condition, one that relates to Jesus' words from the cross and St. Paul's remark in 1 Corinthians. Their powerful intellects notwithstanding, Satan and his angels did act in ignorance. They did so because they did not know God as he is in himself. Their minds, even though angelic, are finite. Unable on their own to grasp the reality of God, they therefore rejected what they did not know. This is not to say that their choice was reasonable—they could have recognized that he was perfectly good—but neither was it irrational.

Here is the core reality if we are to understand the mystery of evil in the human heart. Everything that a human being does is conditioned, both by his state of knowledge and by his desires, which can be either long-lasting or momentary and of short, albeit intense, duration. St. Augustine tells the story of his theft of peaches with his adolescent friends,[10] a theft motivated neither by need nor desire for fruit but simply for the malicious delight of doing something wrong. Augustine was fully aware that he was doing wrong. Far worse than Augustine's prank, in April 2013 a sixteen-year-old boy in Oklahoma shot and killed a jogger because he was "bored."[11] Both incidents were irrational and unexpected. But neither was disconnected from its context and the inner motivations of the perpetrators. In each case, a knowledgeable observer might well have observed that although the act was not expected, it was more or less characteristic of the perpetrator. In each of these cases the agent was an adolescent, and of adolescents we know that they can be remarkably shortsighted, apparently ignorant of the consequences of their acts. Their brains are not yet fully developed. In light of this we may ask whether such a boy can be truly wicked—that is, whether his crime can legitimately be attributed to evil.

To grasp human evil, we must understand that the human person is a spiritual being, one whose interior life "focuses on truth and the good,"[12] and as such his acts cannot be understood in terms of physical interrelationships alone. Like the angels discussed previously, the human person forms his acts according to his understanding of the good. Even the least re-

10. St. Augustine, *Confessions*, Book II, chap. 4.

11. Heide Brandes, "Oklahoma Teen Faces Life Term for Killing Australian Man Out of 'Boredom,'" *Reuters*, April 20, 2015, http://www.reuters.com/article/2015/04/20/us-usa-crime-oklahoma-australia-idUSKBN0NB2AY20150420; accessed June 19, 2015.

12. Wojtyła, *Love and Responsibility*, 5.

flective or intelligent person has interior standards for judging what is true and good. These standards define for him what he is able to recognize as authentically good and therefore normative for himself. However much they may be *influenced* by material factors, these standards, however, are not materially *determined*. The child naturally knows that a father is to be his protector and teacher. From his experience of abuse at the hands of his own father, he may well learn that abusing others is his best way to instill obedience and respect for authority. Nevertheless, reflecting on what he had expected of a father, he may well realize that his approach to the discipline of his own children should differ from his father's; that his way should be marked by gentleness. Plato lived in a culture whose gods were capricious, vindictive, selfish, and often cruel. By reflecting on the moral requirements for any intelligent being, he realized that the tales of the gods could not be true; that whatever gods (or divine beings) might be, they must be noble, truthful, courageous, and temperate. The human will cannot be formed only by physical—that is, organic and environmental—factors; these can only influence it. As spiritual, the will is ultimately and decisively formed only by ideas. Only in virtue of ideas, of spiritual realities, can a will be free.

The implication of the foregoing is that the operation of the will is not observable. One may deliberate about courses of action—forming mental images and schemata, manipulating them in one's mind and comparing results—or one can take note of the environmental factors that affect a proposed course of action—"I plan to play golf, but my wife is frowning about the unpainted hallway." The decision is not taken upon the resolution, "Yes, I will do this," but only upon the initiation of action. The mental processes leading up to the decision may be important, but they do not constitute the decision. Here Kant's account in his *Grounding of the Metaphysics of Morals* falls short, for in his analysis of the will in terms of the practical reason structured by its maxims, he fails to recognize the self-determination by the choice of one's act.

This is not at all to say that the act is irrational or unintelligible. Quite to the contrary. The act, whether chosen after prolonged reflection or on the spur of the moment, is meaningful, expressing what the agent believes (or decides to believe) to be true and good. The soccer player passing suddenly to the player on the wing is behaving as intelligently as the chess player who reflects for seventeen minutes before moving his knight. In Dostoevsky's *Crime and Punishment*, Raskolnikov wrestles with his conscience and plans, doubting and affirming, questioning and resolving, until he arrives at the pawnbroker's apartment, where he settles the inner debate only by murdering her. Then, having chosen to murder, he had immediately to murder again when the simpleton Lizaveta appears unexpectedly and therefore has also to die. How may we understand this? The Cartesian model entails that, for intelligent action to occur, a sequence of mental events necessarily precedes and leads into the physical event. For Kant the will is found entirely in reflection. But this model does not and indeed cannot hold. The act itself is an expression of thought and indeed an interpreter of thought, of the agent's understanding of the truth. Instead of ending his reflections on his own destiny with a thought, "the pawnbroker must die"—note that such a verbal formula can usually be revised—Raskolnikov ends them with a decisive act by which he affirms the values he embraces and the nature of the truth he accepts. Precisely by his acts, the agent affirms and determines the values by which he will live.

By choosing his standard of goodness, the human being defines his own will, which may be good or evil. This may be called his fundamental option, because his act determines and manifests the criteria by which he judges good and evil.

By choosing for evil, his life becomes evil, even if externally it should look good and internally feel good. One's inner disposition toward or against the ultimate good is invisible, both to oneself and to others. Just as the student may be a poor judge of whether he truly understands a science (and so he is subject to the teacher's evaluation), so too is a person a poor judge of his own goodness. Thus, when St. Joan of Arc was asked by the judge at her trial, "Do you know if you are in the grace of God?," she replied only this: "If I am not, may God place me there; if I am, may God so keep me."[13] He can recognize that he is courageous or temperate (at least to some extent) or lazy and thoughtless, but his own fundamental option is invisible to himself. This is why St. Paul can confess, "I do not even judge myself. I am not aware of anything against myself, but I am not thereby acquitted. It is the Lord who judges me."[14]

At this point we may well ask what such a fundamental determination of the will as good or evil has to do with a person's individual acts—specifically how an individual act (a mortal sin) can effect the total determination or redetermination of the will, which is beyond temporal conditions and which remains invisible to the person and, for that matter, ultimately to others. If the will is the inner principle of one's actions and if the principle of the will is the good chosen as ultimate by the will, then clearly the will and its fundamental choice would seem to be prior to the act. Certainly every act follows by way of a kind of inference from one's fundamental values via the practical syllogism.[15] Logically or conceptually the act is consequent upon the value. However, the choice of the value, or one's governing standard of good, may well lie in the choice

13. "Third Public Examination," St. Joan of Arc's Trials, Saint Joan of Arc Center, http://www.stjoan-center.com/Trials/sec03.html; accessed May 17, 2016.
14. 1 Cor 4:3–4.
15. Reimers, *Soul of the Person*, 164–72.

of one's act. By choosing, for example, to betray insignificant details of Thomas More's life to Cromwell, Richard Rich (in Robert Bolt's play) both confirms and embraces the values to which he had been drawn in the months prior. Having just agreed to accept a post from Cromwell in exchange for unspecified future services, Rich comments, "I'm lamenting. I've lost my innocence." To this Cromwell retorts, "You lost that some time ago. If you've only just noticed, it can't have been very important to you."[16] Although he had laid the groundwork in his mind for his moral corruption, dreaming of an important position in court and the perquisites that accompany this, Rich was not a traitor to his friend, nor was he morally compromised until he accepted Cromwell's offer. At that point his ambition, with its consequent rejection of truthfulness and loyalty, became his life's governing principle, a principle that led to his perjuring himself to the condemnation of More and his own promotion to attorney general of Wales. The evil of the act lies in its repudiation, even if implicit, of the divine order of love.

Unlike the fallen angels, the human being, upon sinning, does not instantly become wicked in his entire being. As St. Thomas Aquinas notes, significant remnants of virtue remain in one who has fallen into mortal sin.[17] Therefore one who has fallen into adultery may continue to exercise the virtue of courage in war or amiability in social relationships. He may very well show significant consideration for his wife, watching out for her well-being or carrying out chores. The corruption of the human will is therefore at once instantaneous—indeed, participating in the eternal—and extended in time. The turn from the true good occurs at the moment when the person maliciously chooses what is opposed to his true good. He has turned his will away from and into opposition to the divine Goodness. On the other hand, be-

16. Bolt, *A Man for All Seasons*, 74.
17. *ST* Ia-IIae, q. 65, a. 1, ad 1.

cause the will, or rational appetite, rules the body in a kind of coordination with other appetites, its choice for evil does not immediately affect all those appetites so as to redirect the habits (or virtues) by which those appetites are guided and formed. In this way, we may say that even if one is decisively corrupted, his corruption is not total. In this way, even the most serious sinner may nevertheless "have some good in him."

Love for Whom? Contempt for Whom?

St. Augustine distinguishes his two cities—the City of God and the City of Man—on the bases of their love. Those of the City of God love God even to the contempt of self. Those of the earthly city, by contrast, embrace the love of self, even to the contempt of God. In his book *Sign of Contradiction*, written while he was still a cardinal, Pope John Paul II referred to these two principles as Love and anti-Love.[18] If God is love, then quite logically the choice of self to the contempt of God is the choice against love—it is for anti-love. Those on the King's left at the Last Judgment are those who, ignoring Christ in the least of his brethren, chose against love. And this is malice. God who is goodness itself created us for himself. To choose against him is to choose against goodness.

This is the wickedness of iniquity. If we turn from God, whether we are explicitly aware of it or not, we turn to evil. We embrace iniquity. There is no "pretty good," no "decent" and "nice." In his *Gulag Archipelago*, Alexandr Solzhenitsyn remarks that the most dangerous principle to adopt as a political prisoner of the Soviet system is "survive at all costs."[19] The prisoner who makes this his rule will surely betray others, even to their deaths, thereby becoming of one mind and will with

18. Wojtyła, *Sign of Contradiction* (New York: Seabury Press, 1979), 82–83.
19. Aleksandr Solzhenitsyn, *The Gulag Archipelago: An Experiment in Literary Investigation, III–IV* (New York: Harper and Row, 1975), 603–10.

his and their captors. In the Last Judgment, the damned are surprised: "When did we see you hungry or thirsty, a stranger or naked, sick or in prison, and did not come to your help?" They turned away from love, which means they turned away from God. Rather than to take part in God's work of love, they chose to look out only for themselves and what they deemed good. And this made them wicked.

The Coordination and Magnification of Evil

We have already noted that in the crime of the crucifixion we do not see one master villain attacking and overpowering Jesus. We do not *see* this villain, but we know that he was at work. "Then Satan entered into Judas."[20] "After Judas had taken the bread [from Jesus], Satan entered into him.... As soon as Judas had taken the bread, he went out. Night had fallen."[21] The great crime of deicide was planned and choreographed by Satan himself. Jesus was not the victim of chance mistakes and blind forces. Indeed, he knew exactly what he was up against. His own death was to unmask the wickedness of the devil. In virtue of Christ's sacrificial death, the Holy Spirit is able to bring to light the mystery of evil, convicting the world about sin, judgment, and righteousness.[22]

We do not understand the crucifixion if we pass over the role of Satan, because here the mystery of iniquity is exposed. Although human beings may try to reassure ourselves otherwise, we do not live in a neutral, albeit messy, world where everyone has his foibles and makes mistakes—mistakes that will get sorted out, more or less, in time. Popular culture notwithstanding, the soul's afterlife is not a kind of "heaven" where

20. Lk 22:3.
21. Jn 13:27, 30.
22. Jn 16: 8; see also John Paul II, Encyclical *Dominum et vivificantem*, part 2, §§27–48.

things that went wrong in the earthly life become reconciled, where no one is condemned as truly wicked or evil.[23] Sin is not a kind of mistake, to understand which is to forgive. The reality is that to sin is to make oneself a tool of Satan, to agree to participate in his reign governed by the logic of power, manipulation, or empty pleasure.

The Last Judgment is not about God's inflicting pain on those who broke his rules or who failed to join the right church or say the right kinds of prayers. It is about separating the merciful from those who had chosen against love. God is love,[24] and to choose against love is to choose against God. We can understand how someone might choose against a particular image of God or what another person says about God. But can a person really choose against love? In fact, by choosing self and some good less than God, a human being can choose anti-love. This is the great mystery of iniquity. One can choose self rather than God, convenience rather than the welfare of the hungry, the homeless, the naked, and the imprisoned. The Last Judgment is, in a way, simply Christ's recognition of the choice that one has made of the kingdom of principles by which he will be ruled. The King and Judge offered mercy to all, but those on his left, the "goats," had chosen a kingdom based on power and craftiness. Having rejected the rule of mercy, they find none for themselves.

23. I think here particularly of Mitch Albom's *The Five People You Meet in Heaven* (New York: Hyperion, 2003), but the theme is also common elsewhere in contemporary popular culture.
24. 1 Jn 4:16.

CHAPTER 6

Hell on Earth

It is fair to say that anyone who believes that hell cannot really exist is simply not paying attention. Hell is presaged and, to a limited extent, present on this earth. Disbelief in the reality of hell and evil can be explained by two general mistakes: (1) faulty imagery and (2) blindness to what occurs around us.

Popular imagery of hell tends to be fantastic, if not simply ludicrous. We picture a place of flames (usually bright red on a black background) peopled with horned demons (usually with forked tails) carrying pitchforks. Hell is simply a very hot, painful, disagreeable place where everything hurts. What goes on there has little to do with life here on earth. (Here it is worth noticing that in his *Inferno*, Dante takes a very different approach, making the punishment of the damned correspond to the wrong they had done on earth.) Even if the ludicrous cartoons are rejected, the image of hell as a place where the damned are simply tormented by malevolent demons is also inadequate, suggesting that the judge who should consign people to such a place for simple infractions of his own rules is himself malevolent. One may ask, "If God is all good, then how can he consign his creatures to unending pain?" We can begin to correct this flawed imagery by simply looking around us.

The Ways of This World

In the second book of Kings we read a chilling story of cruelty of the prophet Elisha's encounter with Hazael, a messenger from the king of Aram. Upon meeting him, Elisha breaks into tears.

"Why," Hazael asked, "does my lord weep?" "Because I know," Elisha replied, "all the harm you will do the Israelites: you will burn down their fortresses, put their picked warriors to the sword, dash their little children to pieces, rip open their pregnant women." "But what is your servant?" Hazael said. "How could this dog achieve anything so great?"[1]

Afterward, Hazael returns to his king, murders him, and usurps the throne. Later he will fulfill Elisha's prophecy about the Israelites. This man is frighteningly wicked. When the prophet tells him the atrocities he will commit—destroying fortresses, killing men and children, ripping open the bellies of pregnant women—Hazael puts on mock humility, referring to himself as a "dog." But what is especially revealing is that he refers to these atrocities as something "great." We know, in fact, that ancient kings and warriors could be brutally cruel, with no regard for human life or suffering—as Hazael's behavior manifests so well.

1. 2 Kgs 8:12–13.

Today we take comfort in the fact that we are more civilized; that such treatment of captives and prisoners is truly "ancient history." The Romans, however, were civilized; our civilization is in part an outgrowth of theirs. Dismas hangs on his cross next to Jesus, and just beyond Jesus is the other criminal. Who was responsible for this? These three men, two common criminals and the victim of an envious plot, are crucified under the authority of Rome, whose glories—the Colosseum, the Roman Forum, Circus Maximus, the Via Appia, and so on—we admire even today. Historians tell us that although the ancient Greeks created science and ordered theories of government, the Romans made these things work. Our own legal system—we are proud to be governed by law and not the whim of men—traces its roots to Roman law. This is a great and proud people, one that set the standards for our civilization.

That the Romans executed some criminals is not all that remarkable. Up to the present, governments impose the death penalty. But this kind of execution is especially cruel. At the very beginning of this book we described some of the agonies of crucifixion—the searing pain as the weight of the body pulls the wrists into the nails, the sense of suffocation when the body sags, the intense thirst as the body loses fluids under the hot Mediterranean sun. In one way, Dismas was lucky. He was crucified on the eve of the Sabbath and could not be left hanging there past sundown. And so the soldiers had to break his legs. Normally this did not happen. The condemned were ordinarily left to die slowly—over the course of two or three days in some cases. It was a death so horrible that those who enjoyed Roman citizenship could not be crucified. It was a death for slaves and rebellious foreigners. It was a particularly vicious, cruel, and humiliating way to kill another human being. And the Romans used it. If they were an obscure tribe, living in a harsh and dangerous environment, we might write off this practice of crucifixion as a kind of aberration. People in difficult circumstances might do things we would not. But the Romans were the most civilized people in the Western world. (Of course, the Chinese and Indians had their own civilizations at this same time.) They had art, science, engineering, and literature, government and law, good roads and remarkable aqueducts. And they crucified foreigners and slaves.

Although one could catalogue atrocities from every age, it is well to look at the United States of America. Blues singer Billie Holliday used to end her performances with a haunting song that began:

Southern trees bear strange fruit,
Blood on the leaves and blood at the root,
Black bodies swinging in the southern breeze,
Strange fruit hanging from the poplar trees.[2]

The "strange fruit" were two black men hanging from a tree in Marion, Indiana, in 1930. The executioners who lynched black men and women in the American South and Midwest were ordinary people, decent folks who worked hard and attended church on Sunday. They loved their children and some perhaps appreciated the services of the Negro maid they hired once a week. But we have ample photographic evidence that these ordinary people would turn out in a festive mood for a lynching. We have pictures of proud parents and smiling, happy children standing beneath the tree where hangs the body of two or three men who died (or were still dying) in terror.

The point to stress here is that *we* do terrible things to each other. The situation is not that there exists or once existed a world where incomprehensibly corrupt moral monsters tor-

---

2. Billie Holliday, "Strange Fruit," by Abel Meeropol (pseudonym Lewis Allan) (1939).

tured and killed and then laughed at the sufferings of others. As a general rule, *it is we who are the monsters.* To be sure, not all of us are capable of stringing a man up in a tree and setting fire to his still-living body. One must be trained and hardened through experience to become a torturer. But most of us are capable of approving, helping out, applauding. All that is needed is to know that someone with authority approves and that others in the social environment agree.

Western society has the advantage of laws that are, for the most part, good, in societies where the rules, both formal and informal, keep people from hurting each other too much. We have reasonably good police departments and, by and large, the courts deliver verdicts acceptable to most citizens. These customs and institutions make it possible to live reasonably harmoniously together, and this is a good thing. The danger we face—and this is the reason for these stories and examples—is the temptation to believe that because we are not doing horribly wicked things we are good. When the Nazis overran Poland, destroying so much of that society, some Poles quite readily turned against their Jewish neighbors, thus sharing in the guilt of the invading Germans. But others, despite their fear and desire to stay out of trouble, hid and cared for the Jews near them, and we know that a significant number were saved by good Gentile Poles. It is not being Polish or American or German that makes a person good or evil. Any of us can be wicked. John Paul II wrote, "One man can become the object of use to another. This is the utmost threat to our civilization, especially to the civilization of a materially affluent world."[3]

3. John Paul II, "A Meditation on Givenness," *Communio: International Catholic Review* (Winter 2014): 871–83, 879.

Ordinary Sinners

When we think of evil on earth, we tend to think of the great sinners, history's cruel evildoers—Nero, Hitler, Stalin, Pol Pot —and not of ordinary persons like ourselves and our neighbors. This is dangerously misleading. For simplicity, let us consider Adolf Hitler, who has become almost a modern icon of evil. When we look to see what makes Hitler stand out, it is not necessarily the evil in his heart. Certainly he was a talented man who also had a distinctive opportunity, coming to power during a time of national defeat and humiliation, moral crisis and economic distress. Born twenty years earlier or later, Hitler might well have passed unnoticed by anyone but his neighbors. In other words, the evil of a person's will does not lie in its effectiveness to bring about pain and destruction in the lives of others. It does not consist in his ability to establish tyranny or organize mass-murder. Rather, it lies in his ordination toward himself as god—that is, as the standard of truth and goodness. Such a will can lead to the slaughter of six million Jews or the starvation of ten million Ukrainians, but it can also lead to the destruction of an office colleague's reputation or opportunity for advancement, for the expulsion of a particular person or family from a neighborhood or town, or for the fraudulent legal conviction of an innocent personal adversary. The evil will declares, in harmony with the will of Satan, not that great harm must be done, but that this person's will of itself determines what is good and true and beautiful.

Sin is enslavement. And to bargain with Satan is to fall under his domain. After promising that "the truth will make you free," Jesus continues, "Truly, truly, I say to you, everyone who commits sin is a slave to sin."[4] St. Paul develops this line of thought:

4. Jn 8:32, 34.

Do you not know that if you yield yourselves to any one as obedient slaves, you are slaves of the one whom you obey, whether of sin, which leads to death, or of obedience, which leads to righteousness?[5]

No one thinks of himself as a sinner or a slave, even as he sins. We like to think of ourselves as autonomous, free, and independent. The problem, however, is that human beings are simply not as independent and autonomous as we conceive ourselves to be; that we are profoundly influenced by the spiritual milieu in which we live—and we are most probably more potently influenced by a milieu that claims to have no spiritual influence on us, that claims to be entirely value-free. What I am saying here is that if I am my own god, then I cannot be this highest god, for the principles by which I understand my own divinity come from another who is more intelligent and more powerful than I, even if I do not recognize this dependence.

A spiritual being lives from his interior life, his spiritual life, which focuses on truth and goodness. To recognize this is inevitably first to raise the question, "What is truth?" When Pontius Pilate first raised this question to Jesus,[6] the parameters for situating an answer were not logical or metaphysical but personal and political. The Jewish leaders made their claim and Jesus made his, the crowd was shouting, and Pilate had his responsibilities to Caesar. Jesus' testimony (as well as the entire Jewish way of life) hints at a plane of reality higher than and independent of that of the Roman Empire. Pilate may be reasonably understood to ask where in all this a reliable truth is to be found—in particular a truth that an embattled ambitious Roman procurator could rely on for his own well-being. What, then, is truth? How do we know it? Because we are bodily, temporal beings, we must get truth from others. In principle,

5. Rom 6:16.
6. Jn 18:38.

of course, the individual can verify any particular truth by applying the rules of reason to his perceptions and experiences in the world. However, no human person can infallibly verify all truth for himself. Furthermore, not only must the individual accept most of his knowledge from others, but the very framework and presuppositions of his knowledge are received from others, from his parents, his social environment, and his culture. Werner Heisenberg, whose accomplishments in physics surpassed all but a handful of his contemporaries as he attained an understanding of quantum theory that few can grasp, sufficiently accepted the premises of the Third Reich to enable him to participate in its preliminary efforts to develop a nuclear weapon. We may say that this Nobel Prize winner absorbed his political views from his professional and social environment; his keen understanding of scientific method and mathematical creativity did not enable him to discern the importance of the principles underlying the government under which he lived.

Because we are spatiotemporally limited beings, we necessarily rely on others to know the truth. We cannot claim to be autonomous knowers. Our knowledge must depend on our believing what others teach, tell, or show us. Indeed, one may accurately say that most of our knowledge is a kind of participation in the knowledge of the communities to which we belong. The question of one's relationship with truth, therefore, is a question of whom one ultimately believes on the authority of others. St. John Paul II writes:

In believing we entrust ourselves to the knowledge acquired by other people. . . . Belief is often humanly richer than mere evidence, because it involves an interpersonal relationship and brings into play not only a person's capacity to know but also the deeper capacity to entrust oneself to others, to enter into a relationship with them which is intimate and enduring. . . . Human perfection, then, consists not simply in acquiring an abstract knowledge of the truth, but in a dynamic relationship of faithful self-giving with others.[7]

This is closely related to the question of the good, to the nature of the good that one loves and for the sake of which he makes his choices. St. Thomas Aquinas argues that in fact each human being desires some ultimate good in which he hopes to find his perfection, his personal fulfillment, and his happiness.[8] This ultimate good is what a person lives for. But as rational creatures we must ask what that good is and what the criteria are by which we may recognize it. Immediately we are aware that some values almost impose themselves on us as great, if not yet ultimate, goods. Aquinas summarizes these neatly as the goods of wealth, power, fame and fortune, glory, and pleasure.[9] The very experience of these impresses us with their value as great goods worth our pursuing. A great pleasure, for example, leaves one wanting to experience it again, repeatedly and for a longer time. The ability to exercise real power and see things changed according to one's own will is compellingly desirable, especially if through the force of righteous anger one can right an insult against himself. Experiencing the sensuous and emotional satisfactions of pleasure, honors, glory, and power (keeping in mind that money is a source of power), it is tempting and seems apparently reasonable to direct one's life and principal activities toward the attainment of these goods. However, argues St. Thomas, none of these can reasonably qualify as the highest good. In a nutshell, what Aquinas argues is that all these are acquired from without, always with more or less good fortune, and they do not reflect the goodness of the person who attains them. Whatever is the person's highest good, the good that fulfills and perfects him, must be something that accrues to

---

7. John Paul II, *Fides et ratio*, §32.   8. *ST* Ia-IIae, q. 1, aa. 1–3.
9. *ST* Ia-IIae, q. 2, aa. 1–6.

him not as an ephemeral pleasure that passes as the experience of some temporal good ends, nor as some possession or honor from others. None of these belongs to the person as a rational being capable of choosing the good. St. Thomas's fundamental point in the text at hand is that any reasonable person can recognize that these goods fall short of what must pertain to the perfect good. A thinking person, reflecting attentively, can readily recognize that living for the sake of wealth will never satisfy him, that sensual pleasure, however intense and satisfying it may be in the moment, will pass away, never to be entirely recaptured in its same form. The wise, like Aristotle of old, recognize that the good life is one lived well—which is to say virtuously—by pursuing wisdom, forming solid friendships, establishing a home and family while participating in the life of a healthy community. Aristotle could not quite name the supreme good, although he knew that it must be divine. Aquinas knew that this good can consist only in the vision of God himself and in a kind of imitation of him.

Our problem is so often that we do not intelligently confront the question of the good, but instead follow our desires, emotions, and passions. In the garden, when the serpent proposed to the woman that to eat the fruit would make her wise, she did not question this suggestion: "So when the woman saw that the tree was good for food, and that it was a delight to the eyes, and that the tree was to be desired to make one wise, she took of its fruit and ate."[10] Like a "mark" listening to the barker at a county fair, she believed the words of one whom she did not know and whose promises were too good to be true. Her husband handled the situation even worse. He simply took and ate the fruit that his wife handed him. Eve at least raised an objection, but he said nothing. Of course, this issue is not simply one

10. Gn 3:6.

of thoughtlessness. The will is involved. The promise of great pleasure or the satisfaction of a righteous outburst of anger can be so attractive as to preempt the moment of reflection. It is more attractive to proceed toward the pleasure than to spoil the opportunity for enjoyment by thinking carefully and thoroughly. Nevertheless, reality will out, and the lesser good of pleasure, wealth, power, fame, or glory will prove false and harmful.

In precisely this context we might consider the common first-time adulterer, the one whom we know and whose story we may have seen played out in drama, in literature, and in our own circles. What we all know—what every prospective adulterer or adulteress knows—is that adultery *never* turns out well, that the spouse *almost always* does find out, that the lovers have no future together (not really), that their love will tire and exhaust itself in disappointment and bitterness, and that at home there will be marital and family fights, quite possibly ending in divorce. Anyone paying attention knows that this is how things are. Nevertheless, married men and women slip out to hotels or to other secluded spots in the middle of the afternoon or perhaps an evening when work plausibly might demand absence from home, looking forward to a few hours' pleasure and emotional reaffirmation in each other's arms. The first encounter may well turn out satisfactorily, delivering all that the adulterous couple may have hoped for, but the inevitable consequences will quickly follow—the romance quickly sours; the sex becomes less thrilling, the magic quickly fades, and the relationship ends. Here we are not, strictly speaking, arguing on the level of natural law; certainly there is nothing abstract to such an argument that adultery is bad. In fact, adultery is stupid. This stupidity notwithstanding, men and women frequently engage in extramarital affairs. Some people even adopt adultery as a pattern of life as, despairing of love, they move from brief affair to brief affair, constantly repeating the behavior that once gave the illusion of happiness. In every case, however, we humans are capable of recognizing the truth about our actions and still choosing badly, because we choose the immediate pleasure and the hope of future pleasure rather than tailoring our behavior to what reason shows us to be true.

There is an important point that the example of adultery misses, however. If to enter into an illicit affair is indeed stupid, we may ask why otherwise intelligent people do it. Let me suggest that it is not simply a failure to manage their appetites. (The adulterer may earlier have declined the advances of another and perhaps more sexually desirable partner.) What we see with such a choice is a kind of despair of real happiness. Every human person desires happiness, and not only apparent or temporary happiness, but a happiness that endures and fulfills. Recall that the fullness or perfection of human happiness is found only in the vision of God, the uncreated good. No created—and, hence, limited—good suffices to satisfy the human heart. If one cannot attain this happiness in this life and by one's own efforts, then it is tempting to abandon hope of such a good and devote one's efforts to attaining the best good available. The goods of wealth, especially artificial wealth (money), and sexual pleasure promise such fulfillment. "Here before me, ready to hand and inviting me now, is a promise of more and greater happiness than I had imagined. He (or she) is offering to me a joy that my husband (or wife) and I once had but have now forgotten, a gift I had not hoped for, a gift not only of pleasure but of self-realization. How can I pass it up?" (Let us note in passing, but not irrelevantly, that in our sexually liberated age, the highest human fulfillment is seen to consist precisely in sexual ecstasy.) Even if reason can ascertain that this promise is unrealistic, the vision of happiness remains compelling, and for this reason the desire for emotional and sensual pleasure can take the form of idolatry.

Idolatry has its roots in the desire for happiness, which is the desire for God. John Stuart Mill's characterization of happiness as "pleasure and the absence of pain" fails for precisely the reason that Thomas Aquinas cited, despite Mill's insistence that pleasure is the only thing that people desire for itself alone.[11] Agreeing with Aristotle, Thomas characterizes happiness as "'the complete and sufficient good,' [which] excludes all evil and fulfills all desire."[12] Or we may consider the words of St. Augustine reflecting on his privileged and pleasure-seeking youth.

I came to Carthage, where a cauldron of shameful loves seethed and sounded about me on every side. I was not yet in love, but I was in love with love, and by a more hidden want I hated myself for wanting little. I sought for something to love, for I was in love with love; I hated security, and a path free from snares. For there was a hunger within me from a lack of that inner food, which is yourself, my God. Yet, by that hunger I did not hunger; but was without desire for incorruptible food, not because I was already filled with it, but because the more empty I was, the more distaste I had for it.[13]

There is a peculiar logic here, a kind of flawed syllogism that runs like this:

• I expect true and complete fulfillment from sex (or money or the exercise of my will to power). (Minor Premise)
• Only God can satisfy my desire for true and complete fulfillment. (Major Premise)
• Therefore, sex (or money or exercise of my will to power) must be God, who is the divine power to govern my life. (Conclusion)

Thus does sex, or wealth, or the will to power become exactly an idol. Having granted this, we may discover another syl-

---

11. John Stuart Mill, *Utilitarianism* (Indianapolis: Hackett, 2001), 7.
12. *ST* Ia-IIae, q. 5, aa. 2 and 4.
13. St. Augustine, *Confessions*, Book II, chaps. 1, 77.

logism. God—whatever it is that is a god—tolerates no rivals. A god need not be almighty—Poseidon, the god of the sea, has no problem with the cult of Diana, goddess of the hunt—but in its own sphere, a god must be unrivaled. It may well come to pass that a conflict will arise between lust and the craving for wealth and that the devotee of both will have to choose between them. What is decisive, however, for us who do not worship Olympian gods, is that God himself, the Creator of the world and Savior of human beings, will infringe on the spheres claimed by the idols. In this case his demands become intolerable. To turn away from one's idol or idols amounts to a rejection of that in which one has put his hope for happiness and meaning, even if in fact the idol cannot possibly deliver the hoped-for satisfaction. Augustine witnesses powerfully to this in his *Confessions*, as the quote from Book III foreshadows. He sought joy in pleasures of the flesh, in honors and professional achievements, in beautiful things, but all for naught. It was only in the true God that he found the happiness he craved.

To sin—to turn to idols—is to embrace the culture of death, the culture that puts self and its attachments above love. Why did happy white people stand around the tree with its "strange fruit"? How could the secretaries and soldiers at Auschwitz picnic and party on weekends? How could Kitty Genovese's neighbors turn out the lights and go back to bed? Sin has its culture of solidarity, of complicity. Just as the ordinary Germans who took part in the *Kristallnacht* of November 9–10, 1938, implicated themselves in the Final Solution and Holocaust to come, so do sin and its culture come back to the sinner, saying, "You are with me now. You sold yourself to me. We have a bargain. You can no longer pretend that you are good." Those who lead others in evil know how to compromise the consciences of their followers. Perhaps the baker Schmidt will not kill a Jew. That is too much to expect—now. But he can paste a sign in his shop window. He can throw a rock at the synagogue. On *Kristallnacht* he can join the crowds setting fires and breaking glass in the Jewish neighborhoods. Then what right has he to object to further measures? Václav Havel asks why the shop owner in Communist Czechoslovakia posts the slogan, "Workers of the world, Unite!" in his shop window.[14] Neither he nor the authorities believe the saying. But this is not the point. By posting the slogans, the shop owner implicates himself in the official lie, and by posting the sign he helps to perpetuate it. And so is his conscience compromised.

This is why St. Paul does not speak so much in terms of simply making choices, but rather of kingdoms: God "has delivered us from the dominion of darkness and transferred us to the kingdom of his beloved Son, in whom we have redemption, the forgiveness of our sins."[15] To focus simply on choices is to fragment the moral life. This was good, that was bad, and a third act is on the borderline. If we think (and many moral theologians help us to think this way) of a person's life as simply a succession of choices, then it becomes impossible to characterize a life as a whole as either good or bad, as though stealing notepads from the office today could be counterbalanced by three acts of kindness tomorrow. We may ask, of course, whether it is even pertinent to ask about the goodness or wickedness of a life as a whole. May we not well contend that it is in fact more reasonable to expect one's life to be "pretty good," characterized by more good acts than bad, that moral heroism (whatever that may be) cannot be expected of most people?

What St. Paul (himself building on Christ's words about freedom) says is that by sin we enter into another kingdom. In other words, sin is not simply an event in the world, more or

14. Havel, "Power of the Powerless," 27–28.
15. Col 1:13–14.

less unfortunate in its consequences, more or less blamewor-thy according to certain moral rules. Having made an infernal bargain to get what he wanted, the sinner has transferred his loyalties to another god (the idol) to gain the pleasure or profit that God was not willing to give him. And so he has entered into another kingdom. Unless he finds a way out of the king-dom of sin, unless he gets freed from the dominion of sin, he is damned, not because God has damned him but because he has chosen another god.

Hanging there on the cross, the practiced criminal chose the offer of a new kingdom. His partner-in-crime ridiculed the innocent man between them, repeating the coarse insults and bitterness that were doubtless part of every conversation in the community of crime they shared. Dismas surely knew the drill. He should respond in kind—with ridicule and abuse of this so-called King of the Jews. Instead he decided that here at least he could embrace a piece of freedom, to seek a new kingdom, however improbable it may seem. "Jesus, remember me when you come into your kingdom."

The Evil Within

What our sin does to us is perhaps best portrayed in the opening chapters of Genesis. God had made the world, and it was very good.[16] He gave it to the first man and woman. More important-ly, he placed them with each other, which gave them joy. The Lord brought the woman to the man, who exclaimed, "This at last is bone of my bones, and flesh of my flesh!"[17] Their na-kedness before each other was no cause for shame, because they were capable of an innocent and generous love for each other.[18] They knew that in their bodies they could unite so as to become "one flesh," but in their innocence they experienced no urge to

16. See Gn 1:31.   17. Ibid., 2:23.
18. Ibid., 2:25.

dominate, to manipulate, or to exert pressure.[19] They could be genuinely happy together. Then they turned from God. The serpent tempted Eve, and she gave the fruit to her husband, who also ate it. And their eyes were opened. They saw that they were naked, and shame overtook them.

Granted that the story is told in mythical terms, we can clearly see its truths. The world God has given us *is* good. We all do want love and rejoice when we have it. Indeed, we are capable of love—pure, generous, gracious, fair love. Even with the penalties of suffering and death, to which Adam and Eve were not originally subject, we can be happy in this life. Here we might call to mind the scene in the police car toward the end of the Coen Brothers' 1996 film *Fargo*, as the pregnant police officer drives the murderer back to town. After reminding him of the five people (of whom she knew at the time) he had murdered, she comments, "And for what? For a little bit of money. There's more to life than a little money, you know. Don'tcha know that? And here ya are, and it's a beautiful day."[20] Without great wealth we can enjoy the beautiful day. We can have what we need for a happy, good life, "for we brought nothing into the world, and we cannot take anything out of the world; but if we have food and clothing, with these we shall be content."[21]

Let me digress here, but in a way that will turn out to be relevant. Ever since the Internet came into its own, the most lucrative form of e-business has been pornography. According to some estimates, Internet pornography profits have grown by about 40 percent per year since 1997. This is remarkable in the business world. How does it work? Are there that many "dirty old men," sexually obsessed perverts craving dirty pictures, in our societies? No. The customers for Internet pornography are

19. John Paul II, *Man and Woman He Created Them*, 143–45 (4:1–5).
20. *Fargo*, directed by Ethan Coen and Joel Coen (1996).
21. 1 Tm 6:7–8.

ordinary men, often men who would never think to enter an adult bookstore. What happens is that either out of curiosity or just by accident, a man or a boy just entering into pubescence comes across a site with provocative pictures that grab his attention. His initial response may well be shock or surprise and not sexual arousal. He may, however, linger a moment, and this is what the owners of the site hope for. He knows it is wrong, and he is not sexually aroused. But he is intrigued. And so he clicks on a banner or link, just to see. What he sees starts to arouse him, and returning again—most likely still against his better judgment—he surrenders a part of his mind to those images and becomes hooked. He has set himself up psychologically to crave the forbidden images he is finding. But note this: he was not led into the site by lust. He chose to expose himself to evil, to take it in, disregarding the warnings of conscience. This is what Eve did. She chose to eat the fruit that she was not particularly hungry for.

Even as she ate the fruit, Eve began to pay the penalty. Her very act of taking the fruit and biting it invites concupiscence into her soul. It is a choice of her own will against God's, of her foolish pride against his loving wisdom. "She also gave some to her husband, and he ate."[22] Then both realized they were naked, and they hid.

Scripture does not intend for us to think that this first couple was stupid. After all, God had brought Adam the animals for him to name.[23] In a way, Adam was the first zoologist. What seems to have happened is simply an abdication of conscience. If the woman ate the fruit and gave him some, then he should eat it, too. In his excellent but sobering book *Ordinary Men: Reserve Police Battalion 101 and the Final Solution in Poland*, Christopher Browning shows how the civilian members of a

22. Gn 3:6.
23. Ibid., 2:19–20.

reserve police battalion in Hamburg, Germany, became ruthless, cold-blooded killers of Polish Jews, lining their victims up next to graves and machine-gunning them down on command.[24] One of Browning's principal conclusions in his book is that these men really were "ordinary men," not monsters, not crazed Nazi ideologues. For the most part, they turned their consciences over to the authorities who had sent them to Poland, not questioning but doing what they were told. (This is not true of them all. Roughly 20 percent of them refused, and, except for being treated as social outcasts by their fellows, they were not punished.) Adam simply took the fruit and ate. The ordinary men of Police Battalion 101 simply took their weapons from the commander and killed. In neither case did conscience appear to come into play.

Death Camp Meditations

Whoever believes that there cannot be a place as evil as hell is not paying attention. Here let me offer not analysis but rather personal meditations occasioned by visits to the Auschwitz-Birkenau concentration camp (twice) and the Majdanek extermination camp near Lublin, Poland. Certainly one might ask how God could allow such evil to exist. The more realistic question is how we human beings could perform such evils; how we can devote our intelligence to the creation and execution of industrialized murder under conditions in which the victims are stripped of all the marks of their dignity, tormented, humiliated, tortured, starved, worked to death, or killed in mass execution chambers. Adjacent to the gas chamber at Majdanek is a small observation room for a soldier on duty to observe the gassing of the day's chosen inmates to determine when all have finally died, when the procedure was finished. As part of his responsibili-

24. Christopher Browning, *Ordinary Men: Reserve Police Battalion 101 and the Final Solution in Poland* (New York: HarperCollins, 1998).

ties, this young man in the service of his country looks on as his fellow human beings realize in horror that they are being gassed to death, as they claw at each other's naked bodies to try to escape, gradually succumbing to the gas and dying before his eyes. He is one like us, not much different from the soldiers of the Red Army who will eventually discover his observation post or from the Allied soldiers who will land at Normandy. He is an ordinary boy whose training and habits of obedience have made him into a monster.

Concentration camps were not meant simply to kill, but to dehumanize. The panther pounces, tears with claw, bites with fangs, kills, and eats, because it needs to feed itself and its young. But it does not enslave and starve its prey. The sharks surround the school of smaller fish, driving the school into an ever-shrinking sphere so that when the sharks attack, every charge will gain a mouthful of fish. They do not seek to hold their fish in a prison for the sake of working them to death. Animals kill to protect what is their own and to eat the appropriate prey. The camp guard, the slave driver, the tyrant, even the sadistic boss has to degrade the humanity of those under his control. The bases of the prisoner's humanity—his reason and will—must be denied him. But it is not only or even primarily the prisoner whose humanity must be denied. If he insists on his humanity, if he stands up and cries, "I am a man!," then he can be shot. Then he is gone, and anyone who might be tempted to imitate his protest is warned. His guards' humanity must also be denied. Depending on his rank and position, the guard enjoys privileges and comforts, but the one right he may never claim is that to his own conscience, to his own understanding and will. The soldier in the observation room must have his conscience destroyed, hardened, by watching others die in terror. To feel pity for the damned is to be soft, to lack courage; this was, indeed, the charge against those of the Hamburg police battalion who refused to join in the murder of Polish civilians.[25] The source of power becomes also the source of truth.

Commenting on Aristotle's dictum that the effect of law is to make men good, Thomas Aquinas raises the objection that some laws are tyrannical and that "the tyrant does not intend the good of his subjects," and responds:

A tyrannical law, through not being according to reason, is not a law, absolutely speaking, but rather a perversion of law; and yet insofar as it is something in the nature of a law, it aims at the citizens' being good. For all it has in the nature of a law consists in its being an ordinance made by a superior to his subjects, and aims at being obeyed by them, which is to make them good, not simply, but with respect to that particular government.[26]

People are helped to be good by living in well-ordered polities under wise legislators and honest judges. Indeed, it is not simply the laws that make citizens good; the culture by which people live, their respect for each other, and their customs and institutions enable them to live peaceably and harmoniously together. Concerning the tyrant, Aquinas's point is that tyranny corrupts the people's standards of truth and goodness. In the tyrannical regime the citizen—the father or mother, the friend, the minor official of the town or county—is not capable of judging truth or goodness. He is told, indoctrinated what he must believe, think, and do. To enjoy his privileges, among which may be his freedom itself, the subject must deny his own reason and conscience. He must deny his own humanity and subject himself totally to the power over him. And so St. Thomas maintains that the obedient subject is good not "simply, but with respect to that particular government." The soldier in the observation cubicle watching as others die becomes an increasingly good

25. Ibid., 72.
26. *ST* Ia-IIae, q. 92, obj. 4, and reply to objection.

Nazi guard. And if he has nightmares or can no longer face his grandmother's curiosity about his work, then he simply has to pay this price for the good things he enjoys and the esteem of his fellows.

During my wife's and my first visit to Auschwitz, we saw some Israeli visitors walking through the barren field that once held the barracks and gas chambers of Birkenau, repeating Jewish prayers for the dead, consecrating the ground, as it were. Similarly, outside the door of the starvation bunker where Maximilian Kolbe died, having offered his own life to save another prisoner, I watched one of my students, a young woman with painfully bad knees, kneeling on the concrete in prayer. These Israeli Jews and this American Catholic saw fit to turn to God in a place where the image and likeness of God was to be obliterated.

I suggest that the great question before us is not, as Elie Wiesel famously repeated, "Where is God?,"[27] but rather how did we, who are gifted with the power to know the truth and love the good, devise such evil? What has happened to us that human beings like us could turn so cruelly against our brothers and sisters, effectively killing in the hearts of guards and secretaries, soldiers and scientists the social instincts inbred within our race, and working carefully and diligently to destroy the lives of others? Richard Rubenstein writes:

No man can really say that God is dead. How can we know that? Nevertheless, I am compelled to say that we live in a time of the "death of God." This is more a statement about man and his culture than about God. The death of God is a cultural fact. . . . Buber felt this. He spoke of the eclipse of God.[28]

27. Elie Wiesel, *Night* (New York: Bantam, 1982), 61–62.
28. Cited in Balázs M. Mezei, *Religion and Revelation after Auschwitz* (London: Bloomsbury, 2013).

It is pertinent to note that Nazi Germany was ideologically racist, founded on the premise that the Aryan race was superior to all others, and further that of all the racial groups in the world only the Jews have a claim to be the people chosen by God the Creator. This is no doubt why the Jews had to be destroyed, not for their religious beliefs but for their biological unity as a witness to God's prerogatives in human history. For God to have an existing people of his own choosing was an insult to the foundations of the racist Reich.

We must beware, however. The fall of the Third Reich in 1945 did not mark the end of the eclipse of God in the modern world. It simply marked the failure of the crudest form of this eclipse.

If we live according to the ways of the world—showing our power over others by surrendering our minds and souls to the culture of death—then we live under the threat that this power will turn against us. Viciously we learn vice from those around us, and viciously we reinforce their vices. And we all encourage each other that we are happy and good. We can make deals with the devil, choosing his reign rather than the Kingdom of God by choosing the reign that will satisfy our current desires and earthly needs, rather than directing ourselves to the true good under the kingship of Christ. For the sake of myself I make myself a slave of Satan, an increasingly willing collaborator. And in our pride we give reign to the flesh so that we become incapable of loving others and become embittered and dissatisfied. Having surrendered to the world, the devil, and the flesh, we live an increasingly desperate life in an increasingly hellish world.

The Prodigal Son wanted only to enjoy himself, to feast and enjoy the pleasures of a carefree wealthy scion.[29] In fact,

29. Lk 15:11–32.

he got everything he wanted, and it proved empty. Fortunately for him, his money ran out, and in desperation he turned back to his father. Slopping pigs and envying them their full bellies brought him back to his senses. Too often we are less fortunate. Our money holds out, and we can seek consolation for our inner emptiness in the plaudits of the world, the security of the devil's rule, and the satisfaction of the flesh. And more and more our lives become hellish.

CHAPTER 7

Damnation

Here is a great paradox. The damned are not treated unjustly.
They chose to turn from God, and so they are cast out from
his presence. And yet, if Michelangelo is right—and our Lord's
words give us reason to believe he is—they are surprised and
dismayed by their fate. It is one thing to give up eternal happiness. I have talked with well-educated people who have no use
for heaven. As one man, an artist and university professor, told
me, "This life is good. When it is over I don't need a heavenly
cake for dessert."[1] If to my correspondent hell simply means
losing out on some extra heavenly pleasures and amusements, it
is not that great a loss. If I have lived happily in this life without
God, I can get on well enough without him in the next (if there
is a next, which such persons doubt). This rather lighthearted

1. Private exchange of letters with T. L., September 1999.

attitude reflects a superficial understanding of the afterlife that is based on a superficial understanding of *this earthly life.*

Let us be clear once again: in speaking of heaven and hell, the Christian faith does not propose a system of rewards and punishments based on keeping God's rules. *Do what God has mysteriously decreed and he will pay you off with delights in his heavenly Paradise. Do what God forbids (or leave out what he wants) and you pay forever in a hellish den of torment.* This is a false vision of what heaven and hell are about.

Just as what we call "heaven" is really a state of perfect fulfillment and happiness, "hell" is the name for eternal damnation, which is a state that, like happiness, pertains only to the spiritual. A material being, be it a rock or a house or a dog, can be damaged or destroyed. If we speak of the condemnation of a house, we mean only that an appropriate authority has slated it to be destroyed. A miscreant animal, such as a dog that attacks humans without provocation, is destroyed (or put down), but not condemned, and this for two reasons. First, the dog is not aware of its impending fate. He does not realize that the veterinarian intends to take its life with the needle he holds. Death is not something that an animal experiences. All that it experiences are the events leading up to its death. Second, there is no true guilt and no awareness of a sentence based on guilt. Acting on instinct, a dog perceives a nearby child to be a threat and attacks. The event is tragic, and the parents may demand that it be destroyed, but the extent of justice involved concerns the dog's owners, not the animal itself. A human being, however, is aware of his punishment—that it is impending, that he is held to deserve it, and that it is in response to acts for which he is held responsible.

The condemned human being is aware that he is to lose his life. He is to be no more. Earthly death is the end of the human person's physical life and activity. Whatever he may want to do, whatever plans he had hoped to undertake, whatever he may enjoy is lost to him after his execution. Of course, one may readily accept such loss. The prisoner loyal to the cause for which he was arrested may accept his condemnation rather than betray his comrades. The martyr accepts death rather than deny his God. What such a one loves transcends this life, and so it makes sense to lose his life for the sake of what he loves.

Someone damned eternally loses more. The idols in which he believed could promise only temporal goods, goods pertaining to the body and its existence in the physical world. Eternal condemnation means that no meaning is left, that one's existence is entirely insignificant, that his life has no point. All is indeed lost. The spiritual life is focused on truth and goodness,[2] and if truth and goodness go lost, then the person's spirit has no anchor.

To put this another way, a human life is a sign of reality, a sign of the world and of reality as a whole. To live according to reality is to live in truth, and one who lives according to reality makes himself a kind of sign of the truth, even if to only a limited extent. What God offers to every person (which he offered to every angel, as well) is the vision of himself, a direct participation in his own life and knowledge. To see God as he is, which vision can be attained only if God grants this gift, constitutes the ultimate satisfaction. The person enjoying this vision is fulfilled because all that he is—his entire being—is in perfect accord with the One who is the source of reality, who is being-itself. He is himself conformed to the perfect truth.

Failure of the Damned

The damned person has failed, but it is a peculiar kind of failure. He has failed to attain what he was made for but did not want. He did not care to seek God, and so his failure to reach

2. Wojtyła, *Love and Responsibility*, 7.

God is not a great disappointment, at least not immediately. Furthermore, he may well have been a great success in his lifetime, achieving all the goals he had identified as important. We may think of Don Corleone, who, having turned his successful crime empire over to his son, dies playing with his grandson in the garden.[3] For a historical example we can think of Josef Stalin, whose armies overran nations, who murdered millions and sent millions more into slave labor camps, and who died peacefully in his bed. Both were wicked men who lived wicked lives. And both were successful. They achieved what they lived for and died happy.

After death, however, earthly success means nothing. Lacking his voice, his frown—not to mention his armies and secret police—Stalin became powerless the moment he died. No plan of his will went into effect. Having achieved the status of absolute power, so that in his lifetime he personified the Soviet Union, he became a nonentity in death. His successor, Nikita Khrushchev, could change his policies and even attack his "cult of personality" (as indeed he did), and Stalin was powerless to stop him. Death mocks all our efforts, even those that are worthy. Thomas Aquinas died before finishing the *Summa theologiae*. Mozart's *Requiem* was completed by another hand. How many parents have died without knowing their grandchildren? In this way we are all doomed to failure ... unless we can find a goal, an aim in life, a good that transcends death itself.

Death of the Soul

Let us look more closely at what damnation means for a spiritual being. The scriptures speak of a resurrection to the "second death" for the damned.[4] How can this be? What can it

3. *The Godfather*, directed by Francis Ford Coppola (1972).
4. Rv 20:14.

mean? Whether we speak of a building or a convicted criminal, condemnation is a sentence to destruction. If the soul is immortal and indestructible, then to speak of its destruction or "second death" seems paradoxical or perhaps even metaphorical. If we understand better the relationship between spirit and matter, however, the issue becomes clearer. To live is in some way to have the power to sustain one's existence. Plants do this by sinking their roots toward water and turning their leaves toward the sun. Animals do this by seeking food, fleeing from or fighting against enemies, and preserving their kind by procreating young of their species. Living things behave according to patterns or habits that will sustain them in existence. The life of the human person goes beyond this. Endowed with the power to reason and understand the truth, the person is capable of forming habits of his own, of adapting his patterns of behavior even more effectively to insure his survival and that of his kind. Thus human beings can live in any climate, from the tropics to the arctic, and not only in Africa, where we originated. Furthermore, human beings can record their experiences for future generations, passing on what they have learned to their children and their children's children. This power of reason, of understanding the truth of things, enables human beings to envision not only useful changes in the immediate environment ("How can we bring water more easily to the village?"), but also a whole new world or even a different kind of world. We see these in ancient myths of the gods and demigods with their super-worldly homes on Olympus or Valhalla, as well as in contemporary fantasy and science fiction (*Lord of the Rings* or *Star Trek*). Not only can we dream of new kinds of world, but we can plan for new ways of living, envisioning how to live in outer space or on Mars, contemplating new ways to govern ourselves, to educate our young, and to form our civilization's culture. Whether we speak of human life on the individual, familial, communal, or civilizational level, human life is shaped and sustained not so much by habits acquired "naturally" from our interactions with nature but by those formed rationally. Reason is not simply another mental capacity "added on" to perceptions and animal instincts, but instead forms the life of the human being and community. The human being lives by reason—even at his most irrational and perplexing, man is rational.

Because reason is intrinsically related to truth, for the mind to be incapable of truth is its destruction. Since the behavior of the spiritual being is formed by its understanding of the truth, the spirit cut off from truth is doomed perpetually to failure in its most fundamental enterprises. This understanding that the human being's most important part is his rational power, which is grounded in the soul,[5] is not well received in our day, when materialistic accounts of human nature and behavior predominate, and, indeed, this present discussion may on the face of it support a materialist interpretation of human nature. After all, if, as we are contending, a corruption of one's ultimate end, a misdirection of one's life-orientation toward an inappropriate end, were to constitute a kind of death of the soul, then surely the misdirected person should experience this. If a hungry man seeks to assuage the discomfort in his belly by smoking more, his suffering will not go away. Indeed, the effect of his smoking on an empty stomach may actually induce mild nausea. By analogy, ought not the misdirected life be uncomfortable or even painful? Or to put it more briefly, if pain is the signal of something wrong with one's being (as a toothache signals decay), then it is reasonable to expect the misdirected, "dead" life to be painful. Human experience, however, suggests that it is not. A life amply provided with comforts and interesting di-

5. Reimers, *Soul of the Person*, 250–75.

versions, along with interesting and relatively worthwhile tasks to undertake, is experienced as rich enough to satisfy most human beings. If damnation consists, in part at least, in an insufficient or misdirected engagement of the reason with one's life and choices, then it seems not to be all that bad. By comparison, however, we know that if the brain, which is the bodily organ that most evidently manifests rationality, is diseased or damaged, the damage is often not directly evident in pain (such as headaches). The person who, because of some brain injury or ailment, is sliding into mental illness is himself often unaware of that illness. A malfunction of the brain is manifest not in pain but in the inability to live well, to control one's own life appropriately. Similarly, if one's life is misgoverned spiritually by the powers of intellect and will, there need not result any directly painful experience of this misgovernment—we have noted that generally there is not—but the damage is proceeding nonetheless.

Damnation arises from the turning away from one's authentic good and toward an idol. From this it follows that to turn away from truth is death for the intellectual being. We have already seen in chapter 2 that Satan's rejection of God's offer of the vision of the Divine Essence led to his misery and wrath—and to his project of supplanting himself into God's place in the minds and hearts of other rational beings. The human spirit that follows Satan in rejecting God's invitation shares in Satan's faith, but with this important difference. Having rejected God's wisdom, he becomes necessarily subject to Satan's schemes. His life and being are no longer his own, but become subject to the one who would be the merciless god. To come under Satan's regime is comparable to entering a criminal organization. Full of confidence in one's own powers, his intelligence, and strength of will, the criminal neophyte finds himself in a system already formed and governed so as to form him. In his desire for wealth and access to power and pleasure, the young thug comes under the rule of the crime boss, who controls his future by controlling his prospects and his choices. Indeed, our young criminal finds his life more and more narrowly circumscribed by the requirements of the crime family. Should he decide to leave, he finds he cannot, for his life is literally no longer his own. A similar pattern occurs with one who chooses to enter the governing party of a dictatorship. It is interesting that the only lively discussions of Marxism as well as broader cultural themes described in Solzhenitsyn's novel *In the First Circle* are among the *zeks*, not among members of the party hierarchy.[6] In a very real way, those *zeks* are alive, even in their imprisonment, because they can think and care about their own lives, while the officials who hold power over them cannot. These officials must be careful of every word they say, of every thought they might utter, because the wrong word, however careless, can lose them their prerogatives. They must live not their own lives but rather a life that is imposed upon them, according to a truth dictated by others above them. Their suffering takes not the form of direct and immediate pain, but of increasing alienation from self.

The death of the soul is not experienced directly and immediately, but must be seen in its consequences for one's life. The Prodigal Son feels no pangs of remorse or sympathy for his father, whom he has treated cruelly—he asks *now* for what he would ordinarily get when his father dies—and comes to his senses only when his belly is empty.[7] When Satan and his angels refused God's love, they did so instantaneously, as it were, in the perfect clarity of their unclouded intellects. They made their choice in full consciousness of their intention. Because human beings very seldom act with such clarity of intent,

6. Solzhenitsyn, *In the First Circle*, trans. Harry T. Willetts (New York and London: Harper, 2009), 339–42; 386–408. "*Zek*" was the Gulag term for prisoner.

7. Lk 15:11–24.

we may well ask whether a human being can definitively reject God's love and, if so, how he can do this. This is, effectively, the question of mortal sin, of intrinsically evil acts that kill the life of the soul.

Intrinsically Evil Acts

In his encyclical on morality, St. John Paul II writes:

The primary and decisive element for moral judgment is the object of the human act, which establishes whether it is *capable of being ordered to the good and to the ultimate end, which is God.* . . .

Reason attests that there are objects of the human act that are by their nature "incapable of being ordered" to God, because they radically contradict the good of the person made in his image. These are the acts that, in the church's moral tradition, have been termed "intrinsically evil" (*intrinsece malum*): they are such *always and per se*, in other words, on account of their very object.[8]

The importance of this text for our present discussion is St. John Paul II's contention that certain acts are always incompatible with God's goodness—that they cannot be ordered to the love of God. Such acts decisively and definitively orient the person away from God and his love. It is important to note that John Paul II does not speak here in terms of violation of a commandment, or that the essence of evil consists simply in the violation of a divine command. His point is that the act itself (for instance, willful murder) is incompatible with God's love; that whoever chooses, for instance, willfully to murder has set himself against God's love. Even leaving to the side the disobedience to the Fifth Commandment, the act itself sets one against God's love. Furthermore, it is the act itself that orients

8. John Paul II, *Veritatis splendor*, §§79–80.

the person against God's love, regardless of the motivation or further intention.

But is such an interpretation of an act even possible? Granted that an act of willful murder is a serious wrong and ordinarily destructive to human society and peace, is it reasonable to maintain that the murderer has, by that one act—this event in space and time—turned himself definitively against God and his love? St. John Paul II himself addresses this issue.

As we have just seen, reflection on the fundamental option has also led some theologians to undertake a basic revision of the traditional distinction between *mortal* sins and *venial* sins. They insist that the opposition to God's law which causes the loss of sanctifying grace ... could only be the result of an act which engages the person in his totality: in other words, an act of fundamental option.... The gravity of sin, they maintain, ought to be measured by the degree of engagement of the freedom of the person performing an act, rather than by the matter of that act.[9]

Can it not be maintained that a person may generally be ordered to love, even while on one occasion performing this one vicious act? Perhaps he has performed the act only once, and that under duress. Surely it may be argued that this does not engage his total personhood such that he has definitively turned against the love of God. And in one sense this is true, because in many ways the person can continue after performing this act to perform other acts that apparently express a love for God and neighbor.

Such a defense misses the point. How often has a cheating husband tried to explain to his wife that his one-night stand during a business trip "meant nothing, that she is the only woman he really loves"? What she sees, of course, is that he has shared with the other woman that act which uniquely express-

9. Ibid., §69.

es his complete devotion to her as his wife. Even if she comes to forgive him, the wife recognizes his adultery as a profound betrayal of a completely different order than forgetting her birthday.[10] The principle behind the intrinsically evil act is much the same. It constitutes a direct contradiction to the order of love for God. Even if one continues to profess love for God and to perform other acts expressing love for God, the performance of this kind of act constitutes a rejection of God's love and one's love for God. The logic of intrinsically evil acts is absolute. A philosopher thoroughly committed to the importance of truth may lie to his neighbor about his availability to help move some furniture on Saturday without thereby fundamentally discrediting his overall commitment to truth. Willful murder, however, as an act that deprives another human being of the fundamental good of existence, constitutes a direct rejection of love and is therefore intrinsically evil.

Relatives and Absolutes in Clouds of Consciousness

The foregoing analysis notwithstanding, one may well object that with human beings it is never quite that simple. The adulterer may have fallen from fidelity in a moment of psychological weakness—perhaps he was on a particularly demanding and unsuccessful sales trip away from home—and not from a fundamental rejection of his wife's love. Sophie, the eponymous heroine of *Sophie's Choice*, does not hate her daughter, even as she tells the SS officer, "Take my little girl! Take my baby!"— take her to the death camp.[11] Sophie's act was arguably wrong, but she was caught in an unimaginably horrific situation (and let us note that the twentieth century was rich in these) for

---

10. Of course, such a forgetting suggests a thoughtlessness whose consequences can become grave if not addressed.

11. *Sophie's Choice*, directed by Alan J. Pakula (1982).

which no moral preparation is truly adequate. We do not, however, have to appeal to the most extreme cases to see the two problems implicit in this notion of intrinsically evil acts, problems arising from the clouds of human consciousness.

The first of these is that an act is a limited event in time and space, often incited by a new and sudden situation demanding a prompt response. The chess player has the luxury of pondering his next move, but the basketball player must decide in an instant whether to take a shot or pass to a teammate. One's boss, commanding officer, or an agent of the secret police has demanded the personal betrayal of a friend, a command that requires serious violation of the moral law, and the subordinate stands there nervous and afraid under the superior's steely and threatening glare, knowing that he will pay dearly for failing to obey. He consents and, fighting regret and remorse, he reassures himself that he had no real choice, that he is less to blame—much less to blame—than his superior. The decision was taken, the act performed, and now the incident is over. The logic of the *intrinsece malum* may declare him an enemy of love, but his love for God and neighbor has defined his life so far. Can an unreflective decision, limited by space and time, truly define one's fundamental choice for God? Is it reasonable to claim that the direction of the will can change in an instant?

The second problem, closely related to the first, is that one is seldom aware of the axiological implications, the transcendental depths of his act in relation to the will. By an act, a sequence of bodily movements in space and time, the agent has brought about certain changes in the world, changes that he expects to be good. His intention is certainly to bring about something good, but can it reasonably be argued that one spatially and temporally limited act can of itself define one's transcendent choice for the good, his orientation toward the most fundamental values? Ought we not look more broadly at the overall pattern of one's acts to discern the pattern of values he lives by?

The source of both problems is in human bodiliness—the fact that unlike the angel, the human person lives and realizes himself in space and time, so that, as ancient Aristotle pointed out,[12] the goodness of a life is not really known until it is over. The libertine Augustine repented of his ways and became a saint. Rudolph Höss, commandant of the Auschwitz concentration camp, acknowledged and regretted his crimes, expressing the hope that God might forgive him.[13] By contrast, after following Jesus throughout his public life, Judas betrayed him to those who sought his death. What sense can we make of this? Specifically we need to understand more clearly the relationship between body and spirit, between rational and sense appetites.

The state of the spirit is not directly accessible to consciousness. Specifically, the human person has no direct access to the state of his understanding or to the rectitude of his will. This means that no one can judge himself, that he can turn decisively from good to evil without being directly aware of the damage he has done to his will. Specifically, one does not ordinarily perform an act with the express intention to deny one's ordination toward God as his highest good. Indeed, his moral awareness is most likely rather circumscribed: the act pertains to *this* state of affairs, to the specific motivations involved in the situation at hand. This lack of full moral consciousness does not, however, negate the reality of his corruption.

The problem we are addressing here arises from a false

---

12. Aristotle, *Nicomachean Ethics*, Book I, chap. 10, 1101a12–14; Book X, chap. 7, 1177b25.

13. John Jay Hughes, "A Mass Murderer Repents," Seton Hall University School of Theology, March 25, 1998, http://www.shu.edu/academics/theology/upload/mass-murderer-repents.pdf.

model for understanding human action. We may call this the "chess-player" model. The agent has a clearly defined goal in mind to guide his actions—he wants to win a tournament—and a strategy to win that tournament. To attain this end he contemplates every move for a period of time, considering all the possibilities that he can foresee and the consequences of different moves. Then, after sufficient reflection, he chooses a move. By comparison, our adulterous salesman genuinely desires to maintain a successful, loving marriage. He has had perhaps a drink or two more than his usual, and he had not expected the signals of willingness from an attractive woman in the bar. And so he believes that the sexual liaison "just happened." But his excuse is not true. It is not true because the act is never simply the consequence of a process of reflection. Even the chess player's choice of a move is not simply the result of his analysis. The act is the conclusion and verification of the thought.

One of our most common intellectual mistakes—especially in the wake of Descartes—is to assign thought to the spiritual realm and action to the material, the physical. But this is a false model. Every thought is an action, specifically a series of neuron firings in the brain, and—here is the key—every action expresses an idea (which relates to truth), and a love (which relates to good). A person's acts are governed by what he loves, what he desires. No human act is merely an event to which a variety of interpretations may apply. This is the principle behind Thomas Aquinas's astonishing contention that the first sin of a child upon reaching the age of discretion must be a mortal sin. Thomas writes:

Now the first thing that occurs to a man to think about, then, is to deliberate about himself. And if he then direct himself to the due end, he will, by means of grace, receive the remission of original sin: whereas if he does not then direct himself to the due end, as far as he is capable of discretion at that particular age he will sin mortally, through not doing that which is in his power to do. Accordingly thenceforward there cannot be venial sin in him without mortal, until afterwards all sin shall have been remitted to him through grace.[14]

St. Thomas places an enormous moral responsibility on such a child. At the age of seven (or thereabouts) this child sins mortally if he does not, upon becoming aware of himself as a moral agent, direct himself to his "due end," which is God himself. Thomas continues:

The child that is beginning to have the use of reason can refrain from other mortal sins for a time, but it is not free from the aforesaid sin of omission, unless it turns to God as soon as possible. *For the first thing that occurs to a man* who has discretion, is to *think of himself*, and to direct other things *to himself* as to their end, since the end is the first thing in the intention.[15]

With our minds clouded, perhaps by sentiment, we do not ordinarily see primary-school-age children as capable of grave evil, and certainly a child just at the age of discretion enjoys fairly little consistent control over his thoughts, imagination, and actions. The child who "forgot" to clean his room is not thereby bad; he needs to learn how to exercise his duties responsibly. Aquinas can leave plenty of room for the foibles of the preadolescent mind, but this is not the point. Even a child can direct himself to his due end. His failure to do so is not because of ignorance—he need not understand the term "due end"—nor of immaturity, but of will. He is self-centered: "For the first thing that occurs to a man who has discretion, is to think of himself, and to direct other things to himself as to their end." He sees the world as revolving around himself,

---

14. *ST* Ia-IIae, q. 89, a. 6.
15. *ST* Ia-IIae, q. 89, a. 6, ad 3 (emphasis added).

whereas it rightfully revolves around God. Every human being desires the good and loves its highest end. He is responsible to discern that end according to the lights of reason and of faith and to direct himself toward it as best he can with rectitude of will.[16] This is a spiritual movement of which even the child is capable. The seven-year-old who places himself and his wants at the center of his life has offended God. To be sure, Aquinas does not intend to consign all children to hell, for they have their parents to teach them, as well as the sacraments and spiritual resources of the church to direct them toward God. However, the spiritual working of the will in its directedness toward good and of reason in its order toward truth preexist and underlie the particular choices concerning help or harm to others, respect of another's property, use of the sexual faculties, and so on. The choice of that to which one ultimately directs himself is determined by the human spirit, by the will. The choice, as Aquinas's argument suggests, of self instead of God is not constituted by an explicit thought: "Oh, I shall do what pleases me." Rather it is the choice of oneself (or some other idol) as the criterion of all good. Whenever a human person says to himself, whether implicitly or explicitly, "That is good," he does so according to some more or less clear conception of what it means to be good, according to some definitive standard of good. It is this choice to which St. Thomas is referring. Even a child to whom these arguments would be incomprehensible is capable of recognizing that there is something more important than himself. A child can be capable—and we do see this at times—of giving up some great good of his own for the sake of another or for God's sake. All good is good according to some standard, some ultimate good, to which the human person, as a spiritual being, is directed.

16. *ST* Ia-IIae, q. 4, a. 4.

A further truth comes into play here, one that clarifies the importance and role of punishment. Having chosen to act outside of the order of God's love, a person has chosen a different principle than love to govern his life. Consequently his governing value provides no criterion for judging that his behavior is wrong. However, as a bodily being he is subject to bodily factors, and these constitute the basis for punishment. Our adulterer may well wake up the next morning with strong feelings of shame and remorse. These and his wife's anger when she finds out may induce him to acknowledge his wrong, to repent, and to reorient himself. Of course, they do not have to lead him so. He may well justify himself and confirm his choice of wrong. Upon seeing the prisoner Jesus turning to look at him, Peter went out and wept for his cowardly betrayal. St. Augustine wanted wisdom and happiness, but found that sexual profligacy, moderate wealth, and a good reputation led only to misery. He was able to repent. As bodily beings living in space and time, human beings can be guided by the consequences of their actions.

For the acting person the act itself *is* his choice of values. He performs *this* act rather than another because this act realizes the value that he wants. For the adulterous salesman, it may be true that the other woman "means nothing to him" in comparison with his wife, but his own self-pity and desire for pleasure and reassurance are more important to him than his commitment of love for his wife. Similarly, the murderer has by his chosen act set himself against the One who gave the victim his life. His act is not the confirmation of a previous conscious choice to set himself against God. It *is* that choice. Indeed, one who sets out to murder is not by that fact alone yet a murderer. It is only when he pulls the trigger, stabs with the knife, or performs some other killing act that he murders. Until that moment of action, he can choose differently.

The Company of Hell

Ordinarily, we envision hell primarily in terms of physical pain and suffering—one might even imagine fire and devils with pitchforks tormenting poor souls. But it takes more than pain to make a hell. In fact, of itself pain is not *that* bad. It is not *hellish*. We know that many persons who suffer chronic and serious pain describe themselves as happy, granting that they would be happier were their pain to be gone. On the other hand, as we have noted, healthy and comfortable people can live in misery, such misery, in fact, that they take their own lives. The "hell" of hell is not physical pain. The suffering of hell is this: that for eternity the damned must live eternally with Satan subject to his dominion. This is a society of evil, ruled by a murderous, lying, and rapacious ruler.[17] There is neither faithfulness nor justice nor law beyond what Satan himself should decide.

Let us consider some earthly examples. Crime analysts tell us that a common feature of many serial killers is not deprivation, poverty, or mistreatment, but instead a desire for fame. When arrested, the serial killer will characteristically ask the police if his crimes have been the worst they have ever seen. After the Columbine High School shootings in 1999, the initial story on the young killers was that they had been victims of bullying and had been influenced by a "Goth culture." Subsequently, however, we learned that the two killers came from surprisingly normal backgrounds.[18] Their motivation was simply hatred for their fellow students (as well as most of society as a whole), whom they held in contempt. They saw themselves as men capable of doing something bold and important, unlike the inferior beings who surrounded them every day. So that

---

17. See Jn 8:44 and Rv 12:2.
18. *Columbine High School Shootings*, http://www.history.com/topics/columbine-high-school-shootings; accessed December 28, 2015.

April day they launched their rampage, which they climaxed by their own suicides. What then?

We may hope that in that split second between squeezing the trigger of the suicide weapon and the moment of death, either of these young men may have repented. God can act in split seconds. But let us consider Satan's point of view. Here were two who did his work, murdering their fellows, terrorizing a school and traumatizing a community. If Satan is a murderer from the beginning, these boys would seem to be two excellent disciples. Or are they? Would Satan be proud of these young nihilists? I suggest that he would not. From the satanic point of view, the boys were inept, almost failures. Had they not been so eager to make a big name for themselves they could have been much more effective, killing many more students. (We may note, for example, that Seung-Hui Cho, the more methodical and systematic Virginia Tech killer in 2006, was more effective than the boys at Columbine.) In Satan's kingdom are much better killers and sowers of sorrow than the Columbine killers. In hell the nihilistic murdering hero of his own imaginings will find himself and his own evil efforts mocked and ridiculed. Having turned against the world, he will find that hell also hates and rejects him. Satan will not proudly welcome even his most cooperative disciples. The evidence for this is readily evident in the hellish behavior of tyrannical rulers on earth. Whether an actual tyrant over a nation or empire, the leader of a religious cult, the ambitious climber of the corporate ladder, or simply the president of a neighborhood association, the tyrant is never happy for more than a few moments with the dedication and loyalty of those he or she dominates.

And when the brutally selfish financier, the power broker who with his legal and financial power enriches himself while ruining others who have less, arrives in hell, Satan is not impressed. It is one thing to be a force to be reckoned with for five years in Kansas or even for ten years in Chicago, but that means nothing to the rulers of hell. Money and reputation are useless there. In fact, no one there will hear of his or her—women are as susceptible to wickedness as men—cleverness and exploits. The damned are the poor slobs that demons manipulate and oppress.

It is important to stress this because unless we recognize the reality of Satan and the other fallen angels, we can make no sense of the pangs of hell. Those on earth who thought that they could play by Satan's rules will find that those rules are not reliable, that there is no fairness, no reward for loyalty or a sinner's best efforts. Satan is not inclined to reward even his most faithful servants. He does not respect achievement, loyalty, or cleverness, but instead values only that which is of use to him in the moment. And the true virtues, such as generosity or kindness toward children, that a damned person may retain become the subject of satanic ridicule and mockery. We know this because in rejecting God's governing principle, which is his love, Satan has set himself up as a rival to God.

To be in hell, therefore, is to live perpetually under the domination of a resentful, rebellious, but powerful lord who claims complete authority and mastership over one's heart, desires, will, and being. Those whom the King consigns to the place prepared for the devil and his angels find themselves bullied and tormented with no hope of any good. The sweet fruits once offered and for which they gave everything—the pleasures and gratification of a sexual liaison, the glory of ill-gotten worldly fame, the wealth obtained by manipulation and deceit at the expense of the common good, the satisfaction of being dominant over one's fellows—these fruits are gone. The fisherman feeds no worms to the fish in his pail. There is no good for the damned, because according to the logic of hell, Satan is the only good and only Satan deserves anything good. And he will get it from those he has won—no matter what it may cost them.

If this is the way it is among humans, it is so much the worse where angelic beings, who really *are* superior, are concerned. Therefore those in hell—in the place prepared for the devil and his angels—will be treated with special contempt and indignity. If freedom is, in the words of the Second Vatican Council, "an exceptional sign of the divine image in the human being,"[19] then it is especially hateful to Satan. The damned will find their inherent dignity denied and ridiculed, and any assertion of freedom will be harshly and cruelly punished.

The Pains of Hell

Ordinarily when we think of hell it is in terms of great pain. The "Act of Contrition" speaks of dreading "the pains of hell." The scriptures speak of fires of Gehenna,[20] torments of fire and sulfur,[21] and the lake of fire reserved for the damned.[22] Although the lowest part of Dante's Inferno is so cold that the tears of those sent there freeze over their eyes,[23] our traditional view of hell is in terms of fire. So we ask: what is this hell-fire? What is it like? The word used for "hell" in the Gospels is "Gehenna," which is a valley where garbage was dumped and burned outside ancient Jerusalem. The fires of Gehenna are none other than the kinds of fire we see in any dump. Jesus' point in speaking of Gehenna seems to be that those who value their own satisfaction above God will be thrown out of the Holy City into the dump where the garbage is burned. In other words, Jesus is saying that if one turns from God, he has made his life a waste.

The texts from Revelation are much more dramatic, speak-

19. *Gaudium et spes*, §17. 20. Mt 18:9.
21. Rv 14:10. 22. Ibid., 20:10, 14.
23. Dante Alighieri, *Inferno*, Canto 33, 109–17.

ing of a "lake of fire" and of burning sulfur. And of all the books in the New Testament, Revelation is the least susceptible of a literal interpretation. Rather it is full of imagery through which we glimpse God's ultimate intentions for his church and the human race. The burning sulfur of Revelation hearkens back to the "fire and brimstone" that rained down upon Sodom and Gomorrah, which God punished for their great sins.[24] It is a metaphor for God's severe punishment of sin. It is a place where the consuming and purifying fire of God's justice never ceases.

Earlier in this book we looked at the misery of the soul that has abandoned itself to sin. We saw its emptiness, frustration, and despair. The Last Judgment will take place after the dead have been raised, and therefore the damned will be taken to hell in their bodies. Like the saints, they will live forever in their bodies. The blessed in heaven will enjoy *eternal* life, a life that not only never ends, but in which every moment will be filled with life and God's love. The blessed enter into God's eternal life. However, hell is separated from God. It is ruled by demons and filled with bad people. And this regime and populace make it a very bad place. Furthermore, although hell goes on forever, it is not eternal or timeless. Hell is a constant experience of the meaningless passage of time without interruption, without variety, and without any destination. In this respect, Sartre's conception of hell is correct.[25]

In our lives in this present world, there is always something to be thankful for. Think, for example, of the terminally ill person, seated in a chair by the window, where for the final days of her life she can watch the birds come to the feeder. The condemned prisoner on death row may order his favorite

---

24. Gn 14:25–28.
25. Jean Paul Sartre, "No Exit," in *No Exit and Three Other Plays* (New York: Alfred A Knopf, 1989), 46.

meal before he dies. On the TV news report the woman whose house was just destroyed by the tornado expresses thanks that the children are all safe. All these goods come from God. "Every good endowment and every perfect gift is from above, coming down from the Father of lights."[26] Little pleasures—sunshine in the window, the hope that next year will be better than this, the protection of reasonably just laws and effective police, the availability of good food—all these are gifts from God. The wet and shivering soldiers huddled in a trench as artillery shells explode in the night tell jokes or play cards. This life is bearable because there is so much good. Even in the worst predicaments human beings can find some joy, some little pleasure, some friendliness. Even when evil seems to rule, God's goodness keeps coming through to those who look for it.

Because in hell one lives forever, one needs no food. There is no pleasure of eating, no "snack break" to interrupt the tedium of life under Satan. Instead there is torment from demons and other damned persons. In hell the pains of the body are never alleviated, and there is no sympathy. In hell there is no encouragement—only demons to scream that the damned is worthless, a failure, and will eternally be so. Here on earth work may be tedious and hard, but one can turn on the radio and then chat during coffee breaks. There is no music in hell, and there are no breaks. And besides, no one is interested in what the damned have to say, anyway. They were invited to the feast but insisted on going their own way, and now there is nothing but what Satan will allow. And it is vain to hope for anything good.

The truth about pain is that one can live happily with it. Those who work in pediatric cancer facilities tell us that these suffering (and often dying) children can be happy, that they can

26. Jas 1:17.

endure their sufferings and face their own deaths with remarkable serenity if they are loved. I once taught a young woman—Maggie—whose back went bad in her early adolescence and could not be surgically fixed. Unless there is a miracle or some medical breakthrough, Maggie is condemned to a life of chronic pain. But Maggie is happy. She even wrote her term paper for my course on how happiness is possible with chronic pain. Of course, she and others like her would gladly accept relief. Maggie takes her pills and sees her doctors, and she hopes that they can come up with something to fix her back. Nobody wants pain. On the other hand, even a lifetime of pain can be a happy one. It is different than hell.

The "hell" of hell is not in its pains but in the loss of what makes pain bearable. The "hell" of hell is the hateful society that the damned have chosen. It is hatred and contempt of a society without love. The devil and his angels live in eternal fire that is not physical—spirits do not burn—but spiritual. Pure spirits and human souls have this in common: both have an insatiable desire for the perfect good, for God. "You have made us for yourself, and our hearts are restless until they rest in you." Everything about the spirit (whether angelic or human) is destined for God. We may compare restlessness with the fire of love, which wants to give itself completely, to be absorbed in the good it loves, and to take what it loves completely into itself. To love something or someone passionately leaves a person restless, unsettled, distracted from everything else. The spirits in hell still have this power to love, but lacking everything good (or *almost* everything good, as we'll see in the next chapter), they have no focus. The fire that is in them—and in each of us by nature—is out of control, constantly looking for an outlet but, because of its own self-inflicted blindness, unable to find it. The damned want *something*, and there is nothing good. Hell is crushing boredom, because the devil is not going to amuse us with mindless distractions. Those who are raised up to the "second death" will be alive, but living for nothing. The hurt they will feel is that loss of any hope, the futility of having nothing to do today that is worth doing. The fire within consumes the heart and soul in boredom and frustration and depression.

It might be helpful to contrast this with the harsh conditions that Alexandr Solzhenitsyn portrays in his short novel *One Day in the Life of Ivan Denisovich*, which was based on his own experiences and conversations with other prisoners.[27] Ivan is a political prisoner—he had committed no real crime—in a Siberian labor camp under the Soviet regime. He is unjustly condemned to live and work in this bitterly cold camp with barely adequate food and clothing under the watchful eyes of jaded guards who resent their bleak assignment. In many respects we can say that this is hell on earth. Nevertheless, the novel ends on a curiously positive note. Ivan judges it to have been a good day. He had stolen some extra rest early in the morning and then, with a couple of his fellow prisoners, had succeeded in completing the assigned project by applying some ingenuity to their daily task. Hell is not like this. Ivan Denisovich managed to find small pleasures and challenges, hope, and an outlet for creativity even in the harsh cruelty of the Soviet Gulag. The damned enjoy no such pleasures and hopes in hell. They find no camaraderie, which even prison camp cannot prevent. In Auschwitz, saints prayed and doomed mothers sang to their babies. No one sings in hell.

The (In)justice of Hell

Today we resist the whole concept of hell, more so than in earlier times.[28] We do not want to believe that God could possibly

---

27. Solzhenitsyn, *One Day in the Life of Ivan Denisovich* (New York: Farrar, Straus and Giroux, 1991).

28. Ralph Martin, *Will Many Be Saved?: What Vatican II Actually Teaches and Its Implications for the New Evangelization* (Grand Rapids: Eerdmans, 2012).

send people to hell, especially people like me and my friends. There seem to be two main reasons for our resistance to the idea of hell. The first is that we cannot believe that anyone can be so bad as to deserve an eternal severe punishment. Second, we don't believe that a loving God could possibly be so cruel as to damn a person to sorrow, pain, and misery *forever*. It seems so legalistic, so *out of proportion*. Can hell possibly be just?

In his *Utilitarianism*, which presciently presented the governing ethos of the modern liberal democracies of the United Kingdom, the United States, and Western societies in general, John Stuart Mill argues that, far from being a godless philosophy (as his critics had maintained), utilitarianism was particularly in accord with God's plans for humanity because God wants his creatures to be happy.[29] And what does it mean to be happy? Mill explains that happiness is "pleasure and the absence of pain," while unhappiness is "pain and the privation of pleasure." He continues: "Pleasure and freedom from pain are the only things desirable as ends, and … all desirable things … are desirable either for the pleasure inherent in themselves, or as a means to the promotion of pleasure and the prevention of pain."[30] By this, Mill meant "pleasure" to be understood in a broad, humanistic sense, with the focus not so much on sense-pleasures of food, drink, and sex, but on the pleasures of mind, the more refined pleasures of an educated and cultured person. Indeed, Mill saw the task of government and of all those responsible for the formation of public opinion and attitudes to be precisely the formation of such mental qualities among the populace that all the citizenry will prefer the higher pleasures of the mind and have the attitude that each of them is responsible for the happiness of his fellows. This philosophy, or one very like it, has become the dominant one of our civi-

29. Mill, *Utilitarianism*, 22.
30. Ibid., 7.

lization in this age. When we consider the criteria by which we measure the successes and failures of our societies and the performances of our public officials, these criteria are largely those that Mill has proposed in his book. Mill sums up this vision nicely:

The happiness which they [i.e., earlier philosophers] meant is not a life of rapture, but moments of such, in an existence made up of few and transitory pains, many and various pleasures, with a decided predominance of the active over the passive, and having as the foundation of the whole not to expect more from life than it is capable of bestowing.[31]

We cite this because if Mill is right about these two premises—that happiness is essentially pleasure and that God wants us to be happy—then eternal punishment in hell is extreme. If the criteria of right and wrong are founded ultimately on happiness, if a good life is "an existence made up of few and transitory pains, many and various pleasures, with a decided predominance of the active over the passive," then it is hard to see the reason for any punishment, except as a means to deter and restrain those who would cause unhappiness to others. In fact, even if punishment needs to be administered to one who causes pain to others, this has nothing to do with whether the perpetrator is *evil* or *wicked*. The justification for punishment can lie only in the utility for the society as a whole. "Justice remains the appropriate name for certain social utilities which are vastly more important, and therefore more absolute and imperative, than any others are as a class."[32] Punishment can be nothing more than one of those "social utilities" that make for the greatest happiness of all. Furthermore, if what God wants is for his creatures to be happy (in Mill's sense of that term),

31. Ibid., 13.
32. Ibid., 64.

then it is not reasonable that he inflict eternal punishment of his creatures who cross him and disobey his rules. If Mill's conception of justice is right, then the King's consignment of those on his left to eternal damnation can be construed only as a kind of vindictiveness. More appropriate, from Mill's utilitarian perspective, would be the banishment of all the wicked to a kind of well-administered penal colony, where the damned have to do without the best delights of heaven but do not, on the other hand, have to suffer perpetual torments of any sort. In Mill's system, the notion of hell is simply unintelligible, irrational. If the notion of hell offends us, it is because we do not understand rightly what good and evil truly mean and because our understanding of what God wants is philosophically simplistic.

Could God Be So Cruel?

According to our criminal code, those who break certain laws, ordinarily those that directly and seriously harm others, face incarceration. For the sake of common peace and order, society has laws that all are to obey. Is this how we should think of God's law? We have already said that heaven and hell are not the reward and punishment for doing the right or wrong things. Hell is for those who chose themselves—the lust of the flesh, the lust of the eyes, or the pride of life—over God, those who live for some idol. They do not want to live in God's realm. In this respect, by being consigned to hell they get just what they want.

This important point was rather humorously but, it seems to me, accurately illustrated in the 1967 version of the film *Bedazzled*, about an ordinary man who sells his soul to the devil.[33] At the very end, God offers the devil a second chance to get into heaven (this part was not accurate). All he has to do is to

33. *Bedazzled*, directed by Stanley Donen (1967).

praise God. And this the devil cannot do. Even if the understanding of *angelic* natures is flawed, the *human* psychology is accurate. The damned person is simply incapable of praising or thanking or loving God. He has chosen something other than God for his love and praise. He does not want God, and therefore it is perfectly fair and just that he does not get to spend eternity with him. If he does praise God, it is only to meet the admission requirements.

From this we get an insight into the justice and injustice of hell. To turn away from God is to turn not only from his mercy but also his justice. The King will say, "Depart from me, you cursed, into the eternal fire prepared for the devil and his angels." God is only too happy to save us from the devil and his predations.[34] But if someone chooses against God, there is nothing for it but to come under Satan's rule. And Satan is not fair. The devil is not just. God's goodness is so great that it permeates this world we live in, even breaking through chronic pain and into Soviet prison camps. If Satan's power is restrained on earth, in hell it is not—or at least, not much. It may, perhaps, not be fair for one who has simply indulged his lust throughout his life, betraying his marriage vows and the trust of a succession of mistresses, not only to be sexually impotent but to be mocked and ridiculed, to suffer whatever physical indignities the company of hell may inflict upon him. Unfortunately, he has definitively rejected God's just rule and in doing so has accepted Satan's. When wrong was done in Corinth, St. Paul could appeal to the Corinthians to relax their severity toward the offender: "so you should rather turn to forgive and comfort him, or he may be overwhelmed by excessive sorrow";[35] but Satan, whose judgments are formed by the laws of power and loyalty to himself, has no sympathy for those in his realm. Un-

34. Acts 10:38.
35. 2 Cor 2:7.

der his regime there can be no recourse to principles of fairness or legal justice. This is why we see such dismay on the faces of Michelangelo's damned. It is possible to march into prison cocky and with head high. There is fellowship to be found in an earthly prison. But it is not until judgment that the damned realize the implications of their choice. No one can walk jauntily into the clutches of Satan.

There is one qualification to all this. Even in hell there is good. St. Thomas Aquinas tells us that God is everywhere by his presence, power, and essence.[36] He knows what is in hell and sustains in existence every being that is there. In principle, a person condemned to hell could rightfully and reasonably thank God that at least he exists, that he has not lost all hold on reality. God does not subject him to the ultimate penalty of annihilation. And it may well be that in his mercy God somehow restrains Satan's vindictiveness—even in hell—toward many of those who have fallen prey to him. God's goodness is so great that its traces can be found even in hell. Unfortunately, those who are there have so turned against him that they cannot see these traces.

Can a Human Being Deserve Hell?

We have already indicated how and why we may say that a person "deserves" hell. If someone has turned away from God, then in eternity God will not force himself upon him. He is excluded from God's presence, which he did not want anyway. As an abstract or formal argument this makes sense.

To the person confronted with eternity and with the imminent prospect of eternal damnation, however, what is happening appears to be all out of proportion. One may go through life making choices—some good and some not so good—suf-

36. *ST* Ia, q. 8, a. 3.

fering some bad times and having hurt some people, but not intending to be *bad*. Part of the great mystery of our human nature is that we are free to define the rules by which we want to judge ourselves. We can limit the size of the world we live in. God loved Lazarus.[37] He formed Lazarus in his mother's body to be wonderfully made and placed him among his chosen people.[38] Lazarus was not only created in the image and likeness of God, but he had the privilege of being one of Abraham's children. And the Rich Man ignored him. God had created Lazarus and given him to his people as a gift (for each human person is a gift), and the Rich Man couldn't have cared less. Even in the torments of Hades, he did not get the point: "Father Abraham, have mercy on me, and send Lazarus to dip the end of his finger in water and cool my tongue; for I am in anguish in this flame."[39] For the very first time, he has taken notice of Lazarus, who now lies in comfort in Abraham's bosom. However, the Rich Man does not rejoice at the poor man's good fortune— that at last something has gone right for him. All that the Rich Man can see is that, for the first time, Lazarus might be of use to him, and he asks his help. In fact, he doesn't even ask Lazarus himself, but "Father Abraham." If we had known him, most of us would have regarded the Rich Man not as bad, just short-sighted. He was not cruel to Lazarus. He just ignored him. The Rich Man lived in a very small world, small in the sense that it held only a few persons and some valuable things. Its demands were simple. "Be smart, but honest in business. (Christ does not tell us that he had gotten his wealth wrongly.) Be good to your friends, and don't make enemies. Be faithful to your social, political, and religious obligations. Keep your hands off your neighbor's young wife, even if she smiles at you." The Rich

37. In Lk 16.   38. Ps 139.
39. Lk 16:24.

Man may have done many things right. But he did not love God. We know this because he ignored the poor man, created in God's image and born a son of Abraham, and he failed to love him. The Rich Man thought of himself as simply a creature of this world. We could say that he was a Utilitarian Man.

This was never God's plan for spiritual beings with immortal souls. God made us this way so that he could raise us up bodily to live in an eternal communion of love with him. He does not have it in mind that we can choose, "No thanks. I'll take seventy years of comfort here on earth and then just pass away." Utilitarian Man enjoys what he can see, hear, and feel, but does not address the One who made him. God intends this creation, other human beings, and our very lives all to be gifts that will lead us to him, the Perfect Gift. To deny this is to deny our dignity, the dignity of creatures in God's image called to eternal communion with him.[40]

But is it really so bad to be Utilitarian Man? Can we say that it is *wicked* or *evil* to settle for less than God had intended? Might we not draw upon a somewhat weak, but pertinent, analogy: although we may call him *foolish*, do we say that a talented young person is *wicked* to pass up a good education for the sake of some lesser good? If the human person were nothing but a consumer of pleasures and experiences, then such an analogy might hold. But as rational, free beings—as beings ordered by nature to the truth and goodness—we have greater responsibilities than this. St. John Paul II reminds us of our two fundamental human responsibilities. First, as ancient Socrates exhorts us, is self-knowledge.[41] The inscription over the portal of the Temple at Delphi, "Know thyself," is a fundamental challenge to every human being, for the person does not receive his essence fully defined in such a way that nature itself

40. *Gaudium et spes*, §19.
41. John Paul II, *Fides et ratio*, §1.

tells him who he is and what he is supposed to do. The life of the deer is determined by its genes and the forces in its environment. The human being's life is before him as a project. From the age of five, the child looks ahead to the answer to the question, "what will I be, when I grow up?" To answer this question, which is the question of the meaning of his life, he must come to an authentic self-knowledge. His second responsibility, which is like the first, is to seek out and embrace the highest good, the good that is the source and exemplar of every good, which is God himself.

To understand the wickedness of turning away from God we have to understand how our principles function, how human beings "work." Human beings need principles, loyalties, or commitments. Jesus speaks of this when he says that no one who does not hate mother and father, husband and wife, children, and indeed his own self, can follow him.[42] He demands that our ultimate loyalty be to him. When Scarlett O'Hara vowed, "As God is my witness they're not going to lick me. I'm going to live through this and when it's all over, I'll never be hungry again. No, nor any of my folk. If I have to lie, steal, cheat or kill. As God is my witness, I'll never be hungry again," she adopted a life-principle that led her to exploit the workers in her factory and to drive away the good man who truly loved her.[43] She became a conniving, wicked woman. Not everyone chooses like St. Edith Stein to give her life entirely to Christ or, like Scarlett O'Hara standing on the hilltop, to vow "as God is my witness" to do whatever is necessary to become rich. Many drift into commitments, choosing pleasure over responsibility, an advantage over friendship, a small lie over honesty. And then comes a serious temptation to theft or adultery or betrayal—in other words, to mortal sin. To sin mortally a person has to choose something

42. Lk 14:26.
43. *Gone with the Wind*, directed by Victor Fleming (1939).

that Christ *could not* have chosen, something that *cannot* lead him to God, something totally incompatible with God's love.

Strictly speaking, no one can drift noncommittally through life without choosing some ultimate direction. The psalmist addresses this succinctly:

> Transgression speaks to the wicked deep in his heart;
> there is no fear of God before his eyes,
> for he flatters himself in his own eyes
> that his iniquity cannot be found out and hated.
> The words of his mouth are mischief and deceit;
> he has ceased to act wisely and do good.
> He plots mischief while on his bed;
> he sets himself in a way that is not good; he spurns not evil.[44]

The *Jerusalem Bible*'s rendition of the first line of the psalm is illuminating: "Sin is the oracle of the wicked in the depths of his heart." This voice of sin is a prophetic speaking that seeks to realize what it speaks. The wicked man is the one who listens not to God ("there is no fear of God"), but to the sin in his heart. How does he do this listening? When he is in bed and unable to sleep, or maybe while driving or walking to his car, he is solving his problem. And the problem is how to move ahead with his selfish plans without getting caught. Sin is in control.

The Drama of the Moral Life

St. John Paul II often spoke of the "drama" of the moral life.[45] The Utilitarian Man leads a tedious and generally boring little life. Richard Cory was such a man, prosperous and "a gentle-

---

44. Ps 36:1–4.

45. John Paul II, Apostolic Letter *Mulieris dignitatem* (Vatican City: Libreria Editrice Vaticana, 1988), §30; Encyclical *Evangelium vitae*, §28; "General Audience" (Vatican City: Libraria Editrice Vaticana, March 28, 2001); Post-Synodal Exhortation *Reconciliation and Penance* (Vatican City: Libreria Editrice Vaticana, 1984); Wojtyła, "Persona e atto," 1043–44.

man from sole to crown, clean favored and imperially slim.... In fine, we thought that he was everything to make us wish that we were in his place." He was such until he "one calm summer night, went home and put a bullet through his head."[46] On the other hand, of course, we see other people who grow old in very modest circumstances, burdened with illness, but who are also genuinely happy. Their lives are about something different than the Utilitarian Man's or Woman's.

We are remarkable beings. The Second Vatican Council wrote,

Now, man is not wrong when he regards himself as superior to bodily concerns, and as more than a speck of nature or a nameless constituent of the city of man. For by his interior qualities he outstrips the whole sum of mere things. He plunges into the depths of reality whenever he enters into his own heart; God, Who probes the heart, awaits him there; there he discerns his proper destiny beneath the eyes of God. Thus, when he recognizes in himself a spiritual and immortal soul, he is not being mocked by a fantasy born only of physical or social influences, but is rather laying hold of the proper truth of the matter.[47]

Although we have bodies, we are spiritual beings, and this means that we are not subject only to the determination of nature. Karol Wojtyła wrote:

The human person, as a distinctly definite subject, establishes contact with other beings precisely through his interiority, whereas the whole "biological" contact, which also belongs to him ... and the sensual contact in the likeness of animals do not constitute for him the characteristic ways of connecting with the world.[48]

---

46. Edwin Arlington Robinson, "Richard Cory," in *Immortal Poems of the English Language*, ed. Oscar Williams (New York: Washington Square Press, 1961), 498.
47. *Gaudium et spes*, §14.
48. Wojtyła, *Love and Responsibility*, 5.

Wojtyła's point is that human contact with the world through the human person's perception, practical interaction, and cognition is not governed by his biological nature—that is, by the mechanisms of sensation and instinct alone. Wallabies and walruses do what they do because they are "designed" by nature to behave in certain ways. Animals feed, fight, and flee according to their instinctive responses to environmental factors. If an animal's natural constitution is badly adapted to its environment then it will die. Perhaps some of its offspring may have characteristics that enable survival, in which case evolution by natural selection may occur. However, it is only the species that evolves and not the individual. By contrast, human beings make contact with the world spiritually, through reason and will. So, it can happen that one person may find a Stradivarius cello to be an interesting old artifact, while another, because of her discipline, practice, and chosen love for music, longs to take it up and play it. The son of a Midwestern attorney may become an Olympic swimmer, while an inhabitant of the tropics pursues chess. In short, the human person is free to order and orient his own life toward goods that he recognizes intellectually and chooses to love. And it is pointless to object that our cellist grew up in a family of music lovers or that the swimmer attended a high school with a strong swimming program. These provide inspiration and opportunity, but do not determine a direction in life. One may be born with acute hearing, perfect pitch, and extraordinary manual dexterity—a combination of prerequisites for playing stringed instruments—without ever undertaking the project of becoming a concert musician. Freedom is the power of self-determination in precisely this way: that as a spiritual being the person can form himself according to some desired ideal.

The project of self-determination unfolds not only on the vocational or occupational level but more importantly on the

moral level, as one chooses his governing moral principles. We
know well that one can be successful in some limited field of
endeavor without being morally excellent; indeed, this is a major theme of *Amadeus*, which presents its eponymous musical
genius as crude and often rude, immature and irresponsible—
hardly the angelic being that simply hearing his music might
suggest.[49] It is precisely here that the deepest and truest drama
of human life unfolds. That a talented and ambitious athlete
be struck down at the height of his career with amyotrophic
lateral sclerosis is dramatic because a rare and unforeseen illness has destroyed his hopes.[50] However, this is a destruction
that comes from beyond his control. Gehrig was able to see the
end of his career with thankfulness—"Yet today I consider myself the luckiest man on the face of this earth." This gratitude
and the love of his wife indicate that Gehrig embraced values
higher than athletic success. At stake in the drama of life is a
moral self-determination that is independent of limited prospects and opportunities. Whether one should pursue an athletic career, one in music, or a less dramatic life, he nevertheless must live morally. That is to say, every human being must
respond to other persons—whether this be in love or in that
hatred constituted by the impulse to use others—and to God.[51]
These obligations are inescapable because we are inescapably
social—every one of us was born of two other persons into a
community of some sort—and creatures of God in his image.
If human goodness is constituted in terms of one's love for his
neighbor and love for God, if the fundamental moral vocation
is to love, then the drama of the moral life is acute. When concert pianist Paul Wittgenstein lost his right arm during World

---

49. It is worth noting that the historical Mozart's character is in fact rendered
accurately by the film.

50. Commonly known as Lou Gehrig's disease, after its most famous victim.

51. Wojtyła, *Love and Responsibility*, 11, 25; John Paul II, *Veritatis splendor*, §§6–9.

War I, he experienced professional tragedy that he could not have avoided.[52] When Shakespeare's Macbeth chooses to murder King Duncan to steal his crown, he chooses an evil direction for his life and makes himself evil, so evil that one icon of evil, the Second Witch, announces his arrival with, "By the pricking of my thumbs, / *Something wicked* this way comes."[53]

To recognize that one has an immortal soul and that his destiny is to be with God is not to be "mocked by fantasy," but to be "laying hold of the proper truth of the matter." We are "superior to bodily concerns."[54] Because the human being is not determined by his nature, the deepest and decisive drama of his life occurs within his own will. The drama of the moral life is a true drama because it is a decisive conflict that can turn out well or badly. We are magnificent beings, called to glory, but also find ourselves in a spiritual struggle that has eternal consequences.

The problem with Utilitarian Man and Woman is that their vision is too narrow. They think too little of themselves. They are called to eternal transcendence but prefer to settle for a few pleasures and some things. "There's more to life than a little money, you know . . . and it's a beautiful day."

Merciful Suffering

If the adulteress is lucky, her husband will find out. The embezzler is better off getting caught. This is something we all learned in childhood, even if we did not like it. When the child is caught doing something wrong and Mom punishes him, it really does make him a better person. "Discipline your son while there is hope: do not set your heart on his destruction."[55]

---

52. It should be mentioned, however, that he proved quite creative in creating music (and in transcribing the music of others) for the left hand alone.

53. William Shakespeare, *Macbeth*, act 4, scene 1 (emphasis added).

54. *Gaudium et spes*, no. 14.

55. Prv 19:18; cf. Sir 30:1–2.

Most of us have known someone who, as a child, was never disciplined and has turned out selfish and irresponsible—maybe even criminal. As awful and "unfair" as it was to be grounded during basketball season or without a weekly allowance in the middle of summer, we grew up knowing to obey Dad's rules, to restore what we broke, and so on. It is not only our own sufferings that made us better, but the awareness that others suffer, too. When I was a child, we had to eat all our vegetables and be grateful, "because children are starving in China."

In his apostolic letter on suffering, Pope John Paul II said that suffering is always the experience of some evil, the loss of some good.[56] Our sufferings in this life characteristically derive from losing some temporal good ... the body is injured ... we have failed to achieve what we had hoped for. And this experience of suffering almost always leads to two responses. One is to get rid of the evil by taking an aspirin for the headache or bringing the accident victim to the hospital to treat his injuries. The second is to try to come to grips with the evil, to make sense of it. Stricken with some grievous evil, a person immediately asks *why* this happened. What went wrong? Even if nothing can be done to undo the evil, there must be a way to make sense of it. What these experiences do is to force us to look higher for our true good.

Ignatius of Loyola was a dashing young Spaniard—brave, strong, and arrogant and eager to gain glory in war. Seeking glory, he instead found a cannonball. Rather, the cannonball found him and badly injured his leg. For months a sore and very bored Ignatius lay in bed with nothing but his own thoughts and a book of lives of the saints. By the time he was well enough to resume his life, it was on different terms. His injuries caused him great pain and, by permanently crippling him, left him unable

---

56. John Paul II, *Salvifici doloris*, §7.

to pursue his lifelong dream of military glory. He was forced to reconsider the direction of his life. He could have chosen the path of the wastrel, killing his pain with wine and distracting himself with sensual pleasures. He answered the question of his life's meaning by turning to Christ, who led him to found the Society of Jesus.

Dismas had wasted his life, choosing his crimes over honest work and associating with the worst of men. Finally it came to the cross and the excruciating pains of crucifixion. What was left for him? There was one decent thing he could do. He could stick up for the Rabbi hanging on the next cross over. Jesus was good. He did not deserve crucifixion. So for once in his life—and he knew that it would be over soon—Dismas chose something better. Even hanging on a cross and minutes from death, a person can turn around. So Dismas rebukes his former partner in crime. He stands up for the innocent man and even acknowledges that the Rabbi might really come into his kingdom. "Jesus, remember me when you come into your kingdom." In his suffering he finally turned to the one who could show him mercy. "This day you will be with me."

CHAPTER 8

The Fullness of Good

WHEN GOD SHALL BE ALL IN ALL

For the contemporary philosopher of religion and for the "new atheist," God's morality—or lack thereof—constitutes a serious challenge. The God who commands from Mt. Sinai "thou shalt not kill" orders Joshua to kill every man, woman, child, and beast in the city of Jericho.[1] Ivan Karamazov complains to his brother Alyosha that he cannot accept a God who allows innocent children to suffer; that neither the order of the world nor even the punishment of their torturers can atone for the tears of one innocent abused child.[2] How can a good God command what we today rightly identify as a war crime? How

---

1. Jo 6:17. Of course, the harlot Rahab and her household were excepted.
2. Dostoevsky, *Brothers Karamazov*, 123.

can an almighty and omniscient God be identified as "good" if, having it within his infinite power to intervene, he allows children to suffer? If common opinion today, ratified by most of our legal codes, condemns the willful and depraved indifference on the part of one who could readily save another but does not, then how can a God be called "good" if he allows human beings (and animals!) needlessly to suffer? The conceptual problem is this: if we ascribe the predicate "good" to God, then he ought in some way to be recognizable as such. If God is good, then we require that he should at least meet the minimum standard for moral goodness. And it appears that the God revealed in the scriptures does not. Therefore it seems to follow that God is either not what he is claimed to be—omnipotent and omniscient—or he is not good.

Faced with this dilemma, it is tempting to find a defense for God, and to a limited extent these defenses can be illuminating. One of the most serious such defenses is Alvin Plantinga's "Free-Will Defense," which solves the problem by arguing that a world in which free will, and hence morality, is possible is better than one in which it is not, and that therefore this world, in which moral evil is possible, is better than one in which it is not, even if moral evil should result in suffering on the part of some.[3] The world would not be so good if human beings had no freedom. However, the free-will defense has this shortcoming: it fails to address why God permits nonmoral evils, such as tornados, house fire, earthquakes, and mad dogs. In one important way, of course, this objection is not realistic. The laws by which the universe functions and by which the world is a good and intelligible place to live also allow for occasional misfortunes. To have a world without earthquakes we would have to live on a planet without tectonic plates floating on magma.

3. Alvin Plantinga, *God, Freedom, and Evil* (Grand Rapids: Eerdmans, 1977).

Water is good—vital to life and enjoyable to drink—but if one falls into it, he may drown. To get around we must walk, but even a slight unevenness of the ground may cause one to turn his ankle. A completely safe and pain-free world is impossible to imagine. This all makes sense, but one can still ask why God, who is all-wise, could not have created a painless world, creating humans to be beings not susceptible to pain and evil. One could respond that the presence of any evil in the world allows for the opportunity for human beings to practice mercy and compassion on the suffering. This is certainly true, but then we must ask why some must suffer on the outside chance that one of their fellows will be morally ennobled. Our purpose here is not to respond to these arguments or even adequately to summarize them. Rather I point to them as partly worthwhile, but ultimately unsatisfying efforts to justify God in the face of suffering. Alyosha cannot answer Ivan, although Dostoevsky *shows* us Alyosha's answer to the suffering of children, but we will return to that later.

The fundamental reason that such arguments as outlined in the preceding paragraph fail is that they assume that we know what good and evil are. To know that something, be it a radio or a rhinoceros, is good one must know what good is—what such a thing must be like to be good. A radio is intended to receive electromagnetic signals within a certain range of wavelengths and translate them into sounds. If the device does this well and renders the sounds accurately, then the radio is good. We judge radios by how they fulfill their function. But my neighbor's radio in the next room distracts me from my study, and that is bad. As a living being, an animal, the rhinoceros, should live and reproduce its kind. If a rhinoceros is alive and healthy, eating and sleeping and mating well, it is good. Of course, precisely because it is such a good specimen, it may constitute a mortal danger to the explorer. And that is bad. It is good that plants grow, but we pull up the weeds in the garden; they are bad. A thing's goodness or badness seems then to depend on one's point of view. From the scientific point of view, there is no real goodness—only that which human beings ascribe to things.[4] Good has to do with function, end, or goal—with what is desired. "Good" is meaningful only if the end of a thing is known.

From this it follows that we can know the good only to the extent that we can know their ends, their purposes. Furthermore, if a thing has a nature, if it is some *kind* of thing, then its good is determined by that nature. A cheetah is a kind of animal, which is to say, a kind of living being, and therefore it is good for the cheetah to live. To die would seem then to be an evil for the cheetah, but this is not really so. By nature animals live only for a period of time, but not forever. Since cheetahs normally live for eight to twelve years, it is not bad for one to die at the age of eleven. Because the cheetah is a feline animal it is a predator and carnivorous, which means among other things that the goodness of an individual cheetah is determined in part by its effectiveness as a hunter. Even if the scientist, including the zoologist, finds no place for the good in his theories, we can, without falling into fable or mythology, identify what is good or evil where cheetahs are concerned. The kind of goodness sketched here for this one kind of animal is the sort of goodness we encounter all the time. Generally, if we err concerning the good of some particular thing it is because we have erred concerning its nature; we do not know yet well enough what *kind* of thing it is or what is characteristic of that kind.

To get through our lives as individuals and as societies, we identify as best we can (and generally rather well) what is good. We know the goods of our artifacts, because we have designed

4. Adrian Reimers, *Truth about the Good: Moral Norms in the Thought of John Paul II* (Ave Maria, Fla.: Sapientia Press, 2011), 1–29.

them for our purposes, and by knowing natural things (such as cheetahs and chipmunks) we know their goods, too. This applies even to inanimate things. When an electron in an accelerator does not behave as expected, the scientist says that "something is wrong"; either the machine has malfunctioned or the particle concerned is not an electron (perhaps it is a positron). The point here is that we can and do reliably identify the goods of different sorts of things, including goods pertaining to our own lives and being. But we do not yet have the key to goodness itself, to absolute goodness.

"No one is good but God alone."[5] These were Jesus' words to the rich young man who was looking for direction to his life. On this, St. John Paul II remarks, *"Only God can answer the question about what is good, because he is the Good itself."*[6] Here is the key to the question at hand. Having shown that there must exist a first mover that is itself unmoved, a first efficient cause, a being that is necessary of itself, a being that is the cause of the being, goodness and perfection of every other thing, and an intelligent being to which all natural things are directed as their end—and this being we call "God"[7]—Thomas Aquinas goes on to state that "we cannot know what God is," which is to say that knowledge of the divine essence is absolutely beyond the natural power of the human (or any created) intellect.[8] As the first efficient cause of all things, God is the author of the perfection—the goodness—of every created being. From him ultimately comes their goodness. The argument for God's own goodness moves on the formal level, with little for the human imagination to hang onto. It proceeds as follows: in the divine essence there can be no potentiality, which means neither composition nor dependence on any other thing, but complete and

---

5. Mk 10:18.
7. *ST* Ia, q. 2, a. 3.

6. John Paul II, *Veritatis splendor,* §9.
8. *ST* Ia, q. 12, a. 4.

perfect self-sufficiency. Therefore, God is complete and hence perfect in his own being, with which he is identical. And because he is perfect, it follows that he is necessarily good. A Creator or First Cause of all things, he is ultimately the good of everything created.[9] God is by his very essence good.

The implication of the foregoing is inescapable. As the good-in-itself, whose very essence is goodness, God is the ultimate standard of goodness. Whatever is good or may be called good is so in virtue of some relationship with God. The only way that the human mind can fully understand and judge rightly what is good is to know God himself. Therefore the human judgment that this or that is good can necessarily be only partial and provisional. Hence, in the face of the objections that God allowed girls in south Asia to be taken and sold into sex slavery after the 2004 tsunami or that God himself ordered Abraham to kill his son, we must acknowledge that God is good and that furthermore these things, these events, are ordered to his own goodness. We may very well be unable to explain why a good God allows these things and how his goodness is realized in the lives of those girls or Ivan Karamazov's suffering children. All we can say is that the explanation is buried in the mystery of God's wisdom and the predestination of all things to him. This is why the various theories put forth by philosophers of religion fall short—they try to explain the inexplicable. This is the same answer that we find at the end of the book of Job. A God-fearing man who has committed no offense against God suffers grievously, despite his faithfulness, and he calls God to account. He demands to know *why* God has done this to him. Job does not give God an "out" by acknowledging that his omnipotence may not quite cover every eventuality or by allowing that his suffering might serve in some larger plan. Job asks the very pertinent ques-

9. *ST* Ia, q. 6.

tion: why must *I*, Job of Uz, "blameless and upright," suffer the loss of everything? In the end, his question is answered as God speaks to him directly. His words are hardly comforting: "Who is this that darkens counsel by words without knowledge? Gird up your loins like a man, I will question you, and you will declare to me."[10] God then proceeds to challenge Job to match the divine wisdom and power, to explain the mysteries of the earth, the seas, and the heavens. In the end Job is humbled, but not humiliated. He concludes his response to God, "I had heard of thee by the hearing of the ear, but now my eye sees thee; therefore I despise myself, and repent in dust and ashes."[11] Although Job does eventually have his losses restored to him, his true salvation is the vision of God. God himself has answered him. Job "had heard of" God, but only that. He had never met God face-to-face, had never known God personally to turn to him. His salvation is that in responding to him, God had taken him, Job of Uz, seriously and met him on even ground.

Here it is worthwhile to return to Ivan's challenge about the sufferings of children to his younger brother, Alyosha. Dostoevsky has portrayed the youngest Karamazov as a prospective saint. At the start of the novel he is a monk, being trained by the celebrated *staretz* Zossima, who before dying instructs Alyosha to leave the monastery and return to life in the world. At the time, the eldest of the brothers Karamazov, Dimitri, publicly humiliates a poor man whose sickly little boy is the target of bullying and torment by other boys in the town. Alyosha befriends these boys, leading them eventually to true friendship among themselves and especially with the one who had been the object of their persecution. When this child finally dies, he is surrounded by his erstwhile tormentors, who have gathered to support and console him in his suffering. The closing line

10. Jb 38:2–3.
11. Ibid., 42:5–6.

of the novel is spoken by the boys of the village to their friend Alyosha: "Hurrah for Karamazov!" By his engagement and friendship with the boys of the village, Alyosha has implicitly answered his brother Ivan's complaint.

In the face of evil human beings can find no ultimate answer. Her child tragically dead, the Mamá responds, "Dios quiere"— "God wills." Is this a mindless resignation in the face of irrational evil? Although one can look at it that way, this resignation can also be an expression of faith, that although the mind and purposes of God are hidden his workings are for our good and the good of those we love.

If we understand the true nature of goodness, this attitude is quite reasonable. In his treatise on happiness St. Thomas Aquinas gives us a curious and at first glance puzzling explanation of why only the vision of God can be happiness for a human being. After arguing that only the perfection of man's highest part, his intellect, can constitute the fullness of human happiness, Aquinas continues:

> When man knows an effect, and knows that it has a cause, there naturally remains in the man the desire to know about the cause, "what it is. . . ." If therefore the human intellect, knowing the essence of some created effect, knows no more of God than "that He is," the perfection of that intellect does not yet reach simply the First Cause, but there remains in it the natural desire to seek the cause. Wherefore it is not yet perfectly happy. Consequently, for perfect happiness the intellect needs to reach the very Essence of the First Cause. And thus it will have its perfection through union with God as with that object, in which alone man's happiness consists.[12]

This is a strange argument, formally correct and conceptually coherent but also distant from experience. No one, not even the most dedicated Thomist, is likely to respond to the

12. *ST* Ia-IIae, q. 3, a. 8.

question of his most ardent wish and deepest desire of his heart by stating that he longs for his intellect to be united with its highest object. But why does Aquinas insist specifically on the fulfillment of the intellect? The answer is that the intellect is the basis of our engagement with reality and of our operations regarding it. We are, in a way, embodied intellects in motion, because all that we do is founded on our understanding of reality. As we read the full text, which has already been cited in part, we are tempted to read it narrowly in terms of our scientific knowledge of the world. (St Thomas does not help us in this respect when he gives as an example, taken from Aristotle, the mind's wonder at eclipses.) If we think of suffering, however, the point of the answer becomes clearer.

Confronted with evil, the suffering person asks two questions: (1) what can be done to alleviate this? and (2) how, why did this happen? Even if he cannot make the pain stop, he wants to understand why he is subjected to this evil. Indeed, this questioning, this need for some explanation arises also when the evil is not one that a person experiences personally. It can (and should) arise whenever one is confronted with a great evil. The camp at Auschwitz is preserved not simply to remind the human race not to allow genocide, but to enable our and future generations to see the remnants and reflect on the reality of this great evil. The scandal to philosophy is that the question of evil cannot finally be answered; that there is no account of evil that explains how what we experience or know to be evil can in the final analysis be good. What the book of Job and Aquinas's analysis imply is that the sought-for answer can be found only in the depths of the divine wisdom; that only one who sees the essence of God with his intellect can understand the reason behind evil. Only in this vision of the Divine Essence can the evil truly be overcome.

Since the vision of the Divine Essence and the truth within it cannot be had in this life, suffering must remain a mystery. No knowledge, whether philosophical or theological, that may be had of God in this life constitutes a direct knowledge of God; we can know of God that he exists, but we cannot know his nature, his essence. This does not mean, however, that the believer is destitute of knowledge of God. In faith, which St. Thomas Aquinas calls an "initial participation of the supernatural knowledge" that will be ours in glory,[13] the Christian does, in a way, know God. Aquinas continues, "We have [this initial participation] through faith, which by reason of an infused light holds things which are beyond our natural knowledge." This implies that in faith one confronted with suffering and evil can know that God is good, even if he cannot yet see that goodness. This is the faith that St. John of the Cross calls the "dark night of the soul."[14] The simple believer who responds to suffering with "Dios quiere" is not naïve, blindly denying reality and dulling her pain with a religious opiate, but rather expresses a confidence based on a participated knowledge of God, "a conviction of things not seen."[15]

Joy in Hell?

God is the fullness of all good and the ultimate standard of goodness. Turned away from God, nothing that we call "good" is truly good. In the perspective of faith, then, what appears to be not good can be acknowledged to be for the good. Does this mean, then, that we do not know what is good—that our use of this term "good" is nonsensical? Of course not. Here again we encounter the intersection of the relative and the absolute, of the temporal and the eternal, of the corporeal and the spiritual. Relative to our temporal and corporeal nature, we can with

13. Aquinas, *De veritate*, q.14, a. 2.
14. Juan de la Cruz, *Subida de Monte Carmelo*, Lib. II, cap. 2.2; cap. 3.1, ed. Eulogio Pacho (Seville: Apostolado Mariano, 2007).
15. Heb 11:1.

reasonable accuracy know what is good for us—that nutrition, comfort, sexual activity, strenuous defense of life are goods. All these, however, are relative to some higher good, and the highest good is the fullness of all good, God himself. To lose this Good, therefore, is to lose everything good. There is good in hell. Each of the damned, be he human or angelic, has the good of existence. Each has the power of intellect, the ability to know and understand, and will, the power to love the good and choose the means to it. Having turned away from the perfection and fullness of good, however, no good that they enjoy is enjoyable. Their existence, which is a personal and hence spiritual existence (which is focused on truth and the good), has no root, no focus, because they are cut off from the ultimate and foundational truth and goodness. The only "truth" for the damned soul is that which Satan and the others in hell present to him. The only goods there are relative goods that are pointless and readily lost, for Satan himself controls them. There is genuine good in hell, because it is full of God's creatures, but those who find themselves there are incapable of recognizing or appreciating it.

Sorrow in Heaven?

If heaven is full of God's goodness and therefore of unsurpassed joy, then it cannot be a place of sorrow. But if there is a hell, and if hell is occupied, then we encounter a serious problem, one that Anthony Flew noted with "nausea"—namely, that the saved cannot be indifferent to the fate of the damned; that while some are damned, the saved, whose minds and hearts are in harmony with the Divine, must be happy about the damnation of the lost.[16] David Bentley Hart poses the problem especially starkly.

16. Anthony Flew, "Divine Omnipotence and Human Freedom," in *New Essays in Philosophical Theology*, ed. Anthony Flew and Alasdair MacIntyre (New York: Macmillan, 1955), 154.

What after all is a person other than the history of associations, loves, memories, attachments, affinities? Who are we other than all the others who have made us who we are and to whom we belong as much as they to us? We are those others. To say that the sufferings of the damned will either be clouded from the eyes of the blessed, or worse, increase the pitiless bliss of heaven, is also to say that no persons can possibly be saved. For if the memories of others are removed or lost, or one's knowledge of their misery converted into indifference or, God forbid, into greater beatitude, what then remains of one in one's last bliss? Some other being altogether, surely a spiritual anonymity, a vapid spark of pure intellection, the residue of a soul reduced to no one, but not a person, not the person who was.[17]

If Flew is revolted by "the Angelic Doctor's smug contemplation of unspeakable horror,"[18] Hart asks how a person's own happiness cannot be seriously affected by the knowledge that some of those closest to him, with whom his own life has been intimately intertwined, have fallen into eternal damnation. Will not the knowledge that one's own child or spouse has been damned eternally constitute an eternal sorrow? If the person is truly "the history of associations, loves, memories, attachments, affinities" with others, then in truth, when someone significant is damned then a part of oneself is arguably damned. Cardinal Christof Schönborn raises a similar point concerning loved ones who would be damned.[19]

As we begin to consider this problem, we must note that Flew and Hart based their arguments on an appeal to emotion. This is not, of course, entirely illegitimate. Indeed, the emotional blindness of many among the intelligentsia to horror and suffering

17. David Bentley Hart, "God, Creation, and Evil," in *Creation out of Nothing: Origins and Contemporary Significance Conference*, July 5–8, 2015, Notre Dame University.

18. Flew, "Divine Omnipotence and Human Freedom."

19. Christof Schönborn, *We Have Found Mercy: The Mystery of God's Merciful Love* (San Francisco: Ignatius Press, 2012), 133.

may be one of the most serious ailments of this age. Neverthe-less, emotion must ultimately give way to and be formed accord-ing to truth. And of the powers of the human soul, only reason is capable of reliably attaining to truth. Precisely here we must follow reason's guidance, because with the problem of ultimate happiness we find ourselves at the intersection of the temporal with the eternal, and the eternal is quite literally unimaginable. The eternal is not a matter for perception and therefore not for direct feeling. Both Flew and Hart rely necessarily on imagina-tion and emotion, as these thinkers invite us to image persons be-ing subject to horrible tortures. Given the history of the century just passed, its literature (such as Solzhenitsyn's *Gulag Archipelago* or Anne Frank's *Diary of a Young Girl*) and artifacts (such as Aus-chwitz), we can readily call to mind the images of great suffering of the temporally damned. One may well say that such events on earth give us a glimpse of hell, and we are shocked that men with great power inflicted such suffering upon others, even upon those who are unknown to us. The healthy mind recoils from the thought of his beloved suffering such evils. If one cannot imagine with equanimity his wife or child or friend disappearing into a Gulag camp or Auschwitz, then much less can he accept that same person's falling into hell.

Our challenge here is to consider the question according to truth and not according to emotion. The truth about Nazi and Soviet concentration camps is that they were established by human beings to attain certain political and demographic goals and to humiliate and degrade persons whom they deemed de-void of human dignity. Those imprisoned in such places did not deserve their imprisonment and torture. The truth about hell is different. Our starting point must be the truth that God alone is the perfect fullness of good. All that is good is so in relation to him. Strictly speaking, the human mind does not fully grasp what good and evil are. We know the good only by analogy, by the reflections of the perfect good in creatures around us. What applies to each one of us applies also to our neighbor. We are dismayed at the thought of Anne Frank, young and generous, full of love for life, swept up by the Gestapo and taken to death in a Nazi death camp. However, even though when looking at her, we see beauty, love, and goodness evilly condemned, we do not see goodness itself. We do not know the full goodness in Anne Frank's heart, even if we have good reasons to think that she was a person pleasing to God.

But let us now consider a candidate for hell. Such a person in this life may well have good qualities, such a sense of humor, incisive intelligence, or pleasing appearance, and in virtue of these, he may well have made our own life or that of others we know more pleasant in certain ways. Because of the usefulness of his skills or his capacity to create enjoyment, we may have valued his presence in our lives. And so we may remember him fondly. However, according to our hypothesis, he is a candidate for hell, which means that he has turned against the perfect good. He has rejected God and what God stands for. From our limited earthly perspective we can see only that he is useful or helpful to us in some ways; that he has provided enjoyment, but we cannot see that he is good. Therefore we regard him affectionately and after his death may even recall happy memories of him. *So long as you or I am in this life*, we cannot well cope with the knowledge that some friend or relative or indeed (*pace* Flew) any other person is in hell. Concerning the dead we rightfully hope that they will have turned to the God who will save them.

Besides the truth that God is the fullness of all good—he is the Standard by which goods are measured—we must acknowledge also the truth that one damned to hell has become so by rejecting the good. The damned soul has turned away from its true good, away from love and mercy. John Paul II writes:

Man's disobedience, nevertheless, always means a turning away from God, and in a certain sense the closing up of human freedom in his regard. It also means a certain opening of this freedom—of the human mind and will—to the one who is the "father of lies." This act of conscious choice is not only "disobedience" but also involves a certain consent to the motivation which was contained in the first temptation to sin and which is unceasingly renewed during the whole history of man on earth: "For God knows that when you eat of it your eyes will be opened, and you will be like God, knowing good and evil."

Here we find ourselves at the very center of what could be called the "anti-Word"—that is to say the, "anti-truth." For the truth about man becomes falsified—who man is and what are the impassable limits of his being and freedom.[20]

The beloved deceased whose eternity is to be among the damned has chosen against love. He does not love those he left behind, because he died not loving them. An enemy of God, he has chosen also to be an enemy of other human beings. Having rejected love, he has become unlovable. The mother who sees her criminal son marched to the gallows may grieve for his crimes while hoping that there remains within him some spark of goodness that she felt when he nursed at her breast or that impulse of generosity that she had seen in his boyhood. She wants the good that she once knew in him to continue, to revive. She wants the boy, the little boy whom she had loved so dearly, to be good. In this case, however, her judgment is confined to the temporal. She sees only the body to which she gave birth with the same eyes that gazed upon her newborn son. She does not yet see him in his full truth with a spirit deformed by lies. Therefore in her heart she rightly clings to him and prays in hope that he will not be completely lost.

This is not the same situation of the mother who is wel-

---

20. John Paul II, Encyclical *Dominum et vivificantem*, §37.

comed into the Beatific Vision as her son is ordered to depart into the place prepared for the devil and his angels. Does she carry the grief of having lost her son into heaven? Or must she deny her humanity to rejoice with the angels? Here let us return to David Bentley Hart's analysis, specifically to his comment, "What after all is a person other than the history of associations, loves, memories, attachments, affinities? Who are we other than all the others who have made us who we are and to whom we belong as much as they to us?" Although this may contain an important element of truth, in essence it is false. It is certainly true that we are interrelated with others and that each of us is formed personally in relationships with others ... but not in the way that Hart indicates. The primary—indeed, fundamental—relationship is not with other human beings but with God himself. In his discussion of what is needed for happiness, Thomas Aquinas argues that although friends are needed for happiness in this life, they are not for perfect happiness.

But if we speak of perfect happiness which will be in our heavenly Fatherland, the fellowship of friends is not essential (*non requiritur societas amicorum de necessitate*) to happiness, since man has the entire fullness of his perfection in God.[21]

The society of friends will be possible, conducing to the well-being of happiness; we will see friends and loved ones in heaven rejoicing together in God's presence. But because God is himself the fullness of all good, the perfection of being containing within himself all perfections of his creatures, we will not need the society of friends to enhance or complete our own happiness. Thomas clarifies further:

Perfection of charity is essential to happiness, as to the love of God, but not as to the love of neighbor. Wherefore if there were but one

21. *ST* Ia-IIae, q. 4, a. 8.

soul enjoying God, it would be happy, though having no neighbor to love. But supposing one neighbor to be there, love of him results from perfect love of God.[22]

When we love our neighbor, we do so in relation to God. If to love another person is to will his good, then the perfection of love demands that we will and foster his highest good—namely, that the beloved attain to God. And this is precisely the same good that God wishes for him. To love another on different terms is to fail in love, because the human person is called to love as God loves. There is no other way to love. The friendship of earthly life can indeed persist *in patria*, as Aquinas states, but situated perfectly in the context of God's love.

We argued above that "all that the dead person has of himself, in a sense, is the truth he has understood and his love for the goods he has desired."[23] The mother whose son has been damned takes with her into glory her love that she had for her son. If her love was well formed and well directed, it persists in her eternally. That the son is damned is ipso facto proof that he has decisively rejected not only God's love but his mother's as well. (Most likely and to her sorrow in this life, she was probably aware of this rejection before his death.) His refusal to accept God's mercy is also a refusal to love and to accept the love of other human beings. For her part, the mother has not "wasted" her love, for the love she gave her son (assuming that it was a well-ordered love) manifested itself by a kind of reflection and overflow in love for others. If her self, her personality were constituted simply by her human associations, then, whether or not there is a hell, our hypothetical mother is eternally wounded by her son's rejection and ultimate hatred of her (for he is damned, having rejected good and mercy—even to-

22. *ST* Ia-IIae, q. 2, a. 8 ad 3.
23. See the section "The Immortal Soul" in chapter 2 of this work.

ward his mother). She does not need hell to expose the wound.

But does this mother not mourn? The child she bore is lost forever, and surely this loss must affect her, even though she may be eternally enjoying the vision of God. Those who attain the vision of the Divine Essence love God perfectly and enjoy his perfect love. Everything that they see and know, they see in his light. All that they love, they love in relation to him. The mother in our hypothesis gave herself for her son, conceiving and bearing him within her, sacrificing her comfort and perhaps some of her health and beauty. She made the innumerable sacrifices that a mother makes to care for and educate her child. In doing so, she collaborated with God the Creator, who is the primary author of her son's life and being. The mother's emotional dilemma therefore becomes identical with God's, for he too gave life to the son, worked to educate him and care for him. The mother's loss is linked to God's. It follows, therefore, that her heavenly mourning must be very like God's own mourning. Of course, unlike a human being, God cannot be moved by misfortune; indeed misfortune cannot befall him. Therefore God does not experience changes in emotion caused by factors outside himself and beyond his control. God is not "hurt" by those who turn against him. Nothing can mar the perfection of his goodness or detract from the fullness of his happiness. However, it is wrong from this to draw the notion that God is unaffected, dwelling in a frosty divine indifference to human misery. By his own choice and action, God chose to submit himself to the sins of human beings, exposing himself to the rejection of his mercy and love and to the hatred of human beings. God chose the Hebrews and made them his own people, who repeatedly turned against him in rebellion and ingratitude. "O my people, what have I done to you? In what have I wearied you? Answer me!"[24]

24. Mi 6:3.

Jesus came as God's incarnate mercy to Israel and wept over Jerusalem, saying, "Would that even today you knew the things that make for peace!"[25] We falsify the record of revelation if we deny God's sorrow over sin, because too many texts in scripture attest to it. Furthermore, the very concept of mercy itself entails *pity*, a softening of the heart toward another who is in distress. If God is genuinely merciful, then he is, analogically speaking, moved by the distress of those to whom he shows mercy. From this it follows that there must indeed be a kind of divine regret concerning those who go lost.[26] This is a regret that does not, however, militate against the infinite joy within that trinitarian community of love.

Where we go wrong in our analysis of pity for the damned is in our conception of pity as only an emotional response, one characterized by a certain lethargy and preoccupation of our imagination with the state of the one for whom we feel pity. Our experience of emotion in this life is intimately and inextricably tied up with our physical nature, with the heart rate, the flow of hormones in the endocrinal system, in the images created for our minds by the brain as the human organism responds to certain values (or disvalues) touching it. If pity or sorrow is simply an emotional event, then God could have no share in these, and indeed neither would the mother in our hypothesis. God is in this sense beyond emotion. In his simplicity, God is impassible, the fullness of wisdom. More to our current point, the deepest and most fundamental part of the soul is its intellectual part, wherein the intellect forms and guides and the will loves and delights. Our hypothetical mother—and she stands for anyone who loves one of those who are damned—cannot

25. Lk 19:42.
26. And we cannot forget that even if we have no certain knowledge of any human being's having been damned, we do know that one of the most beautiful of the angels is in hell.

be distraught once she has entered into the Beatific Vision, even as she understands somehow that one she had loved is lost. Her soul is marked by the loss, as it were, as she realizes that one to whom she had given her love has rejected it. As Aquinas says, she rests secure in God's justice, not as indifferent to her son's suffering but as recognizing and fully making her own that divine judgment. If she were not to do this, she would herself have rejected the divine mercy and love in favor of her child's rebellion—and because of the sin for which he was condemned, she would not have her son back.

Conclusion

How can a good God damn people to hell for all eternity? This is a great mystery. The answer, which is quite simple, depends on two important facts:

1. The devil and his angels are real.
2. We human beings can be—and often are—genuinely wicked.

God *never had it in mind* that you or I or any other human being should go to hell. Hell is the place created for Satan and his angelic followers, the spirits that rebelled against him. The place God has for human beings is with him. This is a place that Jesus has gone ahead to prepare. Those who have rejected God's love have no place else to go but to hell—that is, to the place ruled by Satan. And the hell of hell is that Satan is in charge.

We delude ourselves if we believe that evil spirits are a

myth. Scripture and the constant teaching of the church are clear. They are real, and it is terrible to be ruled by them.

St. Catherine of Siena said, "All the way to heaven is heaven, because Jesus said, 'I am the Way.'" We might also say by analogy that the way to hell is hell. The merciless life—the life of one who neither gives nor receives true mercy—is a life in hell. Pope St. John Paul II writes that suffering is the experience of an evil,[1] but in an important way this does not correspond to our experience. Certainly when an evil befalls the body in the form of illness or injury, one experiences pain and suffering, and the agony of defeat when the competitor's best efforts fail is very real. The death of someone much loved brings lasting sorrow. However, when afflicted with the greatest evil, the loss of God's presence in our life, the loss of his mercy as the result of our rejection of it, we hardly notice. The psalmist complains that the bodies of the wicked are sleek and sound; suffering does not touch them as they go from triumph to triumph.[2] If to suffer is to experience evil, how can it be that those who choose evil and reject good do not suffer more than those whose bodies are afflicted?

The evil constituted by turning away from the good of union with God is an evil of the spirit and not of the body. Just as one driving east from Cleveland to Chicago (which is to the west) may travel swiftly and comfortably, all the while moving ever farther from his destination, so the person who has directed himself to something other than God may well feel no pain in his body or frustration in his mind. The misdirected driver may, of course, begin to worry uneasily that he may be on the wrong road—perhaps his wife has raised the possibility—and eventually stop to check his map. The misdirected soul may well sense that not all is well in his life, that perhaps he needs

1. John Paul II, Apostolic Letter *Salvifici doloris*, §7.
2. Ps 73:4–5.

to reassess his direction. It may happen, too, that someone else may warn him or at least suggest that the direction of his life is wrong. Such doubts and misgivings do not, however, thrust themselves upon one's consciousness in the way a toothache or bad burn will.

Whether one sees it or not, the road to hell is the road of despair, which is the sickness specific to the spirit.[3] The ultimate end for the human being, the end for which he was created, is communion with God.[4] Because as a spiritual being he is ordered toward truth and the good, if he is not ultimately ordered to God his life can find its meaning only in terms of created goods—and these cannot satisfy. These created goods must consist of pleasant experiences, material possessions, or victorious exercises of power—effectively, idols that demand more and more but satisfy less and less. Precisely in this context it is worth looking at facts, specifically at the fact that phenomenally prosperous and comfortable Americans—one of the wealthiest societies in human history—turn increasingly to amusements and drugs to fill their lives.

The road to hell *is* hell because the person living on that road governs his own life by the same principles that govern hell itself. Instead of a love that gives disinterestedly of self, he on the road to hell increasingly loves a love that consumes and acquires. Instead of living by truth for truth's sake, the hell-bound lives by power and force, by the strength he can exercise against others to compel them to his own will. Instead of seeking the glory of God who in his mercy has promised to share his glory, one bound for hell seeks the honor and glory according to his own measure. The road to hell does not seem

3. Søren Kierkegaard, *Fear and Trembling*, ed., trans. Howard V. Hong and Edna H. Hong (Princeton: Princeton University Press, 1980). The book's thesis, reiterated throughout, is that the sickness unto death is despair.

4. *Gaudium et spes*, §19.

like hell insofar as it does not directly *hurt*. However, being based on a false understanding, this life becomes less and less pleasurable as former sensuous delights leave one unsatisfied and craving more. Praiseworthy achievements go insufficiently noticed by an unappreciative audience, whether this is one's spouse, work colleagues, audiences, or the general public. And in all this hell's ruler provokes and disappoints. His work is well illustrated in the comedy film *Bedazzled*, in which a young man sells his soul to the devil for the sake of winning the affections of a particular woman. The devil grants his every wish—literally—but in every case there is a catch, a detail that meets his request but leaves his desire unfulfilled. Despairing of ever attaining real happiness, the sinner commits himself increasingly to the previously known sources of delight, while sinking deeper into bitterness and despair. The first adulterous encounter was wonderful, an unexpected and perhaps unimagined delight, but, as the relationship quickly decays, recriminations and even disgust set in. Such a one eventually dies and, having failed to turn to the only source of joy, is left naked before the truth of his choices. Then he finds himself in a realm without love, without comfort, without honor, but subject to the whims of those devils who had planned his fall.

You and I (and every other human being) *can become very wicked*. We can be evil beings if we allow ourselves. How often do we hear it said of someone, "Oh, he seems nice enough," or "Yes, she's nice"? We are good at "nice"; at least, most of us are. But we all know well that a coating of "nice" can cover a lot of "nasty." There are many pretty but naïve young women, or rich but foolish investors, who have mistaken charm for character. Ordinary people can and do put themselves ahead of goodness, ahead of God and his love. And this turns out to be hell.

The reason that we are good, if we are good, is because of God's mercy. Christ wants to welcome us into the mansions the Father has prepared for us, and he will do whatever it takes to win us. In fact, he went so far as to suffer a cruel death and die on the cross for us. At that moment—the Good Thief's last chance, really—he offered his mercy to one man. But he also offers it to us, and this mercy can fill our lives. If we can be wicked—and in our hearts we know that we have often been mean, dishonest, venal, and selfish—Jesus saves us from that. His mercy does not mean only that we can get to heaven in the end. It means that we can become worthy of heaven now. This is why in his letters St. Paul called the people he wrote to "saints." Salvation means freedom from sin and from Satan's reign, in this life as well as in eternity. These ordinary Corinthian, Ephesian, Roman, and Thessalonian Christians were holy, saints, even while St. Paul exhorted them to greater sanctity. The mercy of God, the mercy Christ pours out from the cross, is for us today, to make us living saints. Just as the wicked begin to live hell in this life, as saints we can be living the life of heaven. But it hinges on Christ's mercy.

What Christ wants is to tell each one of us, "This day you will be with me in paradise."

Alighieri, Dante. "Inferno." In *The Divine Comedy*, edited and translated by Allen Mandelbaum. New York: Bantam, 1982.

Aquinas, Thomas. *Commentary on the Gospel of St John*. Edited by James A Weisheipl, OP. Translated by Fabian R. Larcher, OP, and James A. Weisheipel, OP. Albany, N.Y.: Magi, 1998.

————. *The Disputed Questions on Truth*. Vol. 1. Translated by Robert W. Mulligan, SJ. Chicago: Henry Regnery, 1952.

————. *The Disputed Questions on Truth*. Vol. 2. Translated by James V. McGlynn, SJ. Chicago: Henry Regnery, 1953.

————. *The Disputed Questions on Truth*. Vol. 3. Translated by Robert W. Schmidt, SJ. Chicago: Henry Regnery, 1954.

————. *On Evil*. Translated by John A. Oesterle and Jean T. Oesterle. Notre Dame, Ind.: University of Notre Dame Press, 1995.

————. *On the Truth of the Catholic Faith: Summa contra Gentiles*. Translated by Anton C. Pegis. Vol. 1, *God*. Garden City, N.Y.: Doubleday, 1955.

————. *Summa theologiae*. In *Great Books of the Western World*, translated by Fathers of the English Dominican Province. Vols. 19–20. Chicago, London, and Toronto: Encyclopedia Britannica, 1952.

Aristotle. *Metaphysics*. Translated by W. D. Ross. Chicago and London: Encyclopedia Britannica, 1952.

————. *Nicomachean Ethics*. Translated by David Ross. Revised by J. L. Ackrill and J. O. Urmson. New York: Oxford University Press, 1988.

————. *Politics.* Translated by C. D. C. Reeve. Indianapolis: Hackett, 1998.

Auden, W. H. "September 1, 1939." In *The Major Poets: English and American*, by Charles Coffin, 518–20. New York: Harcourt, Brace and World, 1954.

Augustine of Hippo. *City of God.* Translated by Marcus Dods. In *Great Books of the Western World.* Vol. 18. Chicago, London, and Toronto: Encyclopedia Britannica, 1952.

————. *Confessions.* Translated by John K. Ryan. New York: Image, 1960.

————. *On the Trinity.* Translated by Rev. Arthur West Hadden. Grand Rapids: Eerdmans, n.d.

Bedazzled. Directed by Stanley Donen. 1967.

Benedict XVI. *Spe salvi.* Encyclical. Vatican City: Libreria Editrice Vaticana, 2007.

Bolt, Robert. *A Man for All Seasons.* New York: Vintage, 1990.

Browning, Christopher. *Ordinary Men: Reserve Police Battalion 101 and the Final Solution in Poland.* New York: HarperCollins, 1998.

Catechism of the Catholic Church. Vatican City: Libreria Editrice Vaticana, 1993.

Dostoevsky, Fyodor. *The Brothers Karamazov.* Edited by Mortimer J. Adler. Translated by Constance Garnett. In *Great Books of the Western World.* Vol 52. Chicago: Encyclopedia Britannica, 1952.

Fargo. Directed by Ethan Coen and Joel Coen. 1996.

Flew, Anthony. "Divine Omnipotence and Human Freedom." In *New Essays in Philosophical Theology*, edited by Anthony Flew and Alasdair MacIntyre, 144–69. New York: Macmillan, 1955.

Gray, D. J. *William Wallace: The King's Enemy.* New York: Barnes and Noble, 1991.

Hart, David Bentley. "God, Creation, and Evil." Presented at *Creation out of Nothing: Origins and Contemporary Significance Conference*, July 5–8, 2015. Notre Dame, Ind.

Havel, Václav. "The Power of the Powerless." In *The Power of the Powerless*, edited by John Keane, 23–96. Armonk, N.Y.: M. E. Sharpe, 1985.

————. "Dear Dr. Husák." In *Open Letters: Selected Prose, 1965–1990*, 50–83. New York: Alfred A Knopf, 1991.

Holliday, Billie. "Strange Fruit." By Abel Meeropol (pseudonym Lewis Allan). 1939.

John Paul II. [See pre-papacy writings under "Wojtyła."] Apostolic Letter *Salvifici doloris*. Vatican City: Libreria Editrice Vaticana, 1984.

———. *Post-Synodal Exhortation Reconciliation and Penance*. Vatican City:
Libreria Editrice Vaticana, 1984.

———. Encyclical *Dominum et vivificantem*. Vatican City: Libreria Editrice Vaticana, 1986.

———. Encyclical *Sollicitudo rei socialis*. Vatican City: Libreria Editrice
Vaticana, 1987.

———. Apostolic Letter *Mulieris dignitatem*. Vatican City: Libreria Editrice Vaticana, 1988.

———. Encyclical *Centesimus annus*. Vatican City: Libreria Editrice
Vaticana, 1992.

———. Encyclical *Veritatis splendor*. Vatican City: Libraria Editrice
Vaticana, 1993.

———. Encyclical *Evangelium vitae*. Vatican City: Libreria Editrice
Vaticana, 1995.

———. Encyclical *Fides et ratio*. Vatican City: Libreria Editrice Vaticana,
1998.

———. "General Audience." Vatican City: Libraria Editrice Vaticana,
March 28, 2001.

———. *Man and Woman He Created Them: A Theology of the Body*. Edited
and translated by Michael Waldstein. Boston: Pauline Books and
Media, 2006.

———. "A Meditation on Givenness." *Communio: International Catholic
Review* (Winter 2014): 871–83.

Juan de la Cruz. *Cantico Espiritual*. Madrid: Avapiés, 1996.

———. *Subida de Monte Carmelo*. Seville: Apostolado Mariano, 2007.

Kierkegaard, Søren. *Either/Or*. Translated by David F. Swenson and Lillian Marvin Swenson. Garden City: Doubleday, 1959.

———. *Sickness unto Death*. Edited and translated by Howard V. Hong
and Edna H. Hong. Princeton: Princeton University Press, 1980.

Locke, John. *Second Treatise of Government*. Indianapolis: Hackett, 1980.

Macdonald, Paul A., Jr. "Hell, the Problem of Evil, and the Perfection of
the Universe." *American Catholic Philosophical Quarterly* 89, no. 4 (Fall
2015): 603–28.

Maritain, Jacques. *The Person and the Common Good*. Translated by John J.
Fitzgerald. Notre Dame, Ind.: University of Notre Dame Press, 1966.

Martin, Ralph. *Will Many Be Saved?: What Vatican II Actually Teaches and Its Implications for the New Evangelization.* Grand Rapids: Eerdmans, 2012.

Marx, Karl, and Friedrich Engels. "Manifesto of the Communist Party." In *The Portable Karl Marx*, edited by Eugene Kamenka, 203–41. New York: Penguin, 1983.

McInerny, Ralph. *Aquinas against the Averroists: On there Being Only One Intellect.* West Lafayette, Ind.: Purdue University Press, 1993.

Mezei, Balázs M. *Religion and Revelation after Auschwitz.* New York: Bloomsbury, 2013.

Mill, John Stuart. *Utilitarianism.* Indianapolis: Hackett, 2001.

Nault, Jean-Charles, OSB. *The Noonday Devil: Acedia, the Unnamed Evil of Our Times.* San Francisco: Ignatius 2015.

Plantinga, Alvin. *God, Freedom, and Evil.* Grand Rapids: Eerdmans, 1977.

Plato. "Apology." In *The Complete Works of Plato*, translated by Benjamin Jowett. New York and Oxford: Oxford University Press, 2011.

———. "Euthyphro." In *The Complete Works of Plato*, translated by Benjamin Jowett. New York and Oxford: Oxford University Press, 2011.

———. *Phaedo.* Edited and translated by R. Hackforth. Indianapolis: Bobbs-Merrill, 1955.

———. *Republic.* Translated and revised by C. D. C. Reeve and G. M. A. Grube. Indianapolis: Hackett, 1992.

Reimers, Adrian J. *An Analysis of the Concepts of Self-Fulfillment and Self-Realization in the Thought of Karol Wojtyła, Pope John Paul II.* Lewiston, N.Y.: Edwin Mellen Press, 2001.

———. "The Significance of Suffering." *National Catholic Bioethics Quarterly* (Spring 2003).

———. *The Soul of the Person.* Washington, D.C.: The Catholic University of America Press, 2006.

———. *Truth about the Good: Moral Norms in the Thought of John Paul II.* Ave Maria, Fla.: Sapientia Press, 2011.

———. "The Structure of Suffering." In *Cierpienie, Umieranie, Śmierć: Wyzwania i dylematy ludzkiego losu w kontekście sytuacji granicznich* [Suffering, Dying, Death: Challenges and Dilemmas of Human Destiny in the Context of Boundary Situations], edited by P. Dancák, M. Rembierz, and R. Sieroń, 27–42. Stalowa Wola, Poland: KUL, 2013.

Robinson, Edwin Arlington. "Richard Cory." In *Immortal Poems of the English Language*, edited by Oscar Williams, 498. New York: Washington Square Press, 1961.

Ryle, Gilbert. *The Concept of Mind*. New York: Routledge, 1949.

Sartre, Jean Paul. "No Exit." In *No Exit and Three Other Plays*. New York: Alfred A Knopf, 1989.

Schönborn, Christof Cardinal. *We Have Found Mercy: The Mystery of God's Merciful Love*. San Francisco: Ignatius Press, 2012.

Second Vatican Council. *Pastoral Constitution on the Church in the Modern World*. *Gaudium et spes*. Vatican City: Libreria Editrice Vaticana, 1965.

Shakespeare, William. *Julius Caesar*. In *The Complete Works of Shakespeare*, edited by W. J. Craig. New York: Oxford University Press, 1919.

———. *Macbeth*. In *The Complete Works of Shakespeare*, edited by W. J. Craig. New York: Oxford University Press, 1919.

Solzhenitsyn, Aleksandr. *The Gulag Archipelago: An Experiment in Literary Investigation, III–IV*. New York: Harper and Row, 1975.

———. *One Day in the Life of Ivan Denisovich*. New York: Farrar, Straus and Giroux, 1991.

———. *In the First Circle*. Translated by Harry T. Willetts. New York and London: Harper, 2009.

Sophie's Choice. Directed by Alan J. Pakula. 1982.

Van Inwagen, Peter. *The Problem of Evil: The Gifford Lectures Delivered in the University of St. Andrews in 2003*. Oxford: Clarendon Press, 2006.

Wagner, Richard. *Libretti, Tristan und Isolde*. 1859. http://www.rwagner .net/libretti/tristan/e-tristan-a2s2.html. Accessed June 9, 2015.

Wiesel, Elie. *Night*. New York: Bantam, 1982.

Wojtyła, Karol. *Sign of Contradiction*. New York: Seabury Press, 1979.

———. "Person: Subject and Community." In *Person and Community: Selected Essays*, translated by Teresa Sandok, OSM, 219–61. New York: Peter Lang, 1993.

———. "Thomistic Personalism." In *Person and Community: Selected Essays*, translated by Teresa Sandok, 167–75. New York and San Francisco: Peter Lang, 1993.

———. *Persona e atto*. In *Metafisica della persona: Tutte le opere filosofiche e saggi integrativi*, translated by Giuseppe Girenti and Patricja Mikulska, 831–1216. Milan: Bompiani, 2003.

———. *Love and Responsibility*. Translated by Grzegorz Ignatik. Boston: Pauline Books, 2013.

INDEX

Abel, 55
Abraham, 58, 130, 209–10, 224
Absalom, 105
acedia, 109
Adam, 8, 11, 54, 56, 91, 171–73
adultery, adulterer, 18, 29, 89, 104,
  151, 165–66, 189, 192, 195, 211, 216,
  242
aeviternity, aeviternal, 18
Albom, Mitch, 154n23
Alighieri, Dante, 74, 81–82, 89, 91, 105,
  106n43, 140, 155, 199
Amadeus (movie), 215
America, American, 5, 48, 62, 126,
  129–31, 138–39, 158, 176, 241
Amnon, 105
angel, 6, 11, 12–13, 15–18, 20–22,
  29–31, 34–39, 41, 46, 48, 51, 53–54,
  56, 60–61, 66, 89–90, 120, 122, 124,
  143–47, 151, 181, 186, 191, 198–99,
  202, 207, 229, 234, 237n26, 239
anger, 95, 97, 100, 107–8, 111, 163, 165,
  195
Apollo, 70–71, 79
Aquinas, Thomas, x, 8, 18–20, 24n23,
  30, 32n33, 40, 49, 51, 53n25, 60, 67,
  72, 74, 78, 91n21, 98n27, 99, 100n30,
  101n31, 103–4, 124, 130, 134, 151,

163–64, 167, 175, 182, 192–94, 208,
  223, 226–28, 234, 238
Aristotle, 8–9, 14, 17–18, 23, 35, 38, 40,
  50–52, 71–77, 79–81, 103, 164, 167,
  175, 191, 227
art, 9, 16, 26
atheism, atheist, 73, 77, 98, 219
Auden, W. H., 5, 110
Augustine, St., 10, 12–13, 69, 83, 88,
  112, 147, 152, 167–68, 191, 195
Auschwitz-Birkenau, 139n1, 168, 173,
  176, 191, 203, 227, 231
Averroes, 49

Babylon, 33, 124–25
beauty, 11, 14 –16, 22, 25–26, 31–32, 63,
  67–68, 82, 84, 90–91, 98, 106, 126,
  146, 232, 236
Bedazzled (movie), 206, 242
Benedict XVI, 84, 115–16
Bolt, Robert, 139, 151
brain, 16, 29, 36–37, 66–67, 76, 116, 147,
  185, 192, 237
Brothers Karamazov, The, 145n9, 219n2,
  225–26
Browning, Christopher, 172–73
Buddha, 77, 80–81

177, 184–85, 192–93, 204, 210, 224,
226–27, 229, 231, 233, 237, 240
money, 101–4, 127–28, 130, 136, 163,
166–67, 171, 178, 198, 216
More, Thomas, 139–40, 151
Mozart, Wolfgang Amadeus, x, 9, 135,
182, 215n49
murder, 32–33, 44, 45, 55–56, 149, 156,
160, 171, 173, 175, 182, 187–89, 195,
197, 216
mysterium iniquitatis (mystery of
iniquity), 138, 140, 142, 144–46,
153–54, 209, 224–25, 227, 239

Nault, Jean-Charles, OSB, 109n46
Nazi, Nazism, 139, 159, 173, 176–77,
231–32
Nero (emperor), 84, 160
Newton, Isaac, 15
Nietzsche, Friedrich, 131–33

One Day in the Life of Ivan Denisovich,
203
opposition, 28, 44, 151, 188
Othello, 45

pagan, 8, 69–70, 74, 79–81, 86, 137
pain, ix, xi, 1, 3, 6, 11, 17, 40, 48,
64, 66, 76, 82, 86, 92–97, 111, 122,
154–57, 160, 167, 176, 184–86, 196,
199, 201–2, 204–5, 207, 217–18, 221,
227–28, 240
paradise, 2–3, 65, 69, 112, 180, 243
Passion of the Christ, The (movie), 141
Paul, St., xiii, 31, 59–60, 77, 85, 107,
114, 143, 146, 150, 160, 169, 207, 243
Peter, St., 44, 84–85, 99, 141–43, 195
phantasm, 36
philosophy, 51, 65, 71, 74, 76, 120,
204, 227
Pilate, 140, 142–43, 161
Plantinga, Alvin, 220
Plato, 14, 21, 30, 50, 69–71, 73, 75–76,
79, 86–88, 102, 103n33, 136, 137n41,
148

pleasure, 17, 23–24, 34, 61, 68, 72, 89,
100, 104, 106–7, 111, 133–34, 136,
143, 154, 163–68, 170, 177, 179, 186,
195, 198, 201, 203–5, 210–11, 216, 218
Pontius Pilate, 140, 142–43, 161
pornography, 133, 171
pride, 16, 21, 29, 31, 43, 87–88, 97–98,
100, 110–11, 129, 132, 172, 177, 206
psychology: demonic, xi, 12, 22, 34,
54, 90, 207
purgatory, 86

reason, reasoning, 7, 15, 19–20, 29, 37,
52, 70, 72–73, 76, 97, 102, 123, 145,
149, 162, 166, 174–75, 183–85, 187,
193–94, 214, 231
resentment, xi, 55, 95
resurrection, 66, 113–15, 117, 182
Ricouer, Paul, 132
Robinson, Edward Arlington, 213n46
Rome, Roman, 3, 58, 60, 84, 112, 141,
157–58, 161, 243
Rubenstein, Richard, 176
Ryle, Gilbert, 16

Sadducees, 113
Sartre, Jean-Paul, 200
Satan, xi–xii, 12, 17–18, 20–22, 28–35,
37–41, 43–44, 46–47, 53–56, 60–61,
79–80, 90–91, 98, 100, 110, 140, 143–
44, 146, 153–54, 160, 177, 185–86,
196–99, 201, 207–8, 229, 239, 243
Schönborn, Christof, 230
science, 27, 52, 67–68, 71, 76, 128, 150,
157–58
Second Coming, 65
Sennacherib, 125
serpent, 43–44, 48, 54–56, 90, 110, 140,
164, 171
sex, 29, 39–40, 89, 97, 104–5, 132–36,
165–67, 171–72, 192, 194–95, 198,
204, 207, 224, 229
Shakespeare, William, 18n12, 45, 216
sin, ix, xi, xiii, 4–5, 11, 18, 20–21, 35,
42, 44–45, 53–56, 61, 69, 80–81, 98,